ALSO BY CAROLE HYATT

The Woman's Selling Game
Women and Work

ALSO BY LINDA GOTTLIEB

Limbo *(coauthor)*

When
Smart People
Fail

by
Carole Hyatt and Linda Gottlieb

Simon and Schuster
New York

Published by Simon and Schuster
A Division of Simon & Schuster, Inc.
Simon & Schuster Building
Rockefeller Center
1230 Avenue of the Americas
New York, New York 10020
SIMON AND SCHUSTER and colophon are registered trademarks of
Simon & Schuster, Inc.
Designed by Irving Perkins Associates
Manufactured in the United States of America
10 9 8 7 6 5 4 3 2 1
Library of Congress Cataloging-in-Publication Data
Hyatt, Carole.
    When smart people fail.

    Bibliography: p
    1. Failure (Psychology) 2. Success. 3. Attitude
(Psychology) I. Gottlieb, Linda. II Title.
BF575.F14H83 1987   158'.1   86–26205
ISBN: 1-4391-5688-3   ISBN: 978-1-4391-5688-9

To Paul Gottlieb, who never failed me.
—L. G.

To the memory of June Esserman, my partner,
my pacer, my friend.
—C. H.

ACKNOWLEDGMENTS

Our thanks to Pam Bernstein, who encouraged us from the beginning, to Julia Coopersmith and Paul Gottlieb for their editorial ideas, to Richard Baron, our computer doctor, and to Dan Erkkila for his patient and intelligent transcription of our tapes.

There is no way we can adequately thank the hundreds of men and women who gave us hours of their time and shared intimacies with us we had no right to expect. Some have allowed us to use their names. Others appear disguised by pseudonyms indicated by an asterisk. All of their stories are real. It is their contribution that is the heart of this book.

—Carole Hyatt and Linda Gottlieb

Contents

"I have had many dreadful experiences in my life—and most have never happened. . . ."
                                        —Old Norwegian Salt

Introduction

The first two failure stories in this book must be our own. They go back a few years, to the time when both of us thought we were invincible.

Carole Hyatt was a successful co-owner of Hyatt/Esserman Research Associates, a marketing and social behavior research firm. Her clients included Fortune 500 corporations, government agencies, and private foundations. Author of *The Woman's Selling Game* and *Women and Work,* she was a sought-after speaker on the lecture circuit. Confident, comfortable with her aggressive drives, she felt in control of her life and sensed little likelihood that anything would derail her steady upward progress.

One day in 1983 Carole Hyatt's partner, a woman in her early fifties, walked into Carole's office complaining of chest pains. Carole telephoned the woman's doctor husband, got her partner hospitalized, and felt enormously relieved that her quick thinking had probably saved her friend's life. Her usual methods—controlling events, remaining calm, taking charge—had resulted in the usual outcome: success. Later that evening, Carole's partner died of a second heart attack in the hospital, and Carole Hyatt's world fell apart:

June's death made me question almost every assumption I ever had. I thought life was predictable if you planned rationally, but June's death was a horrible wild card. I believed in control, but here was an event I couldn't control. My assumptions about the world were crumbling. I felt bruised, vulnerable. And I missed her terribly.

After her death I used to go into her office two or three times a day to tell her things before I remembered what had happened. I was also angry, furious at her for leaving me to face the business alone.

In any partnership you always believe that what your partner does is the easy part and what you do is hard. It was only when June died that I realized how dependent I was on her. I was left with our whole staff, who tried very hard to be helpful, but I never felt more alone. As much as June and I had disagreed, I suddenly discovered it was that disagreement that gave me the energy to make the business grow. Our arguments, I realized, had been creative. With June I had had a peer who knew how to challenge me; now I had only employees, who knew how to execute orders.

It was as if June were my pacer, a runner I took for granted but without whose steady pace I could no longer run. But if I could not function alone, if it took a partner to make me effective, then surely I was an incomplete human being, a failure.

Carole put the business up for sale and received a good price for it. Friends congratulated her on her success. Carole knew differently. She had for the first time begun to doubt herself and her abilities, and that led to a sense of panic that immobilized her. Far from being a success, the sale of the business, to Carole, represented utter failure. She packed up her personal files, turned over the office keys to the new owners, and went home.

I talked to no one about how I felt. I was sure I was the only person who had ever gone through this. People at cocktail parties would ask me what I did. The first few times I just sputtered, then I began to say, "I'm a lunchist." I felt I had lost my entire identity.

Failure does that to you.

At the time Carole Hyatt was running Hyatt/Esserman Research Associates, Linda Gottlieb was senior vice-president of Highgate Pictures, a successful television and educational film company now branching out into feature films. Though not an owner, she had co-founded the company with its president, a man with whom she had worked side by side for almost twenty years, and over those years she had conceived and supervised a large proportion of the company's most profitable product. Producer of a feature for Universal Studios based on her novel, *Limbo,* recipient of numerous Emmys for her television movies, Linda was in active development with Paramount, Twentieth Century-Fox, Tri-Star, and other studios on a broad range of feature film projects. Known for being self-confident and aggressive, she had from earliest times believed in her own abilities. Until she was fired.

It wasn't as if she hadn't seen it coming:

It was like the end of a once beautiful marriage. The same traits my boss once found endearing—my maverick energy, my quick tongue, my toughness at negotiation—suddenly became annoying, abrasive, and insupportable. The truth was that the business was in trouble, and he felt panicky, determined to make a change.

But why did I stay? Why was I so stuck? Why didn't I take matters into my own hands and get out? These are questions which bother me even today. I saw all the signs. Overnight this man's behavior changed, and I dreaded going to work. I think deep down, in the core of my identity, I believed he would never fire me. We had been together for twenty years—the entire lifetime of my eldest child. Together we had built the company from scratch. I believed I *was* that company, that its identity and mine were forever linked. When I was severed from it, my intelligence, which I had always relied upon, was powerless to shield me from the pain. I, who had had the most gold stars on the achievement chart in fifth grade, who had always been first in my class, who had never failed at anything, was fired.

Ashamed, isolated, scared, Linda Gottlieb talked to her good friend Carole Hyatt. It was as if help could come only from someone who had lived through failure. Given to quick solutions, Linda wanted to know what she could do to feel better right away. Carole, who was a year further along in the process, counseled patience. There was a timetable, she had discovered, perhaps even stages one had to live through. "But the panic—how do I deal with the panic?" Linda wanted to know. Carole suggested they have lunch and talk. Linda tried not to think about who would pay.

Over some sushi, Carole asked her friend a simple question. "What are you afraid of? What is your very worst fear?"

It was not an easy question to answer, because the panic was so nameless, so pervasive. Linda thought for several moments. "I think I'm terrified of not having money," she replied. "I have always prided myself on earning a good salary. I can't even think what this will mean for us financially." Carole, who had already dealt with this fear in herself, had an immediate, practical suggestion. "Go home and call your accountant. Pay for a few hours of his time. Give him all your financial data and take a worst-case scenario—let's say you don't make a cent for one whole year. Let him tell you what that would mean to you. Will it mean you have to sell your apartment? That you have to take your children out of college? That you have to borrow money? Or maybe just that you have to cut down somewhat on your style of living?

"What else are you afraid of?" Carole probed.

"That people are talking about me," Linda confessed, "laughing at me."

As they sipped Japanese tea, Carole urged Linda to say out loud all the terrible things she imagined people were saying about her, to hold nothing back, to make the taunts and barbs as awful as she feared in her darkest dreams they might be. Somehow, as the words hovered in the air of a Japanese tearoom, they seemed to evaporate. Having herself said out loud the worst things she could imagine anyone ever saying about her had taken their sting away, robbed them out of their power.

"Now that you've heard all those things out loud," Carole asked, "can you live with them?"

Linda looked at her levelly. "I can."

Linda gladly picked up the tab for lunch. The recovery process was beginning.

• • •

Two things struck both of us at that lunch. The first was that we felt profoundly isolated by what we perceived as our failures. Alone, each of us had been careful to keep up a front, assuring the rest of the world we were just fine. When we discovered we had lived through similar experiences, there was a wave of recognition like that of long-lost veterans of battle throwing their arms around each other. The relief at no longer being alone with failure was enormous. Our second realization was that there seemed to be no guidelines, nowhere we could turn for help. Career counselors could assess career directions, book abounded on how to find your next job, and there was no shortage of advice on the ways to succeed; but what about the territory of failure? Who had charted that? Who could help us understand where we were? Our programming, we realized, had been for success; we had never been taught how to fail.

So we became explorers in the realm of failure. We began by charting our own progress as we refocused our careers, Carole lecturing and giving workshops, Linda signing a producer's contract with MGM and returning to free-lance writing. To the outsider, our journeys looked easy. In fact, they were accompanied by a great deal of inner stress, self-examination, and, finally, clarity and growth. Through it all we tried to be keenly aware of what we were experiencing, of what made us feel better, and of the places where we seemed to get stuck. We reached out to other people, tentatively at first, asking them if they would share their experiences with us. There was, it seemed, a secret army of men and women who had failed, each thinking he or she was the only one. To our astonishment, we discovered in almost every case *they had never talked about it to anyone else.*

We began to ask ourselves questions. What did failure mean in our society? Was there an anatomy to it? Were there predictable stages everyone went through? Were there differences between men and women? Why was failure fatal to some and an important growth stage to others? And could we, by studying the phenomenon of failure, be of help?

We had to place limits on ourselves. First of all we determined to study only career failure, setbacks that occurred in our subjects' work lives, omitting the areas of divorce, broken friendships, and other personal defeats. We decided to include both those people who, like Linda Gottlieb, had suffered obvious failures—being let go from a job, not getting a promotion that was anticipated—as well as those, like Carole Hyatt, whose failed expectations of themselves had led to a self-labeling of failure.

Second, since we had to limit our sample somehow, we decided to focus on middle and upper-middle class, well-educated people with viable job skills. We did this for several reasons. Who was likely to fail the most, we reasoned, if not the people who took the most risks? And those risk-takers, we felt, were likely to have already pushed themselves into the middle class. Furthermore, since we wanted people whose success had come from their own hard work, we determined to avoid those born into power and money. While some of our subjects were clearly upper class because of their incomes, all had to work hard to acquire their silver spoons. On the other hand, we did not want to include people so disadvantaged they were unable to imagine change. This eliminated those on the lower end of the economic scale. We sought people, in other words, who objectively had options. The question was, could they, after failure, take advantage of those options?

In all, we conducted 176 one-on-one, in-depth interviews. We also held several small focus-groups of all men and all women in order to zero in on gender differences as they applied to failure. The people we talked to were predominantly white, with approximately 10 percent black and Hispanic. They ranged in age from twenty-one to eighty-four. The majority of our sample was drawn from large cities—New

York, Los Angeles, Dallas, Pittsburgh, Washington, D.C., Atlanta, and Detroit—with a small percentage living in suburban and rural areas.

In addition to people who had experienced failure, we talked to dozens of professionals in the fields of psychology, psychiatry, sociology, sex therapy, business management, and employment counseling.

We recruited our sample through professionals in the social behavior field, as well as through people we knew. We sought names of those who had clear-cut career failures and those who were "hidden failures," people who appeared successful to the outside world but who believed they were failing. We tried to include a cross section of occupations—from accountants and insurance salesmen to scientists and entertainers—paying particular attention to the professions of politics, acting, and sports, where winning and losing are almost daily occurrences. We also felt it important to include a cross section of employment patterns—from corporate workers to entrepreneurs.

Soon after starting on our research, we discovered a surprising fact: almost *everyone* we talked to, especially the most currently successful people, had experienced some major failure in their past. When we realized this, we decided to include a certain number of well-known figures in our sample. We did this, frankly, to provide clear and recognizable role models: if famous people can survive failure, so can you. But there were certain risks in our choice. Why should the ordinary person care if George McGovern failed, or Polly Bergen, or Walter Cronkite, or Clare Boothe Luce? Such people were famous and in most cases had money; surely they did not feel the same shock and rage and despair as a middle manager being fired after ten years of loyal service. We believed they did. Many interviews later we know this to be true. The emotions all people go through in times of profound emotional upheaval such as death, divorce, or career failure are very much the same. It is only what they *do* with those emotions or how quickly they get through the cycle of them that may be very different.

Why would people talk to us? you may wonder. Wouldn't they want to keep their failures hidden? Often they did. Those in the midst of it, still bruised and uncertain whether they could survive defeat and turn it into success, were reluctant to talk. Others said quite candidly that they feared being associated in any way with the word "failure." Most survivors, however, were quite open. They felt they had gained wisdom they wanted to share.

And then there were the surprises. A friend called one day to say that David Brown, producer of *Jaws, Cocoon,* and many other movies, had heard we were doing a book on failure and asked to be interviewed. We knew David to be an extraordinarily kind, modest man who rarely sought publicity. We also knew him to be one of the great successes of the movie business. The request seemed altogether out of character. We called him immediately.

"David," we said, "as far as we know, your career has been a total success."

He laughed quietly. "Do you know I've been fired from major jobs not once but four times? Do you know how many movies I've made that failed? In fact," he continued, "I consider myself an *expert* on failure, and I think it is important, very important, to share with others any insights I might have."

His generosity of spirit was duplicated over and over again. People allowed us to relive with them moments of their greatest joy and deepest sadness. We were immensely touched by their candor, for to talk of one's success and failure with another is to share a most intimate sense of self.

For both of us the book became a personal odyssey. We began our quest believing we knew clearly what success and failure were, at least as they applied to our work. We were outer-directed, achievement-oriented people, bred to the role from childhood, giving little thought to the process of how we got there. Listening attentively to the voices in this book, entering into the lives of the people we met, we have had our assumptions shaken. We have been helped by what we learned. We hope you will be, too.

PART ONE:
The Nature of Failure

I

The Last Taboo

Probably you have already failed.
If not, you certainly will.

- Did you fail a test in third grade?
- Did you fail to get into the college you wanted?
- Did you fail to get the job you desired?
- Have you lost the job you held?
- Did you fail to climb as high in your career as you had hoped?
- Though others consider you a success, do you consider yourself a failure?

Few of us will not be able to answer "yes" to one or more of these questions. Failure is universal, endemic, part of the human experience. The fact is, we are all failures or will eventually become so.

The reason for this is simple: risk implies failure. If we dare new things—changing a job, creating a work of art, trying to get into a school, falling in love, inventing a new product—we risk failure. It is implicit in the striving for success. The only way to avoid it is never to strive, to remain fixed where we are. But if being fully human means stretching ourselves to find our broadest capabilities, then all of us who constantly explore our potential are constantly poised to fail.

Failure is the most democratic of all clubs, admitting old and young, rich and poor, black and white, chief executive officers and simple clerks. About the only thing its members have in common is their secrecy about belonging. Think what a national convocation of all eligible members of the Failure Club would look like: millions of people crowded tightly together in thousands of rooms across America—all looking down at their feet.

In a world in which divorce, cancer, pornography, child abuse, homosexuality, and incest have all come out of the closet, failure, one of our most universal experiences, remains taboo. Success is what books are written about; failure is almost never discussed. We believe it is time to end the taboo. Those of us who have failed should examine what has happened to us. Those of us who in the midst of success are haunted by the fear of failure should get to know the intimate enemy. The good news is that it is not so terrible. In fact, for many it has proved an important watershed, an opportunity to reassess one's life and move forward with greater clarity. Failure means some loss; but it can also often mean a gain—wisdom.

What do we mean by "failure"?

Failure is a judgment about events. That is all it is. However, it is commonly understood differently.

Let us say you lose your job, or you do not get the promotion you wanted, or your art show gets negative reviews. Most people would label these incidents "failures." In truth, they are all "events," nothing more and nothing less. Losing your job, for instance, may be a a great relief, if you hated the job; in itself it is only an event, not a failure. It becomes a failure if you or someone else viewing it decides it is a failure.

However, the word "failure" has been so closely linked to the events themselves that it has come to mean, in the popular mind, those very events. We have been led to believe that losing one's job, not getting that promotion, not passing the test are in themselves failures. They may or may not be, depending on who judges them. This distinction between your *judgment* of the events and the *events themselves* is one we will come back to later on, because it is of prime importance in giving you the power to reinvent yourself after a defeat.

In this book, we are looking at "failure" in both senses of the word: (1) as a shorthand term for events such as the loss or nonattainment of career goals—so we will refer to losing your job or not getting promoted as "failure"; and (2) in the sense of a judgment you make about yourself—so that "failure" may also mean not living up to your own expectations. The first kind of failure is generally visible—there is no hiding the fact that the play has closed, the business gone bankrupt, or you have been fired; the second kind of failure is often invisible. This "hidden failure" involves an inner dialogue about your own deep self-disappointment; and though no one in the outside world may ever know, to yourself you are a failure.

The forms of failure are varied, but all have one thing in common: they involve a sense of loss. The losses may be of three kinds: (1) self-esteem, (2) money, (3) social status. Job loss, for instance, generally involves all three, whereas failing in the stock market only means the loss of money.

If there is no perceived loss, than we do not experience the event as failure. If, for instance, you lose your membership in a social club because you forget to pay the dues out of disinterest, that is not felt as a failure. You did not invest the club membership with value of any kind, so there was no experience of loss. But if you lose your membership in your company's top sales club, you will no doubt feel you have failed. Eviction from that club means a loss of status among peers, a loss of self-esteem, and probably a financial loss as well. How severe the experience of failure is depends on how many of the three kinds of loss have been sustained.

Meet a few people who have experienced the most common forms of failure.

FIRED!—JOHN CASTELLI*

Of all the forms of failure, getting fired is probably the most painful. It involves every kind of loss—self-esteem, money, and status—and since it is done *to* you, it makes you feel helpless and out of control.

There are many ways of getting fired. In the factory they send you a note with your paycheck; in the corporate world the boss probably calls you in and shuts the door; in the academic world, as often as not they let you figure it out yourself. No one ever told John Castelli he was "fired." They just told him his grant proposal money had not come through and let him take it from there.

John is a good-looking, wiry Italian with intense dark eyes. He has a Ph.D. in organic chemistry and for ten years was a junior faculty research member at an Ivy League medical school. Psychopharmacology was his specialty. In the Castellis' small, rural-Connecticut home, all John's degrees are framed on the wall of the "family room." No wonder—they were hard to come by.

John was a boy from the working class. His father was a carpenter who had struggled hard to educate his son. He used to joke that he couldn't even pronounce what John taught, but whatever it was, it was good—he had a son teaching at that fancy university.

When he got the medical school job, John Castelli thought he had found what he would do for the rest of his life. Not that he loved it—there were those mornings he would get up tossing at five A.M., his wife would ask him what was the matter, and he would say nothing but would be thinking, I'm stagnating, I'm stuck, and I'm scared to move. But it had prestige. When you were the poor Italian growing up in a neighborhood of WASPs, prestige counts. He was a "doctor," after all, and though he never used the title, he felt it gave him a niche in life, a comfortable academic niche. It also gave him a small income, which, along with his wife's salary as a librarian, allowed the Castellis and their two children "three square meals and toys from *Sesame Steet,*" as John puts it.

At the age of thirty-eight, after a decade at the university, John learned that his mentor, the man who sponsored his research, was leaving. Not realizing at first what that meant, he filled out the same grant proposal he had filled out every year for the last ten. But this year, without the prestige of the older man behind him, John Castelli's proposal was turned down. There were no two ways of reading the letter: in university language, John Castelli had been fired.

I felt like a death curse had been placed on me. The message they gave me was quite clear: there was no room at the inn. I was terrified. I had no savings, and not a contingency plan in the world. I was an academic, and even though I hadn't loved it, it was all I knew how to do. I was afraid to tell my wife. I put the letter in my pocket, and walked three miles to the unemployment office. I just stood outside; I couldn't make myself go in.

Eventually John did go into the unemployment office; he had to. That spring and summer he sent out about fifty letters seeking a university job. Months went by. There were no openings. The Castellis got deeper in debt, and John grew increasingly depressed. Having to face his father was a particular agony.

One day, as he was sitting around writing yet another application letter, the woman next door came by and asked if by any chance he knew someone who could paint her house. John's mortgage payments were overdue, and his daughter needed a new winter coat. He changed into his work clothes and picked up a paintbrush.

When the man down the street saw John painting, he asked if by any chance John would have time to put up some living room paneling. As John nailed the planks into the wall, he thought back to his boyhood years when he had often held boards in place against the strain of his father's saw cutting them to measure. His father used to say to him, "When you grow up, you'll use your head, not your hands." John smiled to himself ruefully at the memory.

When people found out I was doing that kind of work, they got in line. I had always been handy, always been good around my own house. Of course, I never thought—all those years I was studying chemistry and passing orals and finally getting a doctorate—I never thought I would end up as a handyman.

John Castelli, Ph.D. in organic chemistry, has rejoined the working class. One of the almost four million people who lost their jobs in 1985 through cutbacks, layoffs, or relocations, John Castelli discovered that mobility can be downward as well as upward. In this he is far from alone.

Not that he is altogether unhappy about the change. Like many of us, John had felt "stuck" at his job. And though he would never have made a move if he had not been pushed, being fired forced him to change careers.

It's not bad, you know. I make about as much as I made in teaching—more, if there's a big storm or something that's caused a lot of damage. I'm thinking of starting my own home-repairs business one day.

If he does, he will be joining the fastest-growing segment of the American economy—the service sector.

Not many people go from university faculty member to handyman to small business owner. But according to recent research, the average American is not as dissimilar to John Castelli as you might think: he or she will switch careers not once but *three times* in the course of a working life.

Sometimes being fired can start you off.

THE FAILED ENTREPRENEUR—MONA ROCKWELL*

By definition, entrepreneurs take risks, so you would expect they would be more prepared for failure than the rest of us. If anything, they are less so. Part of being an entrepreneur is being optimistic, and that optimism almost never includes the possibility of failure. Unlike employed workers who lose their jobs, entrepreneurs suffer an additional insult: they think they did it to themselves.

. . .

When Mona Rockwell failed in business, she did it the way she had done everything else in her life: spectacularly. To begin with, she was beautiful. That was what the Chicago tax attorney first appreciated when he found her on the ski slopes of Aspen. He soon realized, as they talked in front of the fire, that the "girl" (that's how he thought of her) was also smart. She could analyze a business problem; she even seemed interested in his tax cases. On the slopes she was altogether different—a daredevil, a risk junkie, always willing to try a more dangerous trail, thrilled if she succeeded, quick to pick herself up again if she had a fall. She would be a natural in real estate, he thought.

How often does a forty-year-old, slightly paunchy tax attorney get to play Svengali? He decided to set her up.

It took Mona about five minutes to switch from mountains to buildings. She started a small office in downtown Chicago and quickly became known as "the Robin Hood of real estate" because of her honesty and her ability to get little people to invest. As she describes it:

It was sweat equity in those days. We would all pitch in. They would invest, and I would manage the property, taking a piece of the deal. All of a sudden I had four buildings I was running. It grew and grew and grew until I was in partnerships on ten or fifteen buildings.

By the time Mona was in her late twenties, she had over two thousand apartment units, owned major buildings in Arizona, Nebraska, and California, and had acquired the accouterments of power: bigger offices, fancy attorneys, offshore companies, European partners, one hundred employees, and an enormous overhead. The tax attorney who found her on the slopes of Aspen was too small to handle her work or, for that matter, her life. He disappeared from both, and a "big eight" accounting firm was hired. She describes herself in this period:

I was terrifically ambitious, terrifically focused. I worked from six A.M. until two the next morning. My goal was to have ten million dollars in cash by the time I was thirty-five.

Already earning more than half a million dollars a year, she was well on her way.

Her new accounting firm began referring clients to her. When she protested that she was already overextended, they brushed aside her objections. A group of European investors was looking for an American partner who was scrupulously honest and doggedly entrepreneurial. She was that, her accountants knew, and beautiful, too. Introductions were arranged.

This was heady stuff, big-time people who were worldwide, and they chose me. I knew I had too much on my plate, I didn't quite know how I was going to handle this, but there was a part of me that was going to show the world a woman could do it—be feminine and still do very high-level stuff. I also thought I could do something special, with a lot of integrity and social responsibility. My ego was huge.

The project they picked was a large-scale apartment-conversion project in Arizona. It required far more technical experience than Mona had. Problems surfaced almost immediately. The elevators put in by the contractors did not work properly, a hidden plumbing problem resulted in a cost overrun of more than $600,000, and before she knew it, Mona needed millions of dollars more than her original loan.

I started to get a little scared, but the market was still pretty good. Besides, I was so busy there wasn't time to feel much, and the carrot out there was really big. I figured ten different ways we could sell these units. I worked out five different contracts that people could buy on. All I needed was more money from the banks.

But the banks said no. The day it all collapsed was a Thursday, Mona recalls. She was sitting with her European partners and the loan officers around a table, "looking affluent and smart and successful and sexy." The chief loan officer was affable but clear: unless she placed two million dollars in interest reserve in the bank, she would not get the loan. Mona did not have the cash.

The Europeans took her to a fancy restaurant for dinner. She couldn't eat.

I was sick. I knew there was no way to get the money. And I knew what it meant. I had so many different projects going, I was out on all my lines of credit. My senior guy hadn't raised the money he should have on a project in California, and there was an eight-story senior-citizens complex in Nebraska that I had just syndicated, borrowing money to close that deal. I had counted on the loan we were raising to give me breathing space.

The Europeans ate their dessert—for them this was just one project; Mona sipped water and tried to fight back the panic. "I knew it was all over, the whole thing, the whole ten years, the whole dream."

Creditors sued her. She let her staff go, sublet her offices, fired her houseman, sold her two cars, moved out of her house and into a minuscule apartment. Instead of working in an office on Lake Shore Drive, Mona Rockwell now answered dunning notices from her kitchen.

I watched my net worth evaporate from three million dollars to nothing. When people would ask how I was, I'd say, "I think I'm being prepared to survive nuclear war." I felt I had no skill, that it had all been luck, that it had nothing to do with me, that somehow opportunities fell at my feet, but I didn't add anything to those opportunities. I felt I had no self. I *was* my business, and when it crashed, I crashed with it.

Mona Rockwell's decline was as sudden, total, and dazzling as her ascent.

This isn't the end of Mona Rockwell's story. Her self-reinvention and subsequent success form the subject of a later chapter. The point here is that her failure, though particularly flamboyant and public, is quite typical of the entrepreneur.

More new businesses are being formed in America than ever before, and of those new businesses, approximately 50 percent fail within the first five years. Mona is part of one of the most noticeable trends in American business: the growth of entrepreneurship, and female entrepreneurship in particular. According to the Bureau of Labor Statistics, women are starting new businesses at a rate twice as fast as men.

If people like Mona Rockwell had been afraid to fail, the economy would not be as strong as it is.

HIDDEN FAILURE—CLARE BOOTHE LUCE

"I often thought," says Clare Boothe Luce, "that if I were to write an autobiography, my title would be *The Autobiography of a Failure.*" It is a startling statement, coming from one of the seemingly most successful women in America. Author of numerous articles, books, and plays, twice elected to Congress, former ambassador to Italy, Mrs. Luce, still regal at eighty-four, appraises herself with the same tough eye and witty tongue she used in her best-known play, *The Women.*

Failure means you haven't done your best with the talents or opportunities you were given. Very few people ever *do* do the best they can, and they know it—secretly they know it. In our own eyes, we often see ourselves as failures.

I would say my worst failure, paradoxically, was a rather long-drawn-out series of relative successes, none of which were in the theater. In other words, my failure was not to return to the real vocation I had, which was writing. I don't remember from childhood ever really wanting to do or be anything except a writer.

To Mrs. Luce, her "successes" in politics—the two terms in Congress, an offer to run for the Senate, the ambassadorship—inasmuch as they kept her from her true vocation of writing, represented failure. She is typical of those people who, despite the acclaim of the outside world, believe they have somehow failed themselves.

Running for Congress was not her idea, but her husband's. Already a well-known playwright, she was working on a play that today she still believes to be her best when Henry Luce, who regarded the theater as "nightwork," suggested she give it up and run for Congress.

In those days it was hard enough to be a woman and get elected to Congress. But to be also a playwright writing a sexy comedy would have made it impossible for me to win. I had to make a choice, so I withdrew the play. I always thought I would come back to it.

Everyone thought, myself included, that I would lose. This was 1942, the height of F.D.R.'s power, and I was running as a Republican. I thought at least I would be able to write a play about campaigning. To my surprise, I won.

But it did not feel like success. Not even the second term, when her victory was yet more surprising:

In that vast Roosevelt landslide I had become enough of a public figure so that the Vice-President, Henry Wallace, came into my district seventeen times to speak against me. And really to put the cherry on the charlotte russe, as we used to say, when Roosevelt was told at eight o'clock that *he* had won, he came out on the porch at Hyde Park, accepted his victory, and then added that what gave him almost as much satisfaction as his own election was to hear on the radio that "the lady from Connecticut" had been defeated—which at that point was true. . . . Only a bunch of small apple farmers way up in the backwoods of Connecticut came crashing down with about three hundred votes. So I just squeaked in.

But I did not feel successful. It wasn't my production. Politics is not very creative; it's teamwork. It's a little bit like that contest in which there are eight men on one side of a rope and eight on the other. If your team pulls the opposition into the mud puddle, did *you* do it? In a sense, yes: Do you get the credit? No. It goes to the team. But the real trouble is you're never sure whether it mattered that you were on the team or not. Politics isn't a personal creative effort.

After two terms she resigned, longing to write. But now fate intervened. Her only child, a daughter of nineteen, was killed. Within that same year she lost her mother and brother as well.

My appetite for doing anything was for a long time at a very low point. I had to come to grips with my own private confusions and miseries. I felt I needed the discipline of a church, and I was given the grace to become Catholic. But that, too, I found, made it very difficult for me to write—I had a whole new philosophy, a whole new worldview to come to grips with.

So the whole writing thing—which I yearned to return to—accident, chance, the way my husband felt about things conspired to keep me from doing. And after a while I began to say to myself, Maybe you're not a writer. Maybe you'll never be a writer again.

Mrs. Luce settles back against the cushions of her couch and stares out at the Potomac sunset from her apartment at the Watergate. "I don't really understand the word 'success,' " she says. "I know people use it about me, but I don't understand it."

Clare Boothe Luce is a famous example of a widespread phenomenon: *hidden failure.* Hidden failures suffer less from a sharp sense of loss than a chronic sense of disappointment. But they suffer nonetheless, longing somehow to change, often as scared and ashamed as those who have been fired. How many people, laid off jobs through no fault of their own, nevertheless feel they have somehow failed? How many of us feel stuck in jobs we hate, are terrified to risk change, and despise ourselves for doing less than our best? Often at the very moment the world is praising us, we know in some corner of our minds that we have failed our own best hopes.

Some years ago, in the dark of the night, the number-two man at a billion-dollar corporation confessed to his wife that he was certain he was a failure because he was not number one. Can anyone convince him he is wrong?

Unlike the reverses of John Castelli and Mona Rockwell, the failures of people like Clare Boothe Luce and the corporate number-two man are invisible to the outside world. But they are no less real to the people experiencing them. They are self-styled, hidden failures, failures of one's own expectations.

An Army of Failures

No matter how unique you think your experience—being fired, having your own business collapse, not getting the promotion you thought you deserved, or simply failing in your own expectations of yourself—you are not alone. The numbers are legion. And they are growing.

We are all part of a rapidly changing economic picture. Gone are the days when you started at twenty with one employer and retired at sixty-five with a gold watch. *The average American today will work for ten different employers, keep each job only 3.6 years, and change his entire career three times before retirement. Woven into those statistics is a virtual guarantee: at some point everyone is going to fail.*

The corporation, that great "they" that was going to take care of us all, can no longer be relied upon. Beset by the pressures of foreign competition, shifting market demand, mergers and acquisitions, and rapidly changing technology, large companies are taking a long hard look at their employees. When the telephone company, "Ma Bell," an institution as dependable as our mother, fires over twenty thousand employees, is there any security left? Is there anyplace one can work that is risk free?

The answer is clearly no. In a changing economic world, the only security is the self-confidence of knowing we can cope with insecurity. We cannot isolate ourselves from the possibility of failure. What we *can* do is understand we are not alone with it. What we *must* do is learn how to learn from it.

THE WIN/LOSE SOCIETY

The Eskimos have dozens of words for "snow." We have as many euphemisms for "failure." People refer to "setbacks," "snafus," "glitches," "reversals," "gaffes," "recent troubles," "career pauses," "good tries," even "the F word." Why do we have such a phobia about this word?

Americans are the most success-oriented people in the world. This is a country of winners and losers. Advertisements exhort us to "be a winner." Kids in school taunt each other, "You're a *loser!*" One of America's best-loved coaches, Vince Lombardi of the Green Bay Packers, said with well-placed hyperbole, "Winning isn't everything—it's the *only* thing." Lombardi was talking about football; he could have been coaching American life.

This is the land of the computer, a machine that understands zero/one. Like the computer, we measure ourselves: are we the zero, or are we the one? The middle seems no longer to be acceptable. Even being number two isn't good enough. Ned Edwards, the second-ranked squash player in North America, says quite candidly:

Number two is the same as number sixty-two, in a way. You're still losing when you're number two. You can almost taste number one, but you're not there. You know you're not like the rest of the pack because you are good. But you're somewhere in no-man's-land because you're not number one.

Recently the five-year-old son of one of our friends came home from kindergarten and told his father excitedly he had been in a running race at school.

"Who won?" was the father's first question.

"Teacher says we all won," the little boy replied contentedly.

The father, a well-educated and otherwise sensitive man, got down on his hands and knees so he could be at the boy's height. He took him by the shoulders. "Son," he said, "there was only one kid who crossed the finish line first, and there were fifteen kids behind him. Where were you?"

Like this little boy, we receive our messages early. Sports pervade our childhood years. Contests abound, in after-school clubs, on television, on cereal boxes. Whether from boxtop or baseball diamond, the message is the same: Competition is serious and desirable, producing clear winners and losers.

School reinforces the idea. From first grade on, we are exposed to an instrument so pervasive it becomes a metaphor for life: the test. How well we do in school tests shapes in large part our sense of self-worth. Along with sports, this is our most potent exposure to failure and success. Two aspects of it are noteworthy: it appears to be objective, and it is public. The test admits of no two interpretations. Perhaps you got a ninety-five or perhaps you got a sixty, but whatever you got, your abilities were measured, your worth was quantified. No one, after all, is likely to have told you when you failed the math test that you did as well as you could. No one is likely to have pointed out to you that even though you failed the test, you yourself were not a failure, that you had other strengths as well.

Another powerful subliminal message comes from testing: not only is our worth measurable, it is measurable in the eyes of *others*. Rarely, if ever, are we asked in school what *we* think of our own work. We learn that the judgment of ourselves lies outside of us. Furthermore, since testing results are generally publicized, early on we tend to get labeled as winners or losers, successes or failures.

The messages from sports and school are carried over into adult life and form part of the peculiarly American attitude toward success. As it is popularly understood, success in America has four characteristics:

(1) It involves visible accomplishment, actively *doing* something—starting a new company, creating a hit show, winning a game—as opposed to *being* something.
(2) You must do it yourself. This is a country that reveres the self-made person. Inherited wealth does not count. Each succeeding generation of Rockefellers must prove themselves anew.
(3) Its rewards are generally in the form of money. An exception to this is politics, where the winner reaps power, but even here the reward is quantifiable—the more successful you are, the more power you accrue.
(4) The judgment of success is determined by others. New York's colorful mayor, Ed Koch, speaks for all of us when he wonders out loud, "How'm I doin'?" It's as if he, and we, don't know if we are successful until someone else tells us.

Nowhere in the above description of success is there room for the less tangible, inner-oriented achievement. The actor who may have been pleased with his performance but got bad reviews, the team that played better than they have played before but did not win the game, the writer who feels he has written his best poem but no magazine has published it—these are not American success stories. In our zero/one, win/lose society, these efforts are labeled failures.

ORIGINS OF THE SUCCESS/FAILURE ETHIC

As ideas go, failure is rather recent. In the classical world and throughout the Middle Ages, people did not talk of failure. Reversals in their lives were attributed to strong controlling outside forces—bad luck, chance, fortune, the will of God. Failure presupposes risk, being able to move from the niche into which you were born in order to try something new. In the rigid class system of Europe, where you were expected to do what your father had done before you, the notion of personal failure was almost unthinkable.

In addition, the medieval period placed little emphasis on the individual, unique human, and without the glorification of self, there can be no conception of personal success or failure. The architects of the great cathedrals of the Middle Ages neither sought nor received personal fame. The scribes who painstakingly illuminated the medieval manuscripts remained anonymous. Portraiture, the recording of a unique human face, though known in antiquity, did not come back into existence until the Renaissance. Plays were written about Everyman, not one particular man.

The church reemphasized this abnegation of self. "Blessed are the meek," Jesus told us, "for they shall inherit the earth." What a remarkable idea, and how diametrically opposite to current American notions of success and failure. To Jesus, inheriting the earth did not require *doing* anything; it merely required *being* a certain way—not emphasizing oneself. No wonder Christian paintings, manuscripts, and cathedral plans were unsigned.

The Renaissance, along with its great art, bequeathed us a concept basic to the idea of success: glory. Dante, Petrarch, and the Renaissance poets were stars of their time, proud of their achievements. Ordinary people, too, sought glory, not in the afterlife, but now. A merchant class was formed, living by their wits, prizing not land or titles but money. In countless Renaissance portraits, these newly successful businessmen proudly show off the jewels, clothing, and furniture they accumulated.

In the individualism of the Renaissance, the growth of commerce, and later in the antiorthodoxy of the Protestant Reformation, the seeds of the success/failure ethic were sown. But in Europe an entrenched class system prevented those seeds from taking root.

The New World was a different matter. Here everyone was a newcomer. On the American frontier, whether in New England or the later burgeoning West, there were no classes. You could come here an indentured servant, become a freeman, grab a parcel of land, and with luck maybe even end up a wealthy man. Devoid of a feudal aristocracy, America invented a new upper class with only one entry requirement: money. And since the accumulation of money was open to all, a pervasive American dream was born: upward mobility.

Puritan leaders inveighed against the sins of luxury, but even their own Calvinist theology taught that God had given every man a calling. If a man did his calling so well as to amass wealth from it, was that not a sign of God's favor? Besides, how could Puritan leaders tell their followers to accept poverty when the richest land in the world lay just outside their doors?

In a uniquely American mix, godliness and commerce became forever intertwined. The Protestant ethic was born. The business of

America was to be business. And the Lord not only didn't mind—He smiled upon it.

A new hero sprang forth: the self-made man. This self-made man, this uniquely American invention, could go out and enjoy life, liberty, and the pursuit of wealth guilt free. God Himself had sanctioned it, and the prize for success was something that could never have been his in Europe: immediate entry into the upper class. With the Puritans, the success/failure ethic was born. They are the ancestors of today's fast-track professionals.

To understand just how revolutionary this idea is, consider how success and failure are viewed in a few other countries. British television commentator and writer Melvyn Bragg remarked recently:

The English love failures. We hug them to our bosoms, give them a few quid if they need it, don't mind a bit if they're down and out. Of course we admire wealth, but only if it comes from two sources: what you inherit at birth, or what you win by luck. This is a nation that spends twice as much on gambling as on national defense. We're deeply suspicious of the self-made man. Earned wealth? Over here it seems a bit dirty.

If you have ever tried to put together a deal in England, you know the truth of Melvyn Bragg's statement. The English tend to greet American business enthusiasm with a mixture of awe and curled lip. To be so openly energetic in the pursuit of money simply isn't done.

In France, the legacy of a feudal aristocracy has left that nation with a similar disdain for trade. The businessman in France does not enjoy the same prestige as in America. He can never be in the top ranks of French society merely by making money, so why strive around the clock. Why think big? Thinking comfortably is sufficient. One's sense of self in France, and in many countries in Europe, comes more from family roots than from business success.

In the Far East, the attitude is also strikingly different from ours. This world is but a passing stage, so why strive so hard while here? Wisdom, not money, represents success, and worldly failure has no stigma. In Japan, in fact, the greatest heroes of legend are those who *failed* in battle. It is the way they faced failure, not the way they attained success, that makes them heroes.

In America it is a different matter.

THE BEST/WORST COUNTRY IN WHICH TO FAIL

Because of the special emphasis we place on success, America is the cruelest country in which to fail. Successes are trumpeted and failures spotlighted in a land where discretion has never been a national virtue. Almost no information is sacred here. In such a publicly win/lose society, defeat can be crippling.

Prizefighter Gerry Cooney, a brawny, dark-haired Irish boy, rose spectacularly in the ranks of boxing without a defeat to his name until 1982, when he challenged champion Larry Holmes for the world heavyweight title. In an event broadcast worldwide, Gerry Cooney lost. "I failed!" he says. "I had never done that before in my life, but at this big mega-thing, this worldwide event, I failed. I felt like I had let everyone down." Cooney was so traumatized by the loss, he went into a severe depression and was unable to fight again for almost two years. In a society where winning is all, when you lose, you lose everything. Defeat becomes a kind of death.

But America is also the best place in the world in which to fail. Since status does not depend on birth, there is always the possibility of remaking yourself. This is the land where you can go from rags to riches to rags—and still hope to go back to riches. Second only in popularity to the saga of the self-made man is the saga of the comeback. Richard Nixon is an American invention.

Nolan Bushnell founded the game empire of Atari and then a restaurant chain called Pizza Time Theatres. After the latter company collapsed around him, he commented:

We're probably the most accepting of failure of any nation. The idea that someone could fail in Europe and pick themselves up again and get a major job is almost inconceivable. People are afraid to take risks in England or France—not because they're afraid of losing money, but because they're afraid of losing prestige. They feel once their Tiffany-glass reputations are shattered, they can't be put back together.

In America we know better. The media are always looking for a story. They love "wins," but when someone stumbles, that's a story, too. In what other country, when you failed, could you go back to the venture-capital community and have them say, "He's probably learned a lesson"?

THE POSITIVE POWER OF FAILURE

Few of us recognize the benefits of failure. We try instead to shield ourselves from it, and because we are phobic, we pass that phobia on to our children. A high-achieving couple we know had a son who was not performing up to the standards of the private school in which he was enrolled. His work was slapdash, often unfinished, and he was on the brink of failing. Immediately the parents changed the boy's school. Within months, the same scenario occurred. Again they moved the boy. By the time their son graduated from high school, he had been in four different schools. Technically he had never "failed"—they hadn't given him a chance. Some years later this same boy began work as a researcher at NBC's news department, largely through his father's connections. In his first big report he did his usual careless job, except this time there was no one to shield him. He was fired. After a year of deep depression he now works as a stock boy in a sheet music company. This way he can never fail. The messages he got from his parents were clear: (1) We don't accept failure; and (2) We don't think you are strong enough to survive defeat.

It is important to fail and important to give our children permission to fail. Learning early that you can survive defeat makes you tougher and more resilient for the rest of your life. That is the lesson this boy's parents cheated him out of.

Furthermore, only by risking failure are we likely to accomplish anything. Recently, baseball player Reggie Jackson surpassed Ted Williams's home run record, but in doing that, he also surpassed Babe Ruth's record of strikeouts. The same gigantic, powerful swings that led to home runs also led frequently to strikeouts. There is no accomplishment without risk.

Failure also gives us a unique opportunity to learn. It is no accident that students at the Harvard Business School study unsuccessful companies. Success is enjoyable but rarely tells us much. Some years ago, a producer at CBS News did a one-hour show that made the front page of the *New York Times. Mrs. Kennedy's Tour of the White House* was one of the television's highest-rated documentaries. The producer and the network believed they had discovered a magic formula: famous people showing the audience famous places equaled success. The network quickly committed for ten more shows. The second much-heralded epic was entitled *Queen Frederika's Tour of the Parthenon.* It got some of the lowest ratings in television. By midafternoon the other nine shows had been canceled. The first show had worked not because of the concept, but simply because the audience wanted to see Mrs. Kennedy. It took the failure of the second show to make clear the reason for the success of the first.

Probably the one area of American life where failure is regarded positively is science. Dr. Keith Reemstma, chief of surgery at Columbia Presbyterian Hospital, has been trying unsuccessfully for years to cure diabetes through transplant technology. He has had nothing but failures. How does he keep going? "I never think of what I do as failure," he says. "It's just an incomplete result. I always have in my mind what I am trying to accomplish, and each experiment tells me a little more about what I have done wrong." Unlike the worlds of business, sports, politics, and academics, science understands failure for what it is: the outcome to an event, the result of an experiment, a chance to correct mistakes and move on.

Failure gives you options. Think of driving from your home to a friend's house in another town. If you are successful getting there, nothing has happened on the way; you have simply gotten into your car and driven uninterrupted to your destination. Now think what happens if you run out of gas on a country road halfway there. Suddenly many options are open to you. You might decide to sit and wait for help. But you could also walk to a larger road and flag a motorist, hike to the nearest gas station, or go to a nearby house and ask to use the telephone. Perhaps you might even take a walk in the fields. On your walk, you might well decide to trade in your car. Whatever you do—unless you sit still and do nothing—the result is change: you have either met new people (the gas station attendant, the person in the house), had a pleasant new experience (the walk in the field), or come to a decision (to get rid of the car). The "failure" of your trip has given you many more options than the "successful" drive would have done.

ENDING THE TABOO

Mark Ringheiser* is a New York architect who runs his own firm. Some years ago he was having serious financial difficulties. "I felt like I was hearing the droning of the plane just before it crashed," he says of this period. One day he ran into a fellow architect on the streets, who asked Mark how things were going. In a moment of candor, Mark described a recent disastrous mistake he had made in pricing a job, an error that cost him all his profits. The other architect said he had made similar mistakes but had figured out how to correct them. He told Mark in some detail how he did it. "I stood there listening to the guy and realized I was getting about $100,000 of free advice," Mark says.

As a result of that chance meeting Mark put together an informal network of independent architects, which meets every few months. The rules are simple. All information—including financial information—is public. And at each meeting everybody tells two stories, one success and one failure.

Mark Ringheiser and his colleagues did what too few of us are willing to do: end the silence about failure in order to learn from it.

It is important to understand what failure is ... and what it isn't. Success and failure are not polar opposites; they are parts of a continuum. One can lead to the other with great ease. Neither is likely to be permanent; the irony is we believe both will last forever.

A story told by actress Barbara Barrie illustrates the point. After being nominated for an Academy Award for her role in the motion picture *Breaking Away,* Barbara was down in Georgia shooting the television series that grew out of the film. She was the star, already having had a long career in stage and film. The young boys in the cast, all unknowns, were enjoying their first taste of success, thirteen episodes of a major network series. After six shows the network canceled all their contracts. Barbara recalls the long drive out to the airport with the boys.

We were all talking about our plans. One of them said, "I have an interview for a Broadway play." The second one piped up, "I'm meeting with a major director for the lead in a movie." The third announced his agent insisted he come out to Hollywood immediately, while he was "hot." Then they turned to me and asked what I would be doing next. "Monday morning I'm going to the unemployment line on Ninetieth and Broadway," I told them. There was dead silence in the car.

What they didn't understand was that over the course of a career you're up and you're down many times. When you're down you think you'll never work again, so you cover it up—like they were doing—and when you're on top you think that that, too, will last forever. After a while, when you've been up and down enough times, you understand that both conditions are part of you, that the ups and the downs are both just stages you go through. If you're at all willing to risk in your career, you'll have some successes and some failures. That's what they didn't yet know.

WHAT IS FAILURE?

Failure is a judgment about an event.
  It is a word used to define a stage.
  It is not a condemnation of character.
  It is not a permanent condition.
  It is not a fatal flaw.
  It is not a contagious social disease.
  It is a judgment about an event. How well you cope with that event in large part determines what kind of person you become. The point to remember here is that *it is the way you cope with failure that shapes you, not the failure itself.*
  To say we learn from defeat is a truism. But somehow we have been expected to do our learning in isolation, each of us swallowing bitter little pills of wisdom in silence, keeping our own counsel and muddling through sadder and wiser. We have propagated the myth that failure is too terrible to talk about. Perhaps our fear is that if we tell our children and our friends, they might love us less.
  Yet the people who have told their stories in this book have been willing to break the conspiracy of silence. For all of them defeat has been a powerful, formative experience, one from which they believe they have grown. Because of this they agreed to share what they learned with others.
  In the end, real strength comes from knowing we can survive.

II ————

The Anatomy of Failure

No matter how many times people tell you that in the long run you will be stronger, in the short run there are few things worse than feeling you have failed. You feel pummeled, destroyed, violated, betrayed, terrified, angry, guilty, depressed, vengeful, lethargic, impotent—and occasionally relieved and resolute. Your defenses have been shattered. Armies of warring emotions now seem to be trampling over what was once an intact you. Your mood swings wildly from hope to despair. It is a time of great confusion.

In fact, you have sustained a severe blow, properly termed by psychiatrists a "narcissistic loss"—a loss of your very sense of self. And the more closely you identified yourself with the job or endeavor that failed, the greater that loss. A television newscaster fired by the network sums it up: "People said not to take it so personally, and I said, 'Are you kidding? It was *my* head, *my* voice, *my* face—*me*—they fired *me!*'"

In this sense career failure is unlike any other loss: it is a sudden, brutal destruction of self-esteem. Even the death of a loved one does not attack *our* ego; painful as it is, mourning for another does not obliterate our sense of self. Career failure often does.

Frequently this time period is remembered as being wildly disordered. Actually it is not. Failure seems to trigger a series of stages as distinct and predictable as the stages of dying described by Kübler-Ross in her book *On Death and Dying*, or the stages of mourning so brilliantly analyzed by psychiatrist John Bowlby. The stages we refer to appear to be "negative" ones in that they are painful, tumultuous, and seemingly unhelpful. However, these "negative" phases of failure actually perform a positive function. Like the steps in mourning, to which they are in many ways similar, the stages of failure force us to accept our loss and prepare us for the task of rebuilding.

They are:

(1) Shock
(2) Fear
(3) Anger and blame
(4) Shame
(5) Despair

The speed at which people pass through these phases varies greatly. Polly Bacca, a state senator from Colorado, shattered by the loss of her first election, spent a solitary weekend in the mountains battling all these emotions and in three days had completed the process. Henry Horwitt, a middle manager pushed out of an entertainment conglomerate, took more than a year. Still others seem never to complete the cycle, remaining stuck in their own failures, victims of disordered mourning, vainly seeking what is forever gone.

We are aware that some of the stages seem to and often do overlap—particularly fear, anger, and shame. However, since for many people they happen sequentially, we have treated them separately. Here, then, is the anatomy of failure.

THE STAGES

(1) Shock

It happens so fast! One day you're on all the network news programs, the Secret Service is escorting you in and out of public events, the bands are playing, and enormous crowds are cheering; and then an overwhelming sense of loneliness just takes over the day after a defeat. All the bands stop, the cheering stops, and you're alone in the world. I was stunned by it.

George McGovern is the speaker, describing his loss to President Nixon. Although McGovern was intellectually prepared to lose, emotionally he was completely unprepared. The size of his defeat, losing forty-nine out of fifty states, simply overwhelmed him. How could he interpret it as anything but a very personal rejection? Later his intellect would take over, but, as he says, "It took a couple of years to do this, to see that the voters were not rejecting me personally as much as they were responding to political trends, forces, and conditions over which I had no control."

George McGovern is a sophisticated man, an experienced politician who understood his risks. Yet despite his intellect, despite his exposure to polls, despite what his *mind* told him, when failure struck, it produced in George McGovern the same gut-wrenching shock that it would in a steelworker who suddenly learned his factory was closing. No one is immune to shock.

Patricia Soliman is a statuesque woman whose clear-eyed intelligence is evident in her face. She talks quickly, thinks quickly, and has relied all her life on a first-rate mind as her principal navigating tool. But when she was edged out as president of the publishing house she had built, like George McGovern, she found her intelligence largely useless. In the face of simple, raw shock, her mind gave way.

It was like the worst possible surgery, with no preparation and no anesthesia. I was heartbroken by the betrayal, physically assaulted by the pain of internalizing that betrayal and being unable to say, "I'm dying."

Patricia Soliman had some inkling of her own demise when the company brought in a new player whom she perceived as a wild card. But Sharon Timmer, vice-president of a large cosmetics company, genuinely thought she was indispensable. On the day she confidently asked for a raise, her boss fired her instead.

My first feeling was that something had died, but I couldn't quite place what. It was like the dream you have of walking naked into a room. I was strangely cheerful, not at all angry—in a trance, really.

The first reaction to sudden loss is disbelief, shock, numbness. You know you have been hit ("something had died, but I couldn't quite place what"), but the mind blocks the pain. It is even possible to be cheerful, as Sharon Timmer was, and to continue briefly as if nothing has happened. Patricia Soliman reports being "puffed up with pride" at how well she handled herself the day of the firing. "I said to myself, 'Patricia, you did this the way a man would.' I cleaned up every single piece of paper on my desk with consummate meticulousness." Sometimes behavior in shock is bizarre. One woman fired from her corporate vice-presidency pulled up to her house in a limousine, bedecked in jewels and furs that she had bought upon learning of her dismissal. "Why not spend everything?" she said to her astonished husband.

The mind denies what it cannot process.

Then something happens, usually a random event that punctures the numbness, and the second stage of shock sets in. Reactions are often physical. Patricia Soliman was receiving a champagne toast from her staff at a farewell lunch at the Four Seasons. An elegant woman who never showed emotion in public, she was horrified to find herself suddenly weeping, and weeping violently. Embarrassed, she stood up and discovered she could not walk. The doctor who was summoned could find no medical explanation; he prescribed a cane. Within days she developed breathing difficulties. Another doctor was called in. Apparently she had contracted a rare and exotic lung infection. With hindsight, she says:

The shock factor was so terrific that I didn't realize I couldn't walk until I couldn't walk. I didn't realize I couldn't breathe until I couldn't breathe. I had these incredible physical responses to this trauma which I thought I was handling so brilliantly. I flew out to California to see my husband, and I had to be taken off the plane in a wheelchair. For ten days I was literally crippled. I call it my "near death experience."

In a sense Patricia Soliman *was* near death. When you *are* your job and someone destroys that job, they have in a very real way destroyed *you*.

Shock, the first stage of failure, is thus characterized by an initial state of numbness and disbelief, giving way to the awareness of a terrible blow.

As in dealing with any terrible blow, at this stage you should do nothing. Absorb the blow. Think of the way you react when a heavy object falls on your foot. You may howl and hold your foot, or you may hop on the other foot to try to make the pain go away, but in either case what you are really doing is absorbing the injury and waiting for the throbbing to recede.

It is always a mistake to make any major decisions during this phase. You may think you are behaving rationally; probably you are not.

When you are in the stage of shock, what you need most is a sympathetic listener, *not* someone who will offer advice. You are not ready to hear it. A man who lost his job at a brokerage firm remembers his fury when his wife attempted to be "helpful."

My wife tried to console me. She said "You don't understand it now, but this is the best thing that could have happened to you. You've been doing this too long, and it's time for you to create something new." I was *wild* with her for saying that. All I wanted was for someone to sympathize with the injustice and be furious *with* me. I didn't want anyone telling me sensible things. All I wanted was someone saying "Those bastards! How did they do that to you?"

Therapist Estelle Rosen puts it succinctly: "Shock is the time when what you need most is a back rub and a big hug."

Psychiatrist Yvette Obadia points out that shock is so traumatic to us that we frequently try to protect ourselves from it ever happening again by making a generalized conclusion. Scarlett O'Hara did this in *Gone With the Wind,* after the shock of near starvation in the siege of Atlanta, when she vowed, "I'll never go hungry again." In Scarlett O'Hara's case the vow may have been appropriate, but over and over again we encountered people who drew inappropriate conclusions while in a state of shock. Elaina Zucker, fired from her job in a large advertising agency, found it so painful that she generalized into the conclusion: "I'll never ever work for a corporation again."

Clare Boothe Luce admitted to this trauma generalization in speaking about the failure of her first play, *Abide with Me.* Today, fifty years later, the pain is still in her voice as she describes how an opening-night critic lambasted her for an ill-advised bow she took.

I remember the words to this day, they were so wounding. The critic said, "The last and most painful thing that happened was that [Clare Boothe Luce] leapt from the wings like a gazelle to answer the calls of 'author, author' which were heard by no one but herself."

I vowed to myself that never again, as long as I lived, would I be in the theater the opening night of the play—if I ever wrote another play. Well, I wrote eight plays altogether, and three of them were smash hits, but I never again went on the opening night.

In her childhood, the young Clare Boothe Luce made a similar protective generalization at another time of shock, when she learned that her father had abandoned her mother:

I saw how my dear little mother coped with failure. She was brave, but she wept rather copiously. My pain at seeing this was so enormous that I vowed when I grew up I would never weep again over a failure. I almost never have.

Clare Boothe Luce's behavior, born during a time of shock, is understandable. At this stage all of us are liable to draw strange conclusions and behave in odd ways. We are struggling to absorb a blow. But whenever shock occurs, it is safer to do absolutely nothing except wait and allow the pain to recede.

(2) Fear

Close on the heels of shock come the terrors, the ghosts that lie in wait to attack the mind at four in the morning. At first, fears may be quite specific and even appropriate ("How will I pay the mortgage?" "How will I meet my children's school bills?" "What will I tell so-and-so when he calls?"), but they can escalate quickly to unmanageable proportions ("What if I *never* work again?" "Suppose nobody ever calls me?").

When it focuses on a specific object, fear is a survival mechanism, alerting the body to danger in much the same way that fever alerts us to illness. But when fear metamorphoses into nameless dread, its use ceases. Specific fear can be useful; exaggerated, unfocused fear is paralyzing.

One of the reasons for a generalized sense of fear is that our faith in an orderly world is shattered. If failure can strike with such seemingly random chance, what other horrors lie in wait? As Sharon Timmer, the fired vice-president of a cosmetics firm, expressed it:

The fear didn't set in for a few days. But then it overwhelmed me. My value system had been challenged. I believed if you did the right things in life, good things happened to you. In work, which is a reward system, this should have been the case. I didn't know why I was catapulted up so fast, and why I was cut down so swiftly. The reasons were capricious. Suddenly the whole world seemed capricious.

Lurking behind the worry of meeting the mortgage payment or the dread of never working again lies a darker, more primitive fear: our own mortality. If you identified yourself as Sharon-Timmer-cosmetics-executive and you were just fired, then the part of you that was Sharon-Timmer-cosmetics-executive is dead. The evaporation of so large a portion of your identity is a disturbing reminder that one day the rest of you is going to die. And—worst of all—not even be remembered. All of us somehow imagine the world will stop with our death, and certainly we hope the people who rejected us will fall apart without us. When our ex-employer functions perfectly well after our departure, however, it is disquieting evidence that not only will we die—our demise may barely be noticed. Failure, then, in an eerie way prefigures our own death. In the deepest sense that is why it elicits fear.

Fears overwhelm by their sheer size and because they are by nature shadowy and intertwined. To people who fail, fear is a hydra-headed enemy, almost impossible to grasp. The task is to break it down into manageable size, to confront only one terror at a time. Instead of worrying about the school bills and the house bills and the job interview and why didn't so-and-so return the phone call and the strains on family life—the mind flits from one terror to the other with no peace—the task is to focus calmly on one fear at a time. By taking fear out of the shadows, where it is always more terrifying than in the light of day, by looking at it not as one giant problem but as a set of discrete issues for which solutions can be found, fear becomes more manageable.

If we let fear get out of control, it turns into panic—a sense of sudden, incapacitating alarm. Panic is the enemy, because it is pervasive and prevents us from acting. It must be quieted at all costs.

Mona Rockwell, the spectacular failure in real estate whom we met in the first chapter, has been through this stage.

When I become afraid now, the first thing I do is try to stand still. I quiet myself from panic. I do this by not running around, not keeping busy. I turn inward. Usually I meditate. I tell myself "You've been here before and you will survive." Before, when I was afraid, I would run harder. I was trying to catch "it," whatever "it" was. Now it's as if I can't run. I have to stop and get in touch with what is important to me.

Fear is uncomfortable, evoking within us the terrors of childhood, reminding us of a time when we were helpless, when monsters lurked in the corners. For some people an inner approach, using meditation, is helpful. For others, confronting their fears, one at a time, brings relief.

(3) Anger and Blame

I gave them one-third of my life and I was betrayed far worse than a faithless lover!

—ex-editor from Boston

Anger filled my belly—it suffused every pore of my body and came out the ends of my hair. I had no place left to put it.

—ex-advertising executive from Detroit

I risked my life, got malaria and dysentery, for the *Chicago Tribune,* and this was how they repaid me!

—William L. Shirer, author

Some people never get angry. They move from fear right into despair. By skipping over anger, these people have a harder time recovering from failure, because anger, as long as it is a passing stage, is healthy. It is a sign you value yourself. A strong ego, dealt a severe blow, reacts strongly.

So appropriate is a sense of outrage that the very people who do the firing *expect* it. Corporations pay vast sums of money to outplacement counselors to defuse employees' anger—that's how scared they are of it. And with reason. Hot anger can lead to destructive action—stealing files, harming a job in progress, bad-mouthing the company to others. It can also lead to sleeplessness, irritability, and a constant sense of frustration. Anger, particularly prolonged anger, is uncomfortable for most people.

When it galvanizes us toward righting a wrong, anger is useful, but in this case the wrong cannot easily be righted. However, if we cannot act, all of us can fantasize.

This is a wonderful stage, when anger transmutes into fantasy. Almost everyone we talked to indulged in it. One man, fired as a comptroller by a boss he had barely tolerated for years, carefully photocopied company payroll checks made out to the boss's houseman. For months he composed letters to the I.R.S., tasting the satisfaction he would enjoy at his boss's personal ruin. So enjoyable was the fantasy that he never actually sent the letters.

Perhaps the best revenge fantasy come from Peter Schifter, a young opera director rather publicly fired from a prestigious production at the Kennedy Center.

The night the opera opened in Washington I was by chance at the Kennedy Center working on another production. I of course knew my way around backstage. Now the climax of the first scene, which is very turgid and serious, is the opening of the dead woman's coffin, causing the soprano to shriek with grief. I decided to climb into the coffin—which I could have done because I knew all the people in the cast—so that when the soprano opened the coffin, I would have been lying there smiling. I was certain she would have shrieked off key and the production would have been ruined. It would have been fabulous. Only a rare bout of good taste stopped me.

For some, the only satisfactory revenge is in achieving greater success. These people tend to be impatient, moving quickly at the stage of anger and blame, rather than going through the whole anatomy of failure. Acting from a desire for revenge is acting for the wrong reasons. The story of William Ivers* is a case in point.

Ivers was the chief executive officer of one of the largest investment banking firms on Wall Street. A brilliant lawyer and fierce competitor, he had to win any game he played, from Scrabble to banking. Unfortunately, he often offended fellow employees less intelligent than he. Ultimately, in a brutal power play, the man behind the investment banking company, whom we shall call M. W., fired Ivers. It was an intolerable insult. Ivers passed quickly through the stages of shock and fear and focused on anger and blame. Clearly this was M. W.'s fault. Never stopping to consider what part he might have played in his own downfall, Ivers moved swiftly to fight back. The only revenge sweet enough would be to build a firm bigger than the one he had left. He would show M. W. who was smarter.

Within months Ivers and a partner started another investment banking firm, designed from the beginning to be big. Big meant a lot of people, however, and not all of them could be as smart as Bill Ivers. Temperamentally suited to running a small company composed of himself and a few other equally bright stars, Ivers created a big company that he could not run smoothly because of his personality. Within a year the new firm failed. Reflecting on it now, Ivers says:

I needed to build up something big to make myself feel better about the way I had been treated. Bigger as opposed to smaller was appealing, and that was probably the wrong set of issues. *I was using this new business as a way of avenging past events.* I felt I had been made to look like a failure, and it angered me. If I had delayed everything a year, I would have made a better decision.

To make a major career move out of hot anger, without completing the full cycle, is to make a major mistake.

Dr. Aaron Esman, professor of clinical psychiatry at Payne Whitney in New York, points out that while inchoate rage can lead to depression, coolly focused rage can be an effective motivational tool.

Jane Seely,* a vice-president of one of the networks for five years, had been told by her boss repeatedly that her contract would be renewed. Relying on that promise, she turned down other jobs. When her boss got kicked to a powerless job upstairs, everyone suffered a sudden memory loss about Jane's contract. They offered her two weeks' severance. A well-liked, attractive forty-year-old brunette, Jane was stunned—men had always taken care of her. After the initial shock, she rallied. "Suddenly I was furious. I had never felt so much anger before. I felt abused, betrayed, disregarded, and hurt." She was also tough-minded. Coolly using her outrage, she hired a lawyer and threatened to sue.

It was the hardest thing I've ever done in my life. I was very used to being the well-behaved girl. But on some level I had the tiniest kernel of knowledge that this was important for me to do, that the fight would change my life. I wanted to produce movies, and I knew that involved confrontation. In my business people want to be associated with somebody willing to fight.

I had no money and my lease was up, so I sold my furniture and moved in with a friend. I felt like a little girl out in the cold, an orphan saying to this big corporation, "You must give me money." Every day I said to myself, I can't do this, I can't do this, and every day I answered myself, You've got to do this, you've got to do this.

In the end, they agreed to give me twenty-eight weeks of salary. But the best part was a call I got from one of the senior people at the network when it was settled. He said, "So when are you coming to California, Jane—I can't wait to see you." I couldn't believe it. I had thrown him against the wall and won, and suddenly he respected me.

For me the fight was restorative. I've been through the battles these guys go through, I survived, and I feel like an equal.

Once your hot anger has subsided, a sense of cool outrage can be extremely useful.

• • •

Not everyone we interviewed was fearful, not everyone was angry, not everyone experienced despair—but every single person we interviewed engaged in blame.

"A madman, a raving, drug-crazed fag, a card-carrying asshole," is how the former sales manager of a women's clothing line described the man who fired him. "A wild card who didn't know fuck-all," says a ladylike ex-publisher about the man she blames for her demise. "A demure little killer in a Peter Pan collar," says a securities analyst of a woman who took her job.

Blame, which at first seems irrational, is a perfectly logical response to an insupportable event. Something or someone had to cause this annihilation of ourselves; the assigment of blame is an attempt to pinpoint causality and therefore keep the world rational.

Sometimes we blame ourselves instead of others, though rarely with any more objectivity. Usually it's an exercise in self-flagellation: How could our judgment have been so wrong? Why were we dumb enough to let this happen to us? The ex-director of corporate benefits for a large company says:

I saw the handwriting on the wall. I watched the first wave get fired and thought, It will never happen to me. I watched the second wave go, and I shut my eyes tight. They got me on the third round. It was my own fault, my own fault! Why was I so stupid? Why didn't I get out in time? Why was my judgment so bad?

The most important thing to note about blame is that, although everybody engages in it, it is almost always inaccurate. While it is everyone's first explanation of events, it is rarely the *full* explanation. Indeed, your boss may have been impossible, or the new man in the company may have been angling for your job, but if you take the time to think coolly, you'll generally find that causality is more complicated. It is true that M.W. was determined to force out Bill Ivers in the earlier scenario, but it is also true that Bill Ivers had managerial weaknesses that contributed mightily to his own downfall. It is true the corporate benefits man probably hung on longer than he should have, but it is also true that he had interpersonal problems that played a part as well. Blame, in other words, will only be your *first* interpretation, and not a very accurate one at that.

Anger, revenge, and blame are temporary and highly useful emotions. Anger and revenge reassert the fact that we are valuable people and are our mind's way of protesting a grievous narcissistic loss. Blame helps us continue to see the world as a place ruled by order rather than chance. These feelings serve a definite function. They become a problem only if they persist.

(4) Shame

I didn't pack up my office right away. I made my wife sneak back into the building with me that night and carry out all my things. I couldn't bear the gaze of my fellow workers.

—Paul Bowers,* dismissed lawyer

For three days I didn't tell Helen Gurley Brown I had been fired from yet another job.

—David Brown, ex–publishing executive

Shame owes its existence to the authority we give *other people* to judge us. If we ourselves were the sole arbiters of our behavior, we might feel *ashamed* of what we did—a personal regret in not living up to an ideal—but we would not feel *shame,* disapproval in the eyes of others. "What will 'they' think of us?" is a question we have been programmed from childhood to ask ourselves. Most of the time we don't even know who "they" are.

The more public the personality, the greater the sense of shame. Shame at disappointing his large public was what destroyed prize-fighter Gerry Cooney far more than his loss to Larry Holmes. "I feel I am a symbol of hope to a lot of people, and I didn't want to let them down," Cooney says. "I don't mind letting myself down so much, but letting down all those other people—I couldn't deal with it." Shame is particularly strong when the nature of our failure is public, as Gerry Cooney's was. When failure is more private, shame is not such a virulent stage.

Actress Polly Bergen, warm, poised, never less than stunningly dressed, has survived two major business failures, one in Oil of Turtle, a company she created, and one in *Not for Women Only,* a show she hosted. The difference in the two experiences illustrates the nature of shame.

Oil of Turtle was created "out of nothing," Polly says, much the way she created herself. The daughter of an illiterate construction worker and a mother who worked "at anything available," Polly swiftly became a movie star but felt that show business was not enough; she wanted to make her mark in "real" business. Using a formula she developed herself, she started Polly Bergen's Oil of Turtle.

I ran the company the first year. I knew where every penny went. I was doing all the traveling, all the promoting—it was a one-woman band, and we were making money. Then suddenly, at $1.5 million I thought I wasn't smart enough to run this business. I guess I have a certain amount of insecurity about not having a higher education, and I always feel the other person is smarter. So I brought in a professional to be the financial person. I left him to do his job and I did mine, but I did mine great and he did his miserably. A year later we were $600,000 in debt. So I fired him, and I blamed myself. I always blame myself.

I was forced to sell in order to get capital. A few years later the company to whom I sold Oil of Turtle sold my company to people I knew would destroy my product. There was nothing I could do. I had no choice but to walk away. Three years later it went bankrupt.

Of this first major failure, Polly says:

I felt like a child had died. I was very hurt. I think my pride was injured to some extent. Even though I had sold the company, I felt somehow or other that I had failed.

Polly Bergen felt many things, but she did not feel shame. Her own harshest judge, she granted no one the authority to make her feel ashamed.

Her experience on *Not for Women Only* was another matter. Polly had replaced Barbara Walters as co-host of the show along with Frank Fields. After a year, Polly decided she wanted to leave. On vacation in Acapulco she picked up a newspaper and started trembling when she read the headline: POLLY BERGEN AXED BY NBC. It wasn't true, but people thought it was, and suddenly she felt ashamed. It seemed as if the very people who admired her were now all looking at her, accusing her of failing.

It was the most devastating thing that ever happened to me. I was powerless to fight it, because the more I protested, the more I seemed to give it credence. This was harder for me than losing my company, because it was *public*. When Oil of Turtle went bankrupt I suffered a great deal, but I suffered privately. The NBC fiasco was a *public* embarrassment. I was frantic that people should think I was fired! It's publicly saying "She wasn't good enough."

Losing Oil of Turtle was a *real* loss, but at least it wasn't embarrassing. Having the public perceive me as a failure on *Not for Women Only* was utterly humiliating.

Today Polly Bergen is running a successful women's shoe and jewelry business. From the Oil of Turtle experience she learned to keep control entirely in her own hands. From the humiliation at *Not for Women Only* she determined to become the most important judge of her own success. She would not let people shame her again.

•   •   •

After failure, everyone approaches you gingerly, cautiously probing the air to see what signals you are sending out. "Are you all right?" they ask nervously. What they really are asking is, "Are you ashamed?"

This is a moment of great opportunity. Your attitude about yourself will determine the way they see you. If you act ashamed and defeated, people will treat you accordingly. If you show you are still whole, people will regard you as such. You want to project the image of a smart, resilient person. Remind yourself that *you are in power here.* You are taking control and programming the way others think of you.

"Failure is not a matter of shame unless you act ashamed. Failure is not a disease that is contagious unless you act as though you are a carrier," says movie producer David Brown.

When something terrible has happened to you, go to lunch at a visible place. Let everybody see you. Don't act phony, but let them see that you are not in hiding in a cave somewhere crying your eyes out. You are there, and you survived. People who fail today are not lepers. They are in legion numbers, because companies fail, politicians have failed, the world has failed. There is no shame in having struck out.

Shame is an unproductive feeling, but one that can only exist if you grant others authority to judge you. If you take back the judgment for yourself, if you like and forgive yourself, you cannot feel shame. No one can make you a victim but you yourself.

If ever there was a time for deception, it is during the stage of shame. Save your true feelings for one or two close friends; when facing the career world, it is smarter to wear a mask. As Jane Seely, the former network vice-president, says, "Never complain, never explain. Smile and show them you're still a player." Broke, unemployed, and terrified, Jane used to force herself to look people in the eye and tell them, with an optimism she did not feel:

I'm a person on a search. I feel open to anything and full of confidence about the future. Leaving the network has given me just the push I needed to explore a lot of other things. We're working out a settlement right now, and I'm going to take my time and enjoy the searching period.

As she was saying this, Jane's lawyers were suing her former employer and she was frantically borrowing money from her family to pay the rent.

To combat a sense of shame, many people, like Jane, develop a short, well-rehearsed speech that emphasizes the future. Manny Fernandez, a fiery-eyed Cuban whiz kid from Silicon Valley, founded a computer firm called Gavilan ("the hottest start-up company in a very hot market") and with considerably less fire in his eyes watched it cool. Immediately he interviewed to become a partner in a similar firm. For weeks he awaited word. Finally one of the principals, an old friend, called and told him, "Manny, we like you very much, so I'm going to level with you—when you become a star again, call us back."

Shocked at the man's bluntness, Manny realized he had somehow been projecting an image of defeat and would have to develop a better public story. He began immediately.

I started taking people to lunch, and I would always tell them the same thing. "I went to the plate and I swung—three pitches—I did the best I could. I didn't kill anyone, and I'm going to be up at bat again. I'm a Cuban and I know baseball. Your arm doesn't get any better if you don't use it. The only thing that ages well sitting still is wine."

Inwardly Manny Fernandez was bleeding, but by the end of lunch he had them laughing. "Watch out for me, I'm a survivor" was his message.

Sometimes people are so fearful of others' opinions, so focused on their own shame, they refuse to take a "lesser" job. They let their own sense of shame get in the way of what might be an opportunity for them.

The people we interviewed who best turned defeat into success were all unafraid to start someplace, even if that place was "lower" than where they had been. Susan Winer is a case in point. For ten years she and her partner ran a successful Chicago-based communications company. When her partner died unexpectedly, the business, and Susan along with it, began to wobble. Painfully, she let her employees go and, feeling very much a failure, wondered what to do next. What she did, quite simply, was start over. She moved into her home, hauled her Xerox machine into the kitchen ("I used it as a serving board after work"), and single-handedly, from the ground up, built a new company. "At first I thought it was beneath me to lick my own postage stamps," she says. "After a while," she continues, smiling, "I took a certain pride in knowing I was tough enough to survive again at the bottom." Today her new company is thriving. "Sometimes," she says, "you have to be willing to go backward before you can go forward. You have to go to zero before you can get back to one."

Activity, at *any* level, begets another activity and is the best antidote to shame.

(5) Despair

My parents had always said, "Nolan, you can do anything you want if you're willing to try hard enough." I found I couldn't try any harder. There was nothing left in me. I felt absolutely exhausted.
—Nolan Bushnell, after the failure of Atari and Pizza Time

I got into a downward spiral I couldn't stop. It was like being on a bicycle that is going so fast you can't get your feet on the pedals—you can only hold on to the handlebars and try to steer. You just hang on for dear life. You can't get control.
—Ron Perkins,* on being fired as a literary agent

He took me into his room, whereupon he collapsed in a chair, silent, despairing—as I had never seen him. He seemed to have no rebellion or even anger left. He . . . simply said, "I'm finished."
—Description by Violet Asquith of Winston Churchill after he was forced out of the Admiralty

There is nothing new about despair. People have experienced it throughout history and literature. Winston Churchill called it his "black dog." You feel lonely, sad, depleted, unable to get out of bed in the morning, overwhelmed at the thought of getting dressed, and devoid of hope for the future.

Despair can strike whether or not you have failed, and many people who fail never know its anguish at all. What, then, is the connection? In his book *Feelings,* psychiatrist Willard Gaylin says:

Depression occurs when we lose confidence in our own coping mechanisms. We become depressed when we are bankrupt of self-esteem and self-confidence, when we no longer have the sense of our own capacities to insure either our actual survival or the worthiness or value of the life which we can sustain.

In other words, you don't necessarily become depressed upon losing your job. You may be shocked, angry, or fearful, but as long as you believe in your own worth (self-esteem) and as long as you believe in your ability to provide a better future (self-confidence), you will not fall into despair. Despair occurs only when there is a massive ego loss with no subsequent ego gain, and no apparent way out.

The more closely your ego is tied up with your job, the more likely you are to experience despair at its loss. If, for instance, you are a painter, and you are married, and you have children, and you also work at the local library, you are unlikely to feel despair if the library lets you go. The library was merely a job; your self-esteem came from other sources as well. If, on the other hand, you believe you *are* your job, then failure makes you feel, as Patricia Soliman says, "invisible, like I had evaporated, that there was no me." No wonder this woman developed breathing and walking difficulties; they were physical symptoms of her despair.

According to Susan Garcia, a New York outplacement counselor, depression usually sets in some sixty to ninety days after the loss of a job, if there are no strong prospects for another position. The good news, however, is that most depression is self-limiting. No matter what you do—whether you see a psychiatrist, go jogging, or do nothing—unless you are seriously mentally ill, after a period of a few months at most, the depression will usually have run its course.

Strangely enough, one of the best ways to hasten the end of this stage of despair is to give in to it and allow yourself to mourn. There is something tragic and noble about death, so we allow for a period of mourning. Being fired is neither noble nor grand, so we don't feel similarly entitled. As a fired electronics engineer says ruefully, "Nobody gave me permission to stop and cry; they only gave me permission to get going and survive."

Professor Benjamin Barber, a political scientist at Rutgers and an astute social observer, likens the necessary process to the Jewish mourning ritual of "sitting *shiva.*"

"Sit *shiva*" on your job for a while. Get together with your friends and talk about it, think about it, take out the old reports you wrote for your boss that you were particularly proud of, take out your letters of commendation. Really do it, so you won't have it lurking in the background. The power of positive thinking simply doesn't work. What works is embracing your loss rather than running away from it. Then one day you emerge, and the grieving is over, and you're ready to go on.

Benjamin Barber's suggestion is exactly in line with the advice of psychiatrist Yvette Obadia. "The task is to sort out the person from his loss," says Dr. Obadia, who has treated many patients suffering the effects of failure. "You have lost something, certainly, but *you* still exist. If you have a loss, it is important you replace it with a gain. The goal is to reown your positive side." One of the ways to limit your ego loss, she suggests, is to remember the successes you had in your former job. Most of us, she points out, "throw the baby out with the bathwater," remembering only the souring of our endeavors, refusing to dwell on their joys. Professor Barber's suggestion of "sitting *shiva,*" fondly remembering our successes in the job we lost, not only lets us mourn in a healthy way but also enables us to retrieve parts of our ego.

During this period of despair, friends can be an important source of comfort. Over and over again our subjects sounded two major themes: they were shocked at the number of friends who deserted them, and they valued anew the friends who saw them through. For Manny Fernandez, ex-president of Gavilan, the need for friends was even more urgent than a job. "What I needed most of all," he says of the days following his company's collapse, "was someone to say, 'Hey, Manny, you're an okay guy.' "

The very best friend you can have in this situation is someone who has survived a similar experience. For Manny Fernandez friendship came in the form of a man he barely knew, the president of a rival electronics company who himself had had a business failure. Because he understood what Manny was going through, he would call every few days, offering advice or just listening.

Almost as helpful as friends during the stage of despair is a change of activity. Nolan Bushnell, Sharon Timmer, and Ron Perkins all started doing volunteer work. Paul Bowers,* a lawyer who was forced out of his firm when he did not make partner, began cooking. Lou Moore, unable to find work as a television producer, gave herself specific household cleaning tasks and checked them off on an "accomplishment list" when she had finished.

Dan Erkkila, a gentle Greenwich Village composer who suffered a double loss—the breakup of a long-standing love affair and savage reviews of a concert of his music—discovered the healing power of activity quite by accident.

I was walking down the street, not able to talk to anybody, when I happened to pass Crazy Andrew, a neighborhood character I had nodded to a few times but never really talked to. He had a great shock of gray hair and a wonderful beard, and he was as wacky as a flock of very wise looney-birds. He took one look at me and said, "We have to talk. Something is terribly wrong with you. Crazy Andrew knows."

He made me tell him what happened, and then he just took charge. First he said, "You can call me any time twenty-four hours a day, and if I don't hear from you at least every two days, I'm calling you." So we went like that, day by day, for a few weeks. Then Crazy Andrew said, "Now I'm going to give you a project, and you must do it. Paint your house. You're going to change your environment. You're going to give yourself a present. Paint your house any color." He smiled crazily at me at this point and said, "I suggest black myself."

Well, I didn't use black, but I did paint. From morning to night, I scraped and plastered and painted and blotted out everything from my mind except the task of painting. In the morning there was an ugly, chipped wall, and by noon there was a smooth completed surface.

I realized later how wise Crazy Andrew was. He had given me exactly what I needed—an activity to fill up the time; and time is really the only buffer between the hurt and the healing.

Some seventy years before Dan Erkkila, another man, equally despondent, found his salvation in painting. For Winston Churchill, it wasn't random house painting: it was art. In 1915, at one of the lowest points in his life after he had been forced out of the Admiralty, Churchill was introduced to painting by his sister-in-law. He embraced it eagerly. Throughout his long life, it soothed his spirit and led him to discover a principle that helped him in his most difficult hours:

Change is the master key. A man can wear out a particular part of his mind by continually using it and tiring it. . . . The tired parts of the mind can be rested and strengthened, not merely by rest, but by using other parts. . . . It is only when new cells are called into activity, when new stars become lords of the ascendant, that relief, repose, refreshment are afforded.

Clearly there is an enormous difference between the compulsive house painting of Dan Erkkila and the oil painting of Winston Churchill; yet it is not a ridiculous comparison. Like the people in this book, Churchill discovered that one of the best ways to overcome despair is to *give up* at least temporarily the serious endeavor that has defeated you and to turn instead to an easier, more accomplishable, *different* activity. "Change," as this great man says, "is the master key."

• • •

The stages of failure are as predictable as the stages of a disease, and just as survivable. The truth is that almost no matter what you do, you will get through these "negative stages." Everyone experiences them; and although they are uncomfortable, they are not permanent. Like most diseases, they pass, leaving you with scars but with the knowledge you have survived.

How long does it take? When will you begin to feel better? People vary greatly. Some hurry their way through, like State Senator Polly Bacca, completing the process in three days. Others are more like mourners after the death of a loved one, taking the biblically prescribed one year to recover. For most people these negative stages of failure take several months.

What is important is to let them happen so that you can get done with them. The only real danger is getting "stuck" in a stage, remaining so fixated on anger, or blame, or shame, for instance, that you do not get on with rebuilding your life. Gerry Cooney, for instance, was caught in the stage of shame, going over and over his scenario like a needle stuck on a record. Other people get stuck in blame. Years after they fail at something, they still talk about "whose fault it was." Instead of using their energies to construct their future, they focus on the past.

What is important, then, is not to be afraid of each stage of failure you experience, but to accept it and to see yourself as moving along on a process. All these "negative stages" have a positive function. Like the stages of mourning, their value lies in bridging the time between hurt and healing. The sooner you get through them, the sooner you can get on with the positive task of reinventing yourself for future success.

It all seems like a lot of work, you say.

You're right. It is.

III _____
The Ripple Effect

Failure rarely remains a private event. Anything so profoundly affecting our sense of self inevitably affects our behavior toward those around us. We fail, and our immediate world feels the shock.

Daily patterns are changed. Suddenly someone who was never home is home all day long. Turmoil often ensues. Even though you love your partner, his or her constant presence may feel like an intrusion. Children become confused and uncertain when a parent who was always in the office now mopes around the house or is ready at odd hours to play ball.

Not only is this person home all day—he or she has less to say. Events at work, formerly a subject of banter, exchange, concern, or humor, are no longer a part of the conversation. Communication between partners becomes stilted; whole areas of discussion are marked "off limits." There is an emotional imbalance in the relationship as one partner struggles to keep up his good humor in the face of the other's depression.

Tensions run high. People fight more. There is more to fight *about*—money, what to tell the children, why the partner is not being more aggressive getting a job, why the partner is depressed all the time, why clothes were left around the house, why there is no sex—in short, about anything there is to fight about in the lexicon of fights. As failure ripples out, intimacy often breaks down.

• • •

Adversity does not necessarily bring two people closer together, as the old cliché would have us believe. Some couples are drawn closer by misfortune, but many others are split apart.

In general, *a woman's success is more disruptive to the relationship than her failure, and a man's failure is more disruptive than his success.* Most men, it seems, are quite able to accept failure in the woman they love, rising to the occasion with support and comfort. Failure in business does not seem to diminish the woman as a love object. Ah, but let a woman succeed, and there is often havoc. So strongly have we been conditioned to accept the image of a powerful, successful man and a supportive but less successful woman, that if the woman becomes the primary wage earner, the couple's emotional balance often begins to go awry.

But this is only part of the story. As we examined our interviews more closely, we saw that the effect of failure on a relationship did not depend only on whether it was the man or the woman who had failed. Far more important—indeed, the key factor in determining the effect of failure—was the original implied contract between the couple.

THE IMPLIED CONTRACT

Whenever we are seriously enough involved with another person to start living together, an implied contract is struck. Often unspoken but always there, it determines who gives what and who gets what—the basic "deal." It has two parts: economic and emotional.

A sample contract between a highly traditional man and wife would be:

Man: "I will earn a good living for us [economic contract] and be strong at all times for you [emotional contract]."

Woman: "I will not work outside the home [economic contract], and I will be the mother to your children and supportive of your needs [emotional contract]."

A modified version of that contract would be:

Man: "I will be the principal earner, with you as secondary wage earner [economic contract]; I will be the sensible one in this family [emotional contract]."

Woman: "My career will be subordinate to yours [economic contract]; I will be the exciting, temperamental one in this family [emotional contract]."

Another, less usual contract would be:

Man: "I am an artist and cannot be looked to for money [economic contract]; I agree to be volatile and exciting [emotional contract]."

Woman: "I will earn the income in this family [economic contract], and I will be emotionally steady so that you can be volatile [emotional contract]."

Generally couples continue to prosper when both parts of their original contract remain intact. However, that rarely occurs. In the course of any vital, long-term relationship, people and events inevitably change. When one part of the contract—either economic or emotional—is upset, renegotiation occurs. Relationships often survive that. But if both parts of the implied contract are broken, it is much more difficult. If, for instance, the traditional male who promised to be an economic and emotional anchor suddenly loses his job, that puts a strain on a relationship; but if along with his job he loses his aggressive self-confidence and becomes passive and depressed, then he has violated both the economic and emotional bases of the contract. The wife, who kept her part of the deal, screams quietly, "No fair!"

Randy Sher, creator of Chevrolet's National Success Strategies for Women, describes the process:

In my first marriage the deal was that I would work for a time, then make babies, stay home and be the doctor's wife. Well, changing the rules is one thing; but changing the whole deal is something else. I could become an excellent tennis player—that was nonthreatening—but when I started in business and became very successful, that was changing the whole deal. In my marriage there was no way this man could manage that. My success led to our divorce.

Here is the point: *Both success and failure are equally disruptive to relationships insofar as they violate the couple's implied contract.*

Although there are as many contracts as there are relationships, we have selected three types against which to show the effects of failure and success:

- The Strong Man/Supportive Woman Contract
- The Strong Man/Dependent Woman Contract
- The "Equal" Contract

The Strong Man/Supportive Woman Contract

At age forty-three, Donald Cummings* has those open-faced good looks that seem to grow out of the Corn Belt, where he was born, and

Barbara,* with her blue eyes and pageboy hairdo, seems a perfect match. When they took their wedding vows in the small town in which they had both grown up, the unspoken contract between them was strikingly similar to the contract intoned by the minister. "For richer, for poorer," Donald and Barbara promised each other; and even though both were confident their lives would only encompass "for richer," Barbara was prepared to be emotionally supportive of her man through a skinny time or two. When they went sailing together, which they did frequently, she would joke with Donald that if things ever got rough, they could always live together on a sailboat—she would follow him anywhere. The daughter of a pastor, she admired the women's movement ("especially Gloria Steinem, she's so pretty") but thought it had little to do with her own life.

Donald Cummings started in local radio after he got out of the air force. Within a few years he was writing, producing, and broadcasting his own daily news show. By the time the babies began to arrive, five of them, one after another, the Cummingses had bought a sprawling colonial house, and life was, in Donald Cummings's words, "almost too comfortable." He longed for something more.

There was still some part of me that was altruistic, that said I wanted to participate in the "great debate" in Washington. Here I had been writing news, but that wasn't the same thing as shaping the debate itself. I longed to be part of that intelligentsia. I saw myself in the nation's capital, working with some senator to shape policy.

He picked the family up and moved to Washington, D.C. Barbara uncomplainingly shoved the diapers and the bicycles and the children into moving vans and cars. But the doors to the "great debate" remained shut. The best Donald could manage was to set himself up as a media consultant, working eighteen to twenty hours a day on one small campaign after another, never seeing his wife or children, scrambling just to pay the rent.

BARBARA: I hated those times. I never told Donald because what was the use? It seemed like he was always gone, always someplace else when I wanted to talk to him. During that year I remember thinking I wasn't really a wife. I was endlessly a mother, but Donald wasn't there, so how could I be a wife?

Although she never complained to him, Barbara felt deprived—not of money, because that was never the crucial issue to her, but of her ability to be supportive of her husband. Part of their traditional contract was that Donald would be there; and no amount of money (though God knows there wasn't much) made up for the fact that he simply wasn't.

The job at the Fortune 500 company came as a godsend. "We've watched your energy," they said, "and we think you're the man to be corporate vice-president in charge of public relations in our main office in Detroit." Donald couldn't believe his luck. Not only did he have a hefty salary and security; on his better days he could almost convince himself that handling press relations for the company's nuclear power plants was a contribution to national policy.

For seven years he stilled his doubts, and in the seventh year he started to have trouble sleeping. He had just turned forty. Maybe it was that, or maybe the disaster at Bhopal, India, was giving him nightmares. Whatever it was, he found himself disagreeing increasingly with the CEO's decisions on how the company should handle the press.

One day his boss called him in and told him to report to a new location next Monday: the outplacement office. The corporation needed someone 200 percent behind them; they were sure he understood. Donald would be given nine months' full pay and all the help they could offer.

Wounded, shocked, initially angry, Donald was nevertheless able after a few days to term his dismissal "a fair call from their point of view." A man who grew up on the prairie, steeped in the tradition of the lone macho man, Donald determined at first to bear his defeat alone.

DONALD: I thought about my grandfather. He was a simple dirt farmer in central Ohio, and he sat up on a tractor and worked his land until he died at eighty-six. He always told us, "As long as you work hard and know what you're doing, you'll make your own way—that's the main thing, make your own way." So I just decided I'd be like my grandfather—not talk too much about this to anyone and make my own way.

I said to the kids, "I'm not working at the corporation anymore." They were real silent for a while. I tried to act very bright, and I said to them, "Let's make an opportunity out of this, let's not look upon it as a tragedy."

I believe a man has to show his family he is strong. What is the value of sharing one's grief? To involve the children would be to inflict an unnecessary hurt on them. I guess I'm private in the way I do these things.

Barbara felt left out by Donald's stance. Normally undemanding, she now begged him to share with her his feelings; and at last he did, pouring out his uncertainties and fears for the future. While he wasn't exactly proposing that they live together on a sailboat, Donald was nevertheless putting their contract to the test. Up until now he had given her "for richer"; how would she cope with "for poorer"?

The answer was that at some deep level Barbara Cummings viewed her husband's failure as a personal opportunity. At last she would be given a chance to fulfill her role in this marriage. In their early years together Donald had been very self-sufficient, and during his political consulting career he was simply absent. But now, now he was home and turning to her. As the months stretched on—three months, six months, two job offers and two refusals as Donald held out for what he wanted—he stopped going into the outplacement office every day. He had sent out all his inquiry letters, and he could always phone in for messages. At home Barbara would buoy up his confidence and then suggest a movie or perhaps a long walk. Crazy as it was, Donald found himself thinking of this time as a sort of romantic interlude. So did Barbara.

BARBARA: We saw more shows during that period than at any other time in our marriage. Sometimes on our walks, we'd play trivia games—like who could we remember from our class in sixth grade—silly things. Sometimes he'd get worried about finding another job, and then I'd remind him of all the stress he used to feel—having to defend the makers of toxic poisons wasn't easy—and I'd say that now he had a chance to let go of those stresses. Sometimes, when we were walking and I would say something like that, he'd hold my hand. We were close, very close.

Not only did Donald's failure not threaten her—it gave her the chance she had always wanted. In this most traditional of marriages, where she had always taken a backseat to her husband, at last she could come forward and shine. His financial role had always been primary; now her emotional role took center stage.

Just short of one year after his dismissal, Donald Cummings landed a job as vice-president in charge of public relations for a large Detroit bank. Back on what he calls "the success treadmill," he is not at all sure he wants to continue the pace until age sixty-five. More and more frequently now, he confesses, he dreams about living on that sailboat he and Barbara used to kid about. From his experience of failure,

Donald learned the joy of leisure. Barbara, as usual, says she is ready to follow him.

The strong man/supportive woman contract is generally not upset by the man's failure and often—as in the case of the Cummingses—is actually strengthened by it.

The Strong Man/Dependent Woman Contract

Monica Flannagan* was no Barbara Cummings. "Supportive" was a word she gave lip service to, but only if it was in the "for richer" period. "Dependent" was the real word one would use to describe Monica.

As to Frank Flannagan,* he willingly, even eagerly, gave up everything he had to marry Monica. It didn't matter to him that his ex-wife got the house, the children, the cars, and whatever meager savings they had accumulated in their high-living suburban life. At fifty-five, Frank Flannagan knew his priorities. He had the two things any man would want: a beautiful dark-eyed wife who worshiped him and a fascinating job as president of a research company. The rest was incidental. After all, Monica provided a house—part of her divorce settlement—and if there was one thing Frank was sure of, it was his own earning power.

At age forty-five Monica Flannagan still had great cheekbones and the smile of a seductress. Twice married, she had picked up a real estate license along the way, not with any clear ambitions, but because that was what suburban ladies did when their children left the nest. A career was not what she had in mind; Monica's marital life had been a search for a man to take care of her. She thought she had found it at last in Frank Flannagan. He was handsome, earned a fine living, and was terrific in bed.

The implied contract between them was clear: Frank was to be an economic and emotional tower of strength; she could earn a little pin money on the side, as long as she told him he was wonderful and was ready to hop between the sheets at a moment's notice. For three years it worked. Then there was a management change in the parent company to which Frank reported. His longtime boss and protector was replaced. The new man gave Frank a choice: did he want to take his pension plan money out in one lump sum when he left, or would he prefer a yearly payout? Stunned but still able to negotiate, Frank maneuvered a lump sum settlement and one year's continuation of salary.

What follows are excerpts from separate conversations with Frank and Monica Flannagan.

FRANK: I think I handled myself relatively intelligently that first year. Monica and I remained very close. She was commiserative, did all the things a good wife should do. She said, "Things will get better, I know it hurts." She really made me think, I know my spouse cares. Our model with each other had always been total disclosure.

MONICA: I was out of my mind with fear. But I tried never to show it. I was the best actress you've ever seen because I figured, Look, he needs more than anything to know I still think he's King Kong. But it cost me inwardly. I had no one to confide my fears to, not only about whether he would ever make it again as a breadwinner, but a certain terror I experienced about my own mortality and sexuality. Being forty-five was a big thing for me. Suddenly I realized I wasn't looking at endless time anymore.

FRANK: I knew it would be difficult to get another job at my level, particularly at my age, so I thought maybe I could catch on as a consultant. I set up an office at home, and every day I would sit behind my desk. It was a symbol of organization to me. That year I made about ten inquiries within my industry and maybe ten outside the industry, but I was rebuffed each time.

MONICA: For the first year he did absolutely nothing. I think he was just hiding and licking his wounds. I got to hate his desk—he would just sit behind it and wait for something to come to him.

Monica Flannagan now had before her eyes a living, breathing man totally at odds with the image of the person she had married. The Frank Flannagan she had left her husband for was a sexy, self-confident man full of ideas for their future together, in whose arms she could curl up at night and tell silly real estate escapades, stories that paled in comparison to the tales of her husband's derring-do. The Frank Flannagan in front of her could barely get out of their now considerably cooler bed, his "office" had become a desk behind which he sat passively, and "business lunch" now meant a sandwich which Monica Flannagan had to prepare. Panic set in.

MONICA: I looked at this man and said, "He's stagnating, he's going nowhere. But I'm still young and alive." At the end of a year I said, "In God's name, stop—get any kind of a job. It doesn't matter what you get, just get something."

FRANK: I thought I shouldn't just run after anything that first year. I wanted a job in my field. One of Monica's shortcomings is when she becomes angry, she will grab on to whatever she thinks can hurt you.

By the end of the first year of unemployment the power balance of their relationship had shifted. Monica was earning the only money in the marriage. A woman who wanted to be taken care of, she now dictated what checks Frank could write, and she detested him for putting her in this position. The heart of the problem was her rage at having to cope with a new psychosexual image of her husband.

MONICA: Finally I said, "Get out from behind that desk! Stop playing the big executive! Get out and do anything. I don't care if you shovel shit. I don't care if you tend bar or go to Bloomingdale's and sell shirts. I can't carry the whole burden alone. And even if I could, I can't look at you! I don't need a wife—I need a partner."

In Monica's eyes, Frank had committed the unpardonable sin: he had become effeminate.

When they married, Frank had felt he and Monica were kindred spirits, both ready to make an adventure of the last third of their lives; now his financial failure was exposing the gaping differences between them.

FRANK: Monica is very uptight about money. I'm not. Or maybe I have more faith in myself than she does. This causes enormous strain. We're quite different personality types in terms of how we roll with the punches.

We swing back and forth from trying to hang together to trying not to. As a couple you can get fed up with one another. It ebbs and flows, but each time it flows, it flows a little farther.

The implied contract of their marriage was falling apart. If Frank Flannagan wanted it to last, he knew he had to do something. One day, after having been unemployed for three years, he opened the local paper, saw an ad for a researcher in an ad agency, and answered it. It was exactly the same position he had held in his first paid job thirty years ago. In between, he had run a company with hundreds of employees and made a six-figure annual income. Now he was grateful for $6.30 an hour.

MONICA: Frank had trouble telling me about it. I think he was ashamed in front of me, though God knows I felt only relief. He said, "We seem to spend so much time with older people that I think it would be good for me not to lose touch with young people, so that's why I've done this. Besides"—and here his voice broke, he was holding back tears—"I expect I'll get some pleasure out of it."

I took him in my arms and said, "Look, you're going to do better, do you believe that?" And he said, "Of course I believe that." And we just held each other.

Today the Flannagans are still together, but on a tacitly renegotiated contract. Because he is working, even in a lesser job, her husband has regained some of his potency in Monica's eyes, and she is able to be more loving. But her own self-image has been forever changed.

MONICA: I never will be satisfied again to measure my success in terms of the man I'm married to. Never mind that you've made your husband a raging success, or that your children have done this or that, or your sister is your friend. You've been an enabler, but there is no job title "Enabler." If my life changed tomorrow and Frank suddenly had megabucks, I would never, never ever give up my own career, because it's me now—it's my identity.

Monica Flannagan had been not a supportive wife; she had been a dependent wife, looking to Frank not only for emotional and financial strength, but for her own social status as well. In Monica's view, that was the contract; and Frank's business failure and subsequent passivity were complete violations of its basic terms. It is hardly unexpected that the primary ripple effect of Frank's failure was the near breakup of their marriage.

The secondary ripple effect, however, was more surprising. It was the belated birth, kicking and screaming all the way, of Monica Flannagan as a powerful woman in her own right.

The "Equal" Contract—Three Stories

The "equal" contract is one many people say they believe in, but few stop to analyze. Most people believe that an equal career contract means two people having equally high-powered, high-earning jobs. However, the true equal contract is different: it is one in which two people give each other equal freedom to pursue whatever career they choose, regardless of who earns more, and equal emotional support no matter who is "up" and who is "down." Obviously, this is hard to attain.

A couple may start out working at more or less equal levels of income and responsibility. As time goes by, his career takes off; she decides to quit for a while and have a child. Then, perhaps years later, she goes back to work and becomes very successful at just the time he flounders. And so it goes. The equal contract is not a fixed, unchanging thing; it is, or should be, an equal-opportunity contract, flexible, allowing for a great deal of change.

What follows are three stories of relationships in which the couples believed they had an equal contract—but when failure occurred, all had to figure out just how "unequal" they were willing to allow their partners to be. Two couples endured; one did not.

The Carters—"A Foot Race with Each Other"

"We didn't fall in love; we got married," says Vicki Carter. "We only fell in love several years ago." She smiles when she makes this disarming admission, the voice pure Tupelo, Mississippi, the setting, a West Side New York apartment. The Carters are no different from thousands of young couples who get married for all the wrong reasons, not knowing yet who they are or what they want out of life. What distinguishes them from the rest is that, through a combination of Baptist social background, pure chance, skilled psychiatry, and a major career setback, they managed to renegotiate their marriage contract and survive.

Vicki and Ron Carter met at the University of Southern Mississippi when Vicki played the piano at one of Ron's voice lessons. They were driven to the altar less by romance than by the twin prods of convention and desperation. "I was thrilled that someone wanted to marry me—I thought I was fat and ugly," Vicki confesses. Ron is somewhat more philosophical.

RON: We both saw ourselves as oddballs, not really content with Mississippi and small towns, wanting something more, not really clear what that was, pretty sure neither wanted to be teachers, though both of us were educated to do that. We thought that somehow, if we got married, we'd find a miraculous way to get out.

They did. Ron was drafted and sent to Fort Bragg, North Carolina. There, by pure dumb luck, this Baptist music teacher was assigned to the army psychiatrist's office. Put to work on an experimental program for heroin addicts coming out of Vietnam, Ron felt the world suddenly opening up to him. "They gave me things to do that I thought were way beyond me, and suddenly I was doing them, and the doctors were telling me I did them well." Ron reenlisted for three more years.

Vicki, who had thought she would be playing hymns in a Tupelo church, took a job playing rock songs in a nightclub near the base. To Ron this was a Las Vegas–type atmosphere, filled with drunks; to Vicki, now earning money and attention for the first time, it was heaven. Without knowing it, both were launched on their career paths, and so far they were moving along in tandem. Believers in the rhetoric of the sixties, they thought theirs would be an equal marriage of two wage earners.

In their second stint at Fort Bragg, Ron and Vicki began to clarify their career goals. Buoyed by the army psychiatrists' evaluation of him, Ron decided to get a doctorate and become a psychologist. Similarly encouraged by praise from a professional theater director who had come down to the base from New York, Vicki began to spin an age-old dream—she would make it on Broadway. The Carters headed north for New York.

Here their paths began to diverge. Within days Vicki had landed a job as musical director of an off-Broadway show. A few months later this Mississippi girl found herself conducting a rollicking black musical called *Eubie*. It, and she, were bound for Broadway.

VICKI: When I came to New York, you could have put me into the pit of any show and let me play one song, and I'd have gone back to Mississippi and said, "I did it." That was my dream. This was way more than anything I had ever imagined. Here I was conducting a show on Broadway—I simply could not believe it.

At the same time Ron suffered the most devastating defeat he had ever known. Totally convinced he would be accepted for the doctorate program, he was stunned to find himself rejected at Columbia, Adelphi, and NYU. Like his wife, he too "simply could not believe it." His whole purpose in coming to New York, the whole purpose of his life since Fort Bragg, had been to get the degree; beyond that he had no plan at all. With his multiple rejections, he felt immobilized, wiped out, his newfound sense of self-esteem shattered. He sat in the apartment and stared at the walls. Vicki was getting singled out for praise in all the reviews of the show; Ron was becoming a "house husband." The economic contract—which they had always thought would be more or less equal—was now wildly weighted toward Vicki. With that shift, the emotional balance of their marriage, never strong to begin with, fell apart.

RON: I became the classic stereotype of the nagging housewife. I'd say, "What took you so long getting home? Dinner's waiting and it's getting cold." Sometimes I'd already be asleep when she came in. I lost all interest in sex. Frankly, I wouldn't have wanted to be around me then.

VICKI: At first I didn't even notice he was depressed, I was so into my own career. But then I would just walk around the apartment hoping he would go away, because he wasn't fun. I was having fun, and I was angry at him for feeling lousy.

RON: I began to take pot shots at her, like I'd say, "Why on earth did you choose that singer?" Most of our social life came through her work. I'd come along, and her friends would say to me, "What do you do?" and I'd say, "I'm taking a few courses," and they'd turn to my wife and say, "Vicki, tell us about your next show." I felt worthless, useless, uninteresting.

VICKI: I got tired of him being uninteresting and uninterested. I felt he was hanging on to me, living vicariously through my career.

What did "equal" mean? That was the question Ron Carter was wrestling with. As he puts it:

RON: I believed I was this expansive person—that I had this understanding with Vicki: "I can let you be what you want to be." But when she was what she wanted to be—and she was really good at it—I couldn't take it at all. I became an absolute wimp, a mouse.

Earlier in their marriage, back at Fort Bragg, Vicki had thought of divorce but had backed away from it—mainly, she confesses, because Ron would have taken half the wedding silver, and as a poor girl in Mississippi she had dreamed all her life of owning silver. Now she was sufficiently desperate to give up even the silver. She climbed into bed one night, turned out all the lights, and whispered in the dark, "I want a divorce."

What Ron Carter did next profoundly surprised his wife: he sat bolt upright in bed, turned on all the lights, and announced that they were going into therapy. In order to pay for it, he started a low-paying job as a teller in a bank. Vicki was thrilled. The upsetting thing to her about her husband's failure was not his lack of income—indeed, she was quite capable of being the principal breadwinner; what upset her was her husband's passivity.

VICKI: I didn't like it when I was the principal earner, because I wanted him, too, to be motivated and ambitious. I wanted Ron to want to become the president of the bank as badly as I wanted to go to Broadway.

Ron Carter did not become the president of the bank, but he is today its vice-president in charge of corporate executive development. He never did get that doctorate in psychology, but he uses what he learned from the army psychiatrist's office and his own years of therapy in his dealings with people at the bank. "Somehow," he says, "I seem to be a walking mediator."

At just about the time Ron was promoted in the bank, *Eubie* closed, and Vicki experienced her own sense of career defeat. The roles were reversed once again. But at that point it didn't matter to either of them. Success or failure could no longer wreck their relationship, because both of them had developed other "legs" to stand on. They had become more balanced. Work had become more important to Ron and less important to Vicki. Failure had forced them to reexamine their relationship, and in the course of it they fell in love.

The Carters, now parents of a young daughter, have a true equal contract, both helping each other to do what each likes to do best. It is a contract always in flux.

RON: I would love to have the chance to be mother to my child, not just a working father. We talk seriously about my dropping out before our child gets out of school.

VICKI: Right now I like free-lancing and taking care of our daughter, but if I got a really fabulous job offer, I think we'd think seriously about Ron staying home and me going out to work.

The ripple effect of failure on this marriage was to nearly wreck it at first and eventually to improve it significantly. "We're sort of in a foot race with each other," Ron explains, looking fondly at his wife, "not as a competition, but as a kind of wonderful leverage off each other."

The Hermans—Wrecked By Success

The marriage of Jerry and Ellen Herman* was a Jewish mother's dream—in fact, two Jewish mothers' dreams, since it was hard to tell at the wedding who was more thrilled, Jerry's mother or Ellen's. Imagine, two law students meeting in the stacks of the University of Michigan Law Library and now getting married—a double success story!

This was a marriage founded on what its partners *thought* was an equal contract: both were going to pass the bar, work the requisite years as associates in law firms, then become high-earning partners. Success was their religion, and both were orthodox. Equality, in their minds, meant equality of success.

Trouble began almost immediately. Jerry, who had graduated a year ahead of Ellen, took the bar exam and failed. This in itself might not have been catastrophic—many people fail the bar the first time—but the same month he received the news, Ellen was appointed to the prestigious *Michigan Law Review*. Jerry wondered why he didn't feel happy for her. Ellen wondered why she didn't call her friends until her husband had left the apartment. Jerry started studying for the bar again. He and Ellen assured each other everything would be fine.

One night as Ellen was cramming for a big exam the next day, the doorbell rang. Four friends were standing outside holding a couple of bottles of wine. Jerry had invited them over for dinner. "I told you!" he said, noting her surprised reaction. "You just forgot. I thought it would be good for you to take a break." Ellen was furious. The following day, she was forced to take her test with very little sleep. She did brilliantly. Vaguely she wondered if Jerry could be trying to sabotage her; but the thought was so uncharitable, so disloyal, she forced it out of her mind.

The next month it resurfaced, again on a day before a big test. As she sat poring over her books trying to concentrate, her husband, to her astonishment, began literally moving the apartment out from under her. They had "too much stuff," he decided. Someone had given him a free U-Haul today of all days, so this was a perfect opportunity to move out some of their things and "give us more room around here." The fight they had that day was loud and long and used up most of Ellen's studying hours.

The second time around, Jerry managed to pass the bar. However, the starting job he got was not at one of Chicago's top law firms, nor even at a good second-string establishment. Ellen told him it didn't matter. She had just gotten a clerkship to a judge, an appointment that virtually assured her a top spot later. Together they would be all right.

Her mother-in-law disagreed. At a carefully arranged lunch in one of Chicago's finer restaurants, Mrs. Herman, Sr., suggested to Mrs. Herman, Jr.—in a spirit she termed "sister to sister"—that Mrs. Herman, Jr., might do well to fail an exam or two in order to make her son feel better. "You know the way men are," said her mother-in-law, her voice trailing off.

Ellen and Jerry Herman got a divorce just short of two years after their marriage.

ELLEN: I realized he didn't really want us to be equals. He wanted me to be the suburban wife in a station wagon, and he could brag, "My wife is better than yours because she has a law degree."

My success was a double threat: not only was I succeeding, but he was failing. If he had been succeeding and I failing, everything would have been fine. In our society a woman can still come home defeated and a man will say, "That's okay, honey." The reverse doesn't seem to be true.

Today Ellen Herman is a highly successful lawyer, but at a cost.

ELLEN: Look at the most competent among us. Many of the top women attorneys are single. We've paid the price of having no husband and no children, whereas our male peers have children and are usually married. I look at the top-flight professional women I know, many of them living alone, and I wonder, Why has it been so hard for us to incorporate success into our lives?

Whatever happened, Ellen wonders, to the equal contract?

The Sieloffs—The Exec and the Cop: A True Equal Contract

Alice Sieloff is the blue-eyed, blond corporate marketing director for Crain Communications in Detroit, earning a six-figure salary; Norman Sieloff is a cop. Alice Sieloff is in charge of all marketing for twenty-six business magazines and suffers occasionally from executive stress; Norman Sieloff, who has worked on high-risk beats and also has a sideline business selling brass knuckles and bulletproof vests to police departments, worries about only one occupational disease—"lead poisoning from flying bullets." Though Alice earns over twice what he does, theirs is a remarkable example of the equal contract at work. Their basic understanding is born of mutual love and respect: each will help the other to do what he or she wants to do in order to be emotionally and economically fulfilled.

Norman would say all that is high flown, and he and Alice never discussed any such thing. Which is true. These aren't people who talk a great deal about their feelings. A lot of it is unspoken.

ALICE: He's always there. If I'm angry, he'll be angry, too, or he'll be concerned about things I'm concerned about. Norman's just always there.

Norman was an ex-marine working as an insurance salesman when they married, and Alice had graduated from college and taken a job at Hudson's Department Store. He assumed she would work "as a professional woman," and he would be an insurance executive. Both were doing well financially and pulling down roughly equal salaries. But though Norman appeared to be successful, he was really an example of a "hidden failure." The insurance job was just "sell, sell, sell," as he puts it. "One day you're a hero because you've made your quota, and the next day you're a bum and have to start all over again." He loathed the pressure and eventually developed ulcers. The outwardly successful insurance salesman describes his inner feelings:

NORMAN: When I got out of the marines I was in real good shape. Now I was failing as far as physical health. It depressed me. I felt short-tempered. In the first years of marriage, a couple of times I put a fist through the wall—things like that.

When the doctor told Norman to switch occupations to something he really liked, Norman confessed he had always wanted to be a cop. Alice, who had never loved Norman for his social status, applauded his decision. She regarded his "failure" as an insurance salesman as an opportunity for him to change and become happier. Meanwhile, she had become pregnant and was let go from Hudson's. Suddenly, with Alice and a baby at home, and a rookie cop's salary instead of an insurance salesman's bonuses, Norman was not so sure he had done the right thing.

NORMAN: That's when I really felt like a failure, because I wasn't coming up with a family income. I remember going to the police academy with peanut-butter-and-jelly sandwiches, sometimes without the jelly. Only our son and the dog ate right. I was losing weight, and I was depressed.

If in his own eyes Norman was failing financially, Alice was failing emotionally, sitting home and feeling depressed. According to the terms of their unspoken equal contract, by which each would help the other to realize himself or herself, something had to be done. Norman took the initiative.

ALICE: Norman saw I was depressed. He said, "You're supposed to wallpaper, do macramé," and there I was all day in my woolly jammies, watching the soap operas. He found an ad in the paper, under Male Help Wanted, and he said, "This is you: 'Aggressive young man, be your own boss.'"

Prodded by her husband, Alice went back to work. Once again their incomes were roughly equal, the total family income had increased, and both were happier.

NORMAN: We get along better if she's working. I think she would go crazy sitting at home. Also, working gets her to dress up and put makeup on, and she's attractive when I see her. She's not just lying around in a bathrobe watching TV.

Three years ago the Sieloffs' understanding of the equal contract was put to a test. Alice accepted a position as marketing director for all of Crain Communications's business publications, a job that made her "the only woman in the executive garage" and upped her salary to more than twice her husband's. It also put her in the company of many socially prominent people. Ironically, at the same time Norman was "stagnating," as he puts it, in the police department, blocked from advancement by—of all things—affirmative action programs that gave women "his stripes." How did Norman and Alice take all this?

NORMAN: I like Alice's friends. I don't feel insecure with them. I'm outgoing and enjoy parties. I don't really like cops that much. You go to a police party and the cops talk about their last big caper and the wives talk about their last baby, and it becomes very boring. I think I enjoy her friends more than I do mine.

ALICE: Why should I be embarrassed because Norman's career is at a level that hasn't grown? If the positions were reversed, he would have no trouble. Society accepts that. I don't believe a man or a woman has to be a high achiever in order to be successful.

What's the secret? In dealing with failure and success, how have the Sieloffs been able to do what the Hermans could not do and the Carters almost got a divorce doing? One answer is that they love and respect each other. But there is another, more intriguing answer, an aspect to their relationship that is probably what has allowed it to endure: *the Sieloffs separate their economic from their emotional lives.* Norman sums it up wonderfully:

NORMAN: Alice has about three personalities. She has a home personality, a big executive personality, and she has her little-girl personality. When she tries that executive personality on me, forget it.

Alice is allowed to be whomever she wants at work, and so is Norman. She can hobnob with the social register, and he can put handcuffs on thieves. That has only to do with how they earn their living. At home, in their intimate life, in the life that nourishes and sustains their marriage, Alice and Norman drop the work mask. Alice, the big executive, becomes Alice the little girl; Norman, the low-paid policeman, becomes Norman the strong, giving husband. Their sexual selves are different from their work selves.

Norman Sieloff looks fondly at his wife and says, "I feel great that Alice is earning all that money. Why not? I need a new boat."

Most of us forget to do what the Sieloffs do so instinctively. We tend to bring our work personalities into our homes, to let our economic contracts impinge upon and color our emotional contracts. By separating those two parts of a relationship, by valuing the emotional contract quite apart from the economic contract, both partners are less threatened by each other's failure and more able to enjoy each other's success.

THE SEXUAL PATTERN

I would never presume to know what a woman goes through after a double mastectomy. But I think that for a man, the loss of a job, particularly a prestigious or public one, causes you to feel something similar. You feel a definite loss of your sexuality.

—Harold Jacobs,* fired museum director

All I wanted to do was feel better, and the one thing I could always count on to make me feel better was sex. You know my dominant memory of that period between jobs? It's not of writing resumes, making phone calls, or going on interviews. It's of screwing, constant screwing.

—Ron Perkins,* fired literary agent

Some do more, and some do less, but all do differently from what they did before. Since the main seat of sexuality is the mind, an ego blow such as failure almost inevitably affects sex.

Do you use sex as a measure of performance? Or do you use sex for pleasure? Most people never stop to ask themselves that question, but the answer is likely to determine how your sex life will be affected by failure. According to the people we interviewed as well as sex therapists with whom we spoke, there are two common patterns, which correspond neatly to the two different orientations to sex—performance or pleasure.

Pattern One: Decreased Sexuality—The Performance Seeker

This is the man or woman who constantly measures himself or herself by performance—in the office as well as in bed. The important issue to this person is not pleasure in the job itself when at work, or pleasure in the give-and-take of lovemaking when in bed; the important issue is results. Satisfaction is measured by how many orgasms were recorded on an ever-present sexual Richter scale. Hugging, kissing, cuddling, stroking—activities that may not lead to orgasms—never make it to the scoreboard. They do not represent pleasure, only incomplete performances.

While performance-oriented women may report a generalized disinterest, a feeling of being "less sexy" after failure, performance-oriented men have more dramatic problems. Dagmar O'Connor, director of the sex therapy clinic at St. Luke's-Roosevelt Hospital in New York, observes:

Men associate performance at work very closely with sexual performance. Men who have difficulties at work often develop sudden sexual problems. Most of the time it is lack of erection. But it could also be that their anxiety leads to premature ejaculation. Retarded ejaculation is less common, but that can happen, too.

Unfortunately, the equation of performance in work and performance in bed tends to create a self-fulfilling prophecy. "I failed at work, so I'll fail in bed" leads almost inevitably to "I *did* fail in bed," swiftly followed by the harshest judgment of all: "Now I am a total failure."

Sometimes decreased sexual activity is due not to the person who failed, but to his or her partner. Monica Flannagan, the dependent woman described earlier in this chapter, found her husband far less sexually attractive when he lost his job. Even though he was not impotent, in her eyes he had become so because he was not aggressively trying to get a job. Sex became a bargaining chip, a favor she would grant or withhold as a means of getting him to act. "You don't do 'X,' you don't get sex," was her message. She, too, was using sex for something other than pleasure.

But losing your job need not mean losing sex at the same time—nobody deserves that. If you are having sexual problems as a result of a career setback, stop and analyze how you are using sex. Chances are you will see two things: 1) sex has become a measure of performance rather than a delight for its own sake; and 2) you have equated your work self with your sexual self. This is a pattern you can change, once you recognize it.

The answer is to get back to the pleasure principle, or as Dagmar O'Connor puts it, to return to your childish self:

Most of the individuals I see are too adult to be sexual. Sexuality is in a way childish. To roll around and have fun with each other is regressive behavior, and we're lucky to have it. Sex is a pleasure task, not a performance task. We always knew that as children, but we lost it. We become too well trained and too adult.

She and other sex therapists suggest that performance-oriented people who are having sexual problems stop trying to perform. They should kiss, caress, and enjoy one another's bodies without always expecting intercourse. In other words, decrease the performance pressure, increase the pleasure level. Eventually, the change in the way you use sex might even be one of the side benefits of losing your job.

Pattern Two: Increased Sexuality—The Pleasure Seeker

There are people, many people, who walk out of their office like whipped dogs and perform in bed like aroused rabbits. Sex for them now assumes heightened importance: it is a tranquilizer, an aphrodisiac, a marvelous escape from worry, a surefire success arena—in short, sex is everything their careers are not. Some of these pleasure seekers use sex for guaranteed comfort, much the same way a child who has been hurt cuddles up to its mother. Others seek in sex a quick-fix ego gain. By going out and making a conquest, by becoming more promiscuous than they were before, they seek assurance that they are lovable, worthy human beings.

Harold Jacobs* reports that when he lost his job as director of a museum:

I would swing violently from compulsive promiscuity, compulsive sex, to disinterest. On the one hand, I felt concerned, almost compelled to reestablish my manhood. On the other hand, I felt disinterested in anything that had to do with the obligation of sex—which, unfortunately, meant my marriage.

When sex felt like work, like an "obligation," Harold Jacobs failed to get aroused. He was using sex as a means of regaining his sense of initiative, of control, of conquest—restoring in bed an ego that had been shattered at work.

This kind of behavior used to be a male prerogative; it no longer is. At one of the women's groups we ran, there was widespread agreement with one participant's candid remarks:

When I've had a setback in my business I don't feel sexy with my husband. Even though he's nurturing and kind, I feel that he sees me as a failure, and I am therefore not at all attracted. A handsome stranger—now that's a different story! He wouldn't know how miserable I was. I could just be this sexy creature and enjoy the fact that someone wanted me passionately in return. It would be a way to get my power back. It would be a successful experience.

I suppose this is new for women. Our opportunities for affairs have increased so dramatically, especially since we started flying first class.

Women, too, as much as men, can turn to increased eroticism after failure.

Whether you are experiencing increased or decreased sexual activity, the important thing is to remember all of this is normal and temporary. Don't panic, and don't be hard on yourself. Sex can be a great source of pleasure and comfort.

You are entitled to both.

CHILDREN AND INSANITY POINTS

The best way to describe the effect of an adult's failure on children is by explaining a theory we have evolved over the years to explain aberrant behavior in our two families. We call it the "theory of insanity points." "Insanity points" are the free-floating crazy bits of behavior all of us exhibit from time to time, and we believe every family has a fixed number of them—say, ten. Two adults and two children in the same family, for instance, would normally each take two and a half points, displaying a roughly equal amount of crazy behavior. But—and here is the essence of the insanity point theory—when a major crisis strikes one member of the family, the other members immediately cede all their points to the stricken person, leaving the rest of the family now startlingly sane. When mother is having a breakdown, for instance, the children stop fighting and father tunes in. Or when one child displays violently antisocial behavior, the other child immediately becomes a paragon of virtue.

While completely unscientific, the insanity point theory is a useful description of what happens when a crisis such as career failure strikes. Although only the adult has suffered the trauma, its effects ripple out to the children. The adult has grabbed all the insanity points in the family, and children either become suddenly "perfect" or "act out" even crazier behavior than their parents as they struggle to regain their former quota of insanity points. Startling family shifts are frequently seen.

A therapist we spoke with reports the story of Lewis M., who lost his job as manager of a large bank and sat gloomily at home, unable to make phone calls, go on interviews, or be emotionally available to his wife and two teenaged children. A rather passive man married to a voluble, outgoing wife, this colorless male peacock now suddenly spread his feathers and demanded attention. By failing at work, he had seized center stage at home, and his misery was not only attention getting, but dominating. Lewis controlled all ten insanity points.

Traditional therapy can often be slow, particularly if the patient's neuroses provide him a starring role. In this case, the family took matters into its own hands, though unconsciously, and in one dazzling move replaced Lewis with another star. One day, without any warning, his teenaged son had a sudden, severe psychotic episode. Under the insanity point theory, this was a brilliant solution to the father's depression. By manifesting a more serious problem than his father, the son had recaptured all ten of his father's points. The reaction was predictable. Lewis M. was galvanized by his son's psychotic actions in a way he had never been by his therapist's talk. He immediately snapped out of his depression. The family therapist comments:

It's almost as though the family were saying . . . "Thank God you weren't working—what would we have done without you?" The child here almost offers himself up as a victim, letting the father off the hook about the loss of his job, and allowing the father now to become the healer in the drama.

Within weeks Lewis M. had found a job, and—not surprisingly—the son's psychotic episode was never repeated.

The above story is an extreme example of the ripple effect of failure on children—extreme, because certainly very few children become psychotic in response to their parents' failures. However, children are sensitive participants in the family drama, and it would be naïve to think they are unaffected by their parents' tensions.

Failure can become a contagious disease, affecting not only children but all intimate relationships. Husbands, wives, children, lovers, all are touched—unless you are aware of the problem and learn how to limit the contagion.

LIMITING THE RIPPLE EFFECT

How can you limit the ripple effect of failure? What is the best way to protect the relationships you care about?

• Recognize that you are in a "crazy" time and therefore become extra-aware of your behavior patterns. Try to analyze the source of your emotions. If you come home angry one day, kick the dog, and the dog howls, you are apt to think that if only you got rid of the dog, your life would be fine; the problem, of course, stems from your own initial anger. Similarly, after a major setback it is very easy to blame and make miserable your husband, your lover, your wife, your mother-in-law, the children, or the superintendent. It's easy to find targets, but the targets are usually only stand-ins. Take a deep breath and try to sort out reality.

• Try also to analyze what kind of implied contract you have been operating under. If failure is likely to wreck that contract, bring it out in the open with your partner. Failure might make it necessary to re-negotiate your contract, and that might just be a good idea.

• Make no major changes in your personal life. Give yourself time. There is a strong tendency when you are frustrated by work to act "de-cisively" in some other area. Resist it. You've just had a change in your career—don't also change your spouse or your house. You may think you are behaving rationally, but you probably are not. Wait until your career future becomes clear before making any hasty personal changes.

• Spare your mate. Get an objective "sounding board" on whom to vent your emotions and career concerns. This could be an outplacement counselor, a therapist, or a close friend, as long as he or she can remain objective. Though you will want to share some of your feelings with your emotional partner, it is unfair to burden him or her with all your concerns. Frankly it gets boring, and it certainly does not promote romance. A good counselor can help you preserve your most important intimate relationship as well as give you clarity about your own situation.

• Communicate honestly and simply with your family. A man we know said to his wife when he lost his job, "I'm taking off my success mask. I feel vulnerable without it, but that's the way it's going to be for a while." Far from being frightened, his wife was deeply pleased that her husband allowed her to see the face of his humanity.

Nothing is more terrifying than silence. That's why the insanity points flew around in the story of Lewis M. earlier in this chapter. That's why Jerry and Ellen Herman's marriage broke up: they never spoke about what was really bothering them.

Perhaps the most sensitive handling of the effects of a career change was done by John Phillips,* currently a New Hampshire stockbroker, who at the age of forty-nine was forced to give up a lucrative New York position, move to New England, and start out again in a small office, sharing a secretary. At the time, he had four children, ranging in age from thirteen to twenty.

I called a family meeting and told them I had decided to leave the firm. I laid out the whole story for them, not just snippets of information. I told them my income was going to go down substantially, and they knew the money I had made in my prior businesses was down the tubes. I said I couldn't guarantee anything at this point because the future was totally unclear, but it was my philosophy that if I left them with nothing but a good education, I'd left them enough. They didn't ask any questions. One by one, they just hugged me, and they cried a little bit.

Over a period of a week or so I then spoke with each individually. My oldest daughter sat on my lap and said I was a wonderful father and had provided everyone with the important things, and that I shouldn't worry so much. I was deeply moved by their support.

While for most people the ripple effect of failure is a negative force, destroying existing relationships, its power can also be positive. As in the case of the Phillipses, a family crisis can be the occasion for a uniquely moving kind of family reunion.

Someone once said there are two types of tragedies, those that come from *not getting* what we want, and those that come from *getting* what we want. Both success and failure disrupt old contracts and force readjustments. Both carry with them ripple effects—neither is easy.

The stress of failure can drive away spouses, make children behave strangely, attack your own health, and threaten friendships. But not if you are aware of what is going on. Not if you are alert to the danger. You can behave unconsciously, as Ellen and Jerry Herman did, acting out anger against your mate for being more successful than you; or you can wake up and behave consciously, as Ron and Vicki Carter finally did when they began talking about what they were feeling.

None of us can escape change, and with change comes inevitable readjustment. But if we are self-aware, if we monitor our own behavior, if we communicate honestly with one another, the effects of change need not be so painful. The key is to understand what is going on. Once we are aware, there is a chance we can help each other through.

IV

The Male/Female Difference

Ask a group of men to write down the first words that come to mind when they hear "failure," and they are likely to write "death," "ruin," "end." Women are likely to write "stuck," "female," "typical." Ask a group of men to associate words with "success," and you might see "powerful," "rich," "glory." Give women the same task, and the words might include "surprised," "conceited," "alone."

In talking with individual men and women, we began to sense different patterns for each sex in perceiving and handling failure. To pursue this idea, we set up several small-group sessions in various cities. At each, we asked eight to ten high-achieving people of the same sex, all of whom had experienced major career setbacks, to explore the impact of failure on their personal lives. Any doubts about whether or not there were discernible differences between men and women vanished the moment we announced this would be a *group* session: suddenly men did not want to come. Willing as they might be to talk to us individually, they had to be coaxed, reassured, and cajoled into discussing "the F word" in front of other men. But that was only the first difference.

It is, of course, always dangerous to make generalizations, and in all our findings there was a wide range of individual differences. Still, in broad outline, based upon the people we interviewed, the following points appeared so consistently as to seem to us inescapable conclusions.

• *Many women who fail consider quitting work; almost none of the men who fail regard this as an option.*

For some women the reason is a long-delayed baby, for some it's the needs of children at home, and for some it is simply a decision to turn their backs on what they perceive to be the ruthlessness of business. But for whatever the reason, many women who fail either do not go back to work or take a long hiatus. A woman who didn't make partner in her law firm, a woman fired from her job in network news, a florist whose business went under—all these fast-track females within one year of their failures became mothers.

Others—single women who did not quit work for motherhood—also abandoned the job market, at least temporarily. "It was so barbaric, so cruel, so cutthroat, so devoid of any respect for the human spirit, that I just wanted to walk away from corporate America and never come back," says Joanne Harding, a thirty-two-year-old black sales executive fired from UPI. For one year she stayed home rather than go back into the arena where she had been mauled, preferring to collect unemployment insurance, cut back on her expenses, and live off her savings.

Another woman, Elaina Zucker, was fired from her job as an account executive in an ad agency. She says:

I felt so burnt out that the thought of going back to work was horrifying to me. At first I thought I had to, but then I thought, Why? Why not become a dropout? Why not *not* work for a while? I wanted to refuel. I had some savings, and I started going to museums, reading books, seeing friends. I didn't feel guilty about it for a minute.

Though many women we talked to had no *economic* choice—they had to work—unlike men, they felt they had a *social* choice. Abandoning the paid work force did not make them social outcasts.

As for men, even when they had savings or wives who could have supported them, none of them over the age of thirty considered not working, even temporarily. "If you fall off your bike, you don't sit on the ground and cry," said one man we talked with. "You pick yourself up and get right back on again—that's what my father told me." A thirty-eight-year-old ex-publicist who recently opened his own restaurant put it this way:

Remember when Roberto Duran went tapioca in the middle of the fight? He was getting the shit beat out of him, and he just put up his gloves and said, "*No más.*" Well, let me tell you he was finished after that—everyone hated him. They hissed and spat at him. You can't just walk away when they're beating you up, you *can't* say "*no más.*"

What is at stake here is not just social acceptability, the fear of being spat upon by your peers; the underlying fear is loss of sexual identity. You can't say *"no más"*—no more—if your virility, your very manhood, depends on your work. Over and over again men sounded that theme. Not to work was to become effeminate, to "go tapioca," to become as soft as pudding or—God forbid—as a limp sexual organ. Though it is less true of younger men, for most men sex and work are intricately linked.

You *can,* however, say *"no más,* thank you" if you're a woman. You may not choose to—the overwhelming majority of women *did* go back to work after failure—but *not* to work was at least a sexually and socially acceptable option.

• *Men returning to work after failure emphasize their "feminine" side; women returning to work after failure emphasize their "masculine" side.*

It's as if everybody wakes up and gets in touch with the missing facet of his or her personality. Men who have been putting in eighteen-hour office days suddenly realize the emptiness of their lives when they have no office to turn to. Trained to kill competitors with never a thought, they now find themselves grateful for the soothing touch of friendship and feel guilt for the first time at the bodies strewn behind in their own climb to success. Men who have listened only to the sound of their own voice because their own voice was always right, suddenly turn their heads and hear the sweet sounds of others.

From his earliest days in Cuba to his success as a whiz-kid entrepreneur in Silicon Valley, Manny Fernandez had spent a lifetime avoiding any show of vulnerability. It meant being weak and unmanly. But when the computer company he created from his own sense of bravura collapsed around him and a man he barely knew called daily to offer comfort, Manny Fernandez found himself touched in ways he had never imagined. A simple act of friendship when he most needed it suddenly crumpled the macho Cuban veneer. Perhaps he had been too closed, too authoritarian in his computer company, he thought. Perhaps there were other ways to relate to people, even as his newfound friend was relating to him.

Manny Fernandez was not out of work for long, and when he did relocate himself, he brought his freshly gained sense of openness to the new company. "Before, I used to ignore everyone else—I was the boss," he explains. "In my next job I started listening to my staff more, really listening to minority positions for the first time."

A Hollywood studio head had a similar awakening after being dismissed. "For the three years I ran that studio I thought everyone was my friend. The day I got fired, I realized I hadn't a friend in the world," he says. This man started a conscious rebuilding program, investing more of himself in friendships, shedding the trappings of a marriage to which he had long been unfaithful, and looking seriously for an adult mate instead of the starlets he had been casually seducing.

Other men we spoke with took up cooking, wine collecting, gardening, and volunteer work. Children, those intimate strangers they had fathered years ago, suddenly became newfound sources of delight. "The baby changes so much day to day," said a sales manager who had ignored his daughter for the first year of her life, "I'm really going to miss her when I go back to work!" As we were talking, his wife looked on, bemused by this middle-aged Columbus discovering the wonders of his own backyard.

Failure seems to force men to confront the "female" side of their natures, and in the confrontation they often discover unexpected rewards.

Women who have failed, on the other hand, don't prattle of flowers and babies. In fact, they tend to feel it was the female side of their nature that led them astray in the first place. A thirty-five-year-old public relations executive put it this way:

I was always trying to smooth things over, to keep everybody happy, to avoid bad feelings. If someone on my staff didn't do his job, I was eternally understanding. I would move people around to cover for his mistake, rather than face the unpleasantness of dismissing him and getting the job done. As a result I had just about the smoothest, happiest staff in town. I was everyone's mommy. They loved me. Right up to the time I was fired.

Enough with trying to please, these women are saying. What has it gotten us to be open and team-oriented when the guys play it close to the vest and take the glory? Time to toughen up. Listen to the ex-vice-president of a housewares company who had been completely open with her male co-worker until he was promoted instead of her:

You want to know what I learned from it all? I learned that business is war, and if you're going into battle, you don't go in showing your weaknesses.

Never reveal inner stuff to people you're doing business with. As far as possible, remain charming, but get tough when you have to get tough.

A new postfailure credo emerges from these women: Separate your emotional life from your work life. For dollars and cents look to the office; for love and approval go back home.

• *Most women have an easier time coping with career failure than most men.*

If you put all your money in one bank, you would be penniless if that bank went under; but if you had only some of your money in the bank, some in stocks, and some in real estate, the loss of your bank savings would not wipe you out. Traditionally, men have been like the one-bank investor, depositing their identity in the single source of work. Women have always spread their risk, investing themselves in family, friendships, community activities, religion, and also their job.

"I'm a Christian, I'm a feminist, I'm an alcoholic, I'm a married woman, I'm a lover of cats, children, and sailing, and I am also an employee of CBS," says Jane Ross, currently handling outplacement for the network. Like most women, Jane Ross stands on many legs, and although she would be extremely upset by the loss of her job, it would only knock out one leg from under her. She could still stand.

Men, on the other hand, particularly those with traditional orientations, often feel they *are* what they do. They stand with the weight of their identity on one leg and are therefore knocked senseless when their careers fail.

Psychiatrist Willard Gaylin points out, "More men commit suicide over the loss of a job than the loss of a wife or child." Divorce can be withstood by these men because marriage is not the wellspring of their identity. It may be an important source of comfort or nourishment, but when asked who they are, men respond with their job label. That is the insupportable loss, destroying their very sense of self.

The reverse is true for women. They are far more likely to be devastated by the breakup of a marriage than by any failure in their career. In almost the mirror image of men, women find work the added source of nourishment, while marriage is the primary source of stability and identity.

Women have another advantage over men in dealing with failure: they are more easily able to express their emotions and can therefore get through the stages of failure more quickly. Twenty-six-year-old Diane Eskins* was a UNICEF coordinator in Colorado responsible for putting together a major fund-raising festival. When it was not as successful as she had hoped, she was shocked, angry, full of self-blame, and then depressed. How did she handle it? "I went home and cried for five or six days," she reports matter-of-factly, "and then I felt better." Lee Basking,* on hearing that she was fired from her editorial job, says, "It was like I was on fire. All I could do was go home and cry in my bed." Not only did these women cry naturally and easily; both were unashamed to share that fact with other members of the group session. Their emotional expression was unselfconscious.

The men we spoke with formed a startling contrast. In one session, we asked the ten men present to name the person in whom they had confided when their careers failed. Eight out of ten said, "No one." One man shared his feelings with his wife, and one with his brother. Twenty-nine-year-old Mark Levine, a plumbing contractor, confessed, "I could never speak to a woman about financial failure. My role is that of the breadwinner. I'm from a low-income Jewish family, and that's what I was brought up to believe."

Phil Fester, a former pop singer now turned building contractor, attended another of our sessions with Jerry Pushkoff, his best friend. As the evening went on, Phil talked with some embarrassment about how "broken up" he had been to abandon his dream of a singing career. Being a building contractor felt like failure to him, he confessed. His friend Jerry, obviously moved by Phil's admission, then described his feelings at losing several million dollars of his investors' money in a real estate deal. "I literally felt myself turning weak, physically weak, like my legs could not support me. I knew I was going to fail."

There was a silence in the room. Then Phil turned to Jerry and asked, "How come you've known me all these years and I've known you all these years, and we've never talked about any of this shit?"

The day after this session the phone rang repeatedly as several of these men thanked us for giving them a rare forum in which to vent their feelings.

How sad that it should be so rare. But not surprising. In *Loss,* his pioneering work on mourning, psychiatrist John Bowlby connects the way an adult deals with loss to the way his parents allowed him to deal with loss as a child.

The injunctions "Don't cry," "Don't be a crybaby," "I won't love you if you cry" can ... do untold harm, especially when uttered in contemptuous tones. Instead of being permitted to share occasions of fear, unhappiness, and grief, an individual treated thus is driven in on himself to bear his sorrows alone.

Men, it seems, do indeed bear their sorrows alone, far more than women. Conditioned from infancy not to be "crybabies," grown-up men who fail suffer a double pain: not only the sharp stab of defeat, but also the dull ache of emotional isolation.

There is one group of men that does not fit this category, a group we have labeled "expressive men": those males who have consciously sought to develop other sides of themselves, who are comfortable with their emotions, and who draw nourishment, as women tend to do, from many sources. They consist of two subcategories, the "aware post-thirty-five-year-old" and the "younger man."

Ex-senator John Brademas, now president of New York University, fits the "aware post-thirty-five-year-old" group, as do many artistic and creative people. Brademas is unusual for his generation in that he stands on many legs.

Who am I? I know who I am. I'm a Christian. I'm an American. I'm of Greek origin. I'm of Anglo-Saxon Protestant origin. Notre Dame was in my life, and so was St. Mary's. I'm a product of public schools. I'm a Harvard man. I was a member of Congress. I believe in the democratic political process.

Brademas's broad definition of himself enables him, more than most men his age, to deal with defeat. He lost two elections before winning his first seat in Congress and took a third trouncing in his reelection bid for the Senate. Through all this, he was able to separate who he was from what he did in a way that not many men of his generation could.

The other group of expressive men are younger males, those below thirty. Their adolescence ran parallel to that of the women's movement and as a result their consciousness was raised. From that movement they drew a clear lesson: Just as women had the same rights as men in the job marketplace, men had the same rights as women in the emotional marketplace. Exposed all their lives to this philosophy, these younger men tend to be more comfortable than their fathers in expressing emotion and more willing to regard work as only part of their identity.

For the moment, women still have an easier time with career failure than men; but as men continue to redefine themselves along less traditional lines, the picture is changing.

• *Success and failure are moral judgments to women and game calls to men.*

Men look at work as war. If they're not fighting the actual Battle of Normandy at the office, at least they're playing a spirited game of "Capture the Flag." Surprise attack is permitted, aggression is encouraged, you always have to watch your back, alliances are necessary but impermanent, maneuvering for advantage is standard procedure, and at the end of the day personal daring still wins the medal. Over and over, men spoke of "playing business." One described the collapse of his franchise chain as "losing my toys." It was all a giant game, one that could hurt terribly if you lost, but—like all games—winning and losing had nothing to do with *morality*. Even if the game turned nasty, rarely were men morally outraged.

Lee Elman, a handsome man in his late forties, talks of being fired from his first job. At a very young age, he had convinced the Chicago-based investment banking firm of Walter E. Heller to let him create an international division based in New York, where he lived. This division became so successful the national headquarters decided to take it over. They offered Lee the chance to move to Chicago. When he declined, they gave him 120 days to find another job. Here is how he describes it:

They said to me, "We'd like you to go to Chicago and become a big wheel, but if you stay in New York, you might as well leave." It was some kind of a blow to me, but after all, it was an internal political thing. They decided to take over the division I had created, and then they felt, since Elman won't come out here, why should we have Elman? They were very nice about it.

But, you might say, they took over the division *he* had created! And then they fired him! How unjust, how unfair! Lee Elman says none of that. His dismissal, though personally upsetting, seemed in no way unjust or immoral to him; it was merely a game call.

Ah, but listen to the women. "The reason I cried so hard, the thing I really couldn't get over," says a young publicist fired from her job, "was that I felt I was coming from 'good,' so why didn't I get 'good' in return?"

Polly Bergen, some thirty years older than this woman, echoes the lament.

I always thought that if you were decent and good and you did for others and you understood their problems, they would be decent and good and understand your problems in return. I found out I was totally wrong. I think the only way to be successful in business is to be the meanest son of a bitch on the block.

Actress Barbara Babcock, who won an Emmy for her work in *Hill Street Blues,* says of her early years of failure:

I had always been raised, from four generations of military, to believe if you merited it, you would get it, that there was justice in this world. But that wasn't happening for me. I learned the world is not just. I learned the theater and film industry is especially not just. That was the most difficult thing for me to contend with.

How are we to understand these cries of moral anguish? Are these women prophets of righteousness in the corrupt wilderness of American business? Are they pricking our consciences in pointing out that morality does not always, or even often, lead to success? Or is there another explanation? What is behind their distress? The story of Nancy Rainer* is instructive.

A documentary film producer in her mid-thirties, Nancy was one of the most disillusioned women we met. She regarded her greatest success—the production of an investigative documentary on the logging industry, which won awards and changed state legislation—as also her greatest failure. She had done all the work, but her superior, a man who encouraged her to give as much as she could to the film, ended up taking the lion's share of credit. Nancy was morally outraged and totally surprised.

When I realized how he had used me, when I was trying to do this documentary that made things right in the world, I was really horrified. I was working on the *film,* and he was thinking of *credit.*

That she resents her efforts being used for someone else's glory is obvious. But Nancy is saying something more complicated and interesting. In her view, the moral component of what you give should determine the moral component of what you receive. Thus, if you "do good" in the business world, you should be rewarded with "good," or in this case success. This is a particularly female assumption, echoed in the words of Barbara Babcock, Polly Bergen, and many other women we interviewed.

Nancy objected violently to her boss's interest in taking credit for the film while her primary concern was the film itself. But look at the situation from her boss's point of view. Of course he was thinking of the credit. As a man he was groomed to think of his own career advancement as a valid objective. And he understood the political reality necessary for that advancement: it depended in large part on the way others perceived him. Therefore, while he may well have been extremely interested in the quality of the film, he was also vitally interested in what the film could do for *him*.

Why didn't Nancy think that way? Why did she feel it was immoral for her boss to consider his own credit? Perhaps it is related to the interesting fact that when asked to associate a word with "success," Nancy, along with two other women in her group, wrote the word "conceited."

Like many women, Nancy was probably groomed from childhood to think of herself as part of a larger social unit rather than an individual achiever. As a daughter, as a sister, she was taught it was the family good that counted. How, then, does she behave when she is in charge of something? What role model does she turn to, since she instinctively rejects the competitive, highly individualistic male success model?

Although there are still very few role models for businesswomen, the one unequivocal success model that exists for women is motherhood. Consider its criteria for success. A mother must give to others, place the good of the whole unit above her own fulfillment, and compromise to keep the largest number of people happy. Her success is never judged by acts of individual brilliance—that would be unthinkable—but rather by the happiness and well-being of those around her.

Without knowing it, without even giving it conscious thought, Nancy and many women like her, we believe, have incorporated the ideal of motherhood as a behavioral model for business. There are few ideals more opposite than corporate American business and altruistic American motherhood. Imagine a mother firing one of her children because he or she did not measure up to the mark, and you immediately see how ludicrous the comparison is.

Nancy Rainer's outrage at the immorality of business was caused by her confusing the standards of motherhood, which rewards selflessness for the sake of the family, with business, which rewards selfishness for the sake of the enterprise. In the family, as long as you are good and moral, you are loved, without having to *do* anything. In business, it helps if you are good and moral; but to be loved and promoted, you certainly have to *do* something. Furthermore, how much you're loved depends more on what you *do* than what you *are*. Business is about performance more than character; family is about character more than performance. Approval from the corporation is quite different from approval from the family.

Unfortunately, women all too often don't make this distinction. They tend unconsciously to use in business the model of mother-and-family, with the result that aggressive, self-promoting, tough-minded behavior—the very behavior that often leads to business success—is, to them, immoral and deeply suspect.

But it is not immoral to be self-seeking, as long as you do your job well. It is not immoral to dismiss employees if they cannot measure up, even though they tried their hardest. If you bring to business the moral overlay of the family, such behavior may strike you as unseemly; but if you bring to business the moral overlay of war and games—as men do—such behavior falls within the rules.

Kim Carruthers* is a scrappy redheaded lady who has jolted the conservative world of the Fortune 100 company where she works. Worldwide public relations director for the company, she generally manages to confound the men around her because, in the words of one of her colleagues, "She just doesn't act like the other women around here." Kim has learned a few simple truths:

Success is a game. Competition is a game. Money is a game. I like to get in and mix it up and take risks playing the game. I enjoy it when they keep promoting me in this conservative old man's kind of world. Women, because of their conditioning, talk about how hard they worked, or that they gave it their best. Well, none of that counts. Business does not even ask that you do your best or work hard. They ask only one question: Did it work?

Not all women can, like Kim Carruthers, change their moral spots to fit the gamesmanship of male-dominated corporations. Some cling to their moral views of business and, if they find the ethics of large corporations intolerable, leave for smaller, often service-oriented enterprises, frequently run by other women. This rise of female entrepreneurship is one of the fastest-growing trends in American business today, much of it caused by women's moral queasiness at the success ethic in male-run corporations.

• *Sex-based differences regarding success and failure are less pronounced in younger people than in older people.*

A quiet, unheralded revolution seems to be going on in the hearts and minds, and eventually in the work places, for people roughly thirty and under. Instead of looking to work primarily to fulfill material needs—to buy the bigger house or the third car—they are demanding that work provide personal fulfillment. In his study *A New Social Contract in the Workplace,* the eminent social behaviorist Daniel Yankelovich points out that the flower children of the sixties, when forced by economic circumstances to go to work in the seventies, discovered to their astonishment that work could be as fulfilling as leisure. In effect they transferred their inner values to the work place and as a result helped give rise to a new work ethic, one in which personal satisfaction rather than material need is the primary motive. Yankelovich calls this philosophy "expressivism."

Younger people share this work ethic, he reports, *regardless of sex.* As a result, younger men and women do not show the same divergence in attitudes to success and failure as their parents. The young men's attitudes are becoming more similar to the way women's attitudes have been all along. No longer are male strivers measuring themselves only by their paychecks. Unlike their fathers, they are saying work has to fulfill them in other ways; and if their formal work does not do this, they are looking to outside sources of contentment—as women have always done. In *Saturday Night Fever,* John Travolta played a blue-collar version of this expressive philosophy, measuring his success not by his salary in the paint store, but by the flash of his feet on the dance floor Saturday nights. A decade earlier, Dustin Hoffman in *The Graduate* didn't have that luxury. The woman he married might find fulfillment through dancing, if she chose; but at the end of the movie young Benjamin still looked to the nose-to-the-grindstone world of business for his success.

A young couple we interviewed, both doctors, took down their Park Avenue shingles and moved to New Mexico. Rural medicine, varied and intensely personal, would be more rewarding, they felt. A Boston couple, the man a twenty-nine-year-old copywriter and the woman a twenty-eight-year-old corporate graphic artist, had a child whom they saw rarely because of the demands of their careers. "We looked at each other one day and decided we were on some kind of crazy treadmill. One of us—I think it was me," said the father, "just bent over and flicked off the switch." Turning their backs on "successful" careers, they bundled up their baby and moved to the Vermont countryside. He is now a free-lance writer, and she illustrates books. Both have less money and more satisfaction.

Regina Herzlinger, professor at the Harvard Business School, clearly sees a growing similarity of values between young men and women M.B.A. candidates. The men, she notes, seem to spend as much time on child care as the women, and the women seem as comfortable as the men with their power drives.

Nowadays more and more men say, "I'm going to take a year off." None of these people in an earlier generation would have taken a year off from work because their colleagues would have said they had a drinking problem or something like that. Today men are much less loyal to their companies and much more loyal to themselves. Part of the sexual revolution is that not only have women been integrated, but so have men, producing a greater androgyny.

As these younger men and women move closer together in attitudes toward work, both should feel a greater sense of liberation. Men and women living together can, in principle, become emotional and financial safety nets for each other; and when that happens, failure need no longer be viewed as devastation. It can now be seen for what it is—simply one outcome to the challenge of risk.

PART TWO

Reinventing Yourself

T he slate has been wiped clean.

You are back to Start.

It's as if one day you walked out of your old house full of furniture, clothes, and mementos, and while you weren't looking, the door slammed shut. You race back to try the door. No use—it's locked. You wheel around. Ahead of you is a blank room. What do you do? In the first stages of failure—the "negative" stages of shock, fear, anger, blame, shame, and despair—you couldn't look at that blank room. You turned your back on it, preferring to gaze at the locked door, missing all the old furniture, dwelling on what was and would never be again.

But that's over. You've stared at the locked door long enough. You've put in your time being shocked and scared and angry and ashamed and blaming. You've done your mourning. It's time to turn around and look at the blank room in front of you. "Blank" can mean devoid of what was, or "blank" can mean ready to be filled anew. The easiest thing to do is move in the old furniture—repeat your pattern— but you do not have to. You are at a point of choice: even though you feel scared, maybe this is the time to discard the old worn-out stuff and refurnish.

Outright failure is one of the most liberating things that can happen. It possesses a clarity that hidden failure lacks. If before you thought, Maybe I should leave, but there are good reasons why I should stay, or, I'll just keep on trying this a little longer—rejoice, you have had a cosmic kick in the pants.

Visible failure has this enormous virtue: it gets you unstuck.

You are free now to reinvent yourself.

What do we mean by reinventing yourself?

The clearest way to explain is to describe a recent encounter we had with a New York cabdriver named Anthony Abruzzi.* While zigzagging through traffic, cursing with the authority of the genuine article, Anthony confessed to us he wasn't really a cabdriver at all; he was a purchasing agent who had lost his $40,000-a-year job. For eleven months he had been answering advertisements and going on interviews looking for a job as a purchasing agent for $40,000 a year. He had turned down jobs for $30,000 because he felt they were "a step down,"

101

preferring to drive a cab and continue to look. By now, he confessed, his marriage was being affected ("In the bedroom? Forget it," was his rueful comment), but still he persisted. "I'm a $40,000-a-year purchasing agent," he explained, "that's what I am." Why didn't he take the $30,000-a-year purchasing agent job? we asked. Or why didn't he look in some other field? "Because I'm a $40,000-a-year purchasing agent," was his reply.

Anthony Abruzzi is doing to himself what many of us do: he is continuing to define himself by what he was in the past. He is using the powerful tool of language to label himself—"I am a purchasing agent"—and the label, by defining him, limits him. He cannot think beyond it. Over and over again he tries to reestablish himself as exactly what he was, repeating the same behavior, even though it is unsuccessful. As a result of the label he has placed on himself, he remains stuck.

Like Anthony Abruzzi, many of us define ourselves by our failures. We do this because we feel we have no choice. We believe there are no options. The reality is that we *do* have options, but only if we let ourselves see them.

Smart people, when they meet with continued resistance, are able to change and adapt. They are able to do what Anthony Abruzzi could not: they are able to *imagine themselves differently.*

Reinventing yourself is the process of discovering you have options, deciding what you want to be, and having the courage to become that person. Reinvention is the process of taking control of your own life again.

Reinventing yourself consists of four stages:

(1) Analyzing what went wrong in order not to repeat the same mistakes.
(2) Reinterpreting your story.
(3) Relabeling yourself.
(4) Expanding your options.

V

Figuring Out What Happened: The Nine Most Common Reasons for Failure

Each time we fail, we believe there were unique circumstances, and in a sense it is true. Each failure *is* specific. But if you were to go back and write down the scenario of your major reversals, listing all the steps involved, chances are you or a trained oberver would be able to detect a pattern. It's like a song in which each verse has different lyrics, but the melody is always the same.

We have picked what we believe are the nine most common reasons why people fail, though these are rarely the reasons people give when asked. All of us constantly reinterpret our failures. At first we blame other people, then sometimes we cite larger economic forces, and only later, if we are really honest, do we look back to see what parts we ourselves may have played. Yet this scrutiny of our defeats is critical. As one of the people we interviewed commented, "Failure is like indigestion. If you don't confront it and learn from it, it comes up again."

Just as there are patterns for success, so there are patterns for failure. The reasons why people fail are often not as clear-cut as the categories we have outlined would imply, and no one scenario may apply exactly to you. But perhaps you can find yourself somewhere in the following patterns.

POOR INTERPERSONAL SKILLS

This is the single biggest reason for career failure. This is the single most important skill to acquire.

Most people who fail for this reason never realize this is the real cause. They frequently talk of "office politics" doing them in. But "office politics" is nothing more than office interactions among people; so if you have trouble with "office politics," you are really having trouble with your interpersonal skills.

Another way to describe interpersonal skills is to call them "social intelligence." You can have great academic intelligence and still lack this crucial way of being smart. Social intelligence consists of

• Being sensitive to others
• Listening to hear the subtext of what is said
• Giving and taking criticism well
• Being emotionally steady
• Building team support

Dick Toffler* did none of these things for five years and got away with it, and in the sixth year his company failed. Toffler was a *wunderkind* who had built an industrial film company out of nothing. In his early thirties, a man who knew exactly what he wanted, Toffler punched the air with his glasses when he talked and had the annoying habit of always being right. He employed ten people, all of whom admired his brains almost as much as they disliked his personality.

As long as he was solely in charge, his unpopularity did not matter. After all, *he* decided what films to make, *he* brought in the money, *he* oversaw the marketing plan; and although he drove everyone around him ruthlessly ("I'm tough on others," he said of himself, "but no tougher than I am on myself"), he was effective.

All that changed when the industrial film industry went into a decline and Toffler realized he had to be producing movies for television if he wanted to stay in business. He went to Hollywood, armed with seven "high-concept" ideas for television movies. In two days he sold three of them. That was the easy part.

To develop scripts and produce movies, Dick Toffler had to interact with people in a way he never had before. Network executives were not subordinates who had to put up with Toffler's abrasive personality. Unlike his employees, they did not need him; in fact, he needed *them*.

Trouble began when the network turned down the five directors he proposed for his first film. Toffler took this as a personal criticism. He phoned Sam Marsden,* the network's vice-president in charge of movies, and exploded. Did the network not value Toffler's opinions? Did they not know his reputation? How *dare* they not trust him to do his job? (He told friends he wasn't going to be "like all those other ass-kissing producers who just caved in to the networks' pressure.") In the end Sam Marsden got him to hire a sixth director, one the network favored. Toffler made it clear he disagreed with the choice and expected the worst.

He got it. The director was more than just slow and disorganized; he disappeared into his trailer on lunch breaks to snort cocaine. Toffler was incensed. The director's behavior was unprofessional and, since Toffler's company would have to pay any overages beyond the network's agreed-upon budget, the director's weaknesses were actually costing Toffler money.

He had a legitimate complaint. However, instead of calmly presenting the situation to the network and getting them to view it as a mutual problem, Toffler committed three unforgivable interpersonal errors. First he loudly and publicly chastised the director, a tactic that pitted the director's allies on the film location against Toffler, destroying any team feeling and, in the ensuing commotion, wasting half a day of shooting.

Mistake number two: He telephoned Sam Marsden at the network and demanded in a highly confrontational way that the director be removed. Instead of searching for a mutually face-saving solution, Toffler was creating a win/lose situation, leaving himself no room for retreat. Marsden, however, indicated he could not fire this director since the man was a close personal friend of his boss. The network vice-president hung up the phone believing Toffler had understood the subtext of his message: "I'm in a tight spot here, so don't embarrass me with my boss." But Dick Toffler, always insensitive to others, had not picked up the cues.

Toffler now committed his third and fatal mistake: He went over Sam's head and phoned Sam's boss. With that one phone call he finished his career at the network. Sam's boss, the senior vice-president, was nothing if not polite. He insisted the director be retained but agreed that if the picture went over budget because of this director, the network would reimburse Toffler.

Dick Toffler believed he had done everything right. His picture was getting made, the network would reimburse him for the costs, and he "had shown them he was tough." At the same time he hung up the phone believing he had won, the senior vice-president of the network was calling Sam Marsden into his office. In no uncertain terms he told him never to do business with the likes of Dick Toffler again. Marsden didn't need convincing.

The network's check for $100,000 arrived promptly ten days after the end of the shoot. It was the last network check Dick Toffler ever got.

You can get along on brilliance for quite a while, as long as you don't have to depend on other people—if you are a philosopher, a composer, a writer, a scientist, or a painter, for instance. But most of our careers involve interaction, and the simple truth is no one wants someone who is "difficult to get along with."

Mortimer Feinberg, a highly respected executive counselor, says, "People will get you; they will help you fail if they think you are aloof and uninterested or using them as instruments." He tells the following anecdote:

The other day I was at Kennedy Airport, checking my golf bags through to Miami, when I noticed a man near me bawling out the porter. He was calling him a son of a bitch, really giving him a rough time. Afterward I went over to the porter and congratulated him on not meeting the man's anger with anger of his own. He looked up at me and said, "I'm nothing but a Christian gentleman." Then he smiled and added, "That man, he's going to Miami, but of course his bags are going to Kalamazoo."

Dick Toffler was as insensitive to the feelings of his employees and network clients as the man in the airport was to the porter. Like the porter who retaliated by sending the bags to Kalamazoo, Sam Marsden, the network vice-president, never lifted a finger to help Dick Toffler because Dick had been abusive to him. Toffler never built a support team; therefore, although he was always technically "right," people were just waiting for him to fail. He had the intellectual I.Q. to succeed; all he lacked was the social I.Q.

Here is a secret about careers: You can get away with unbelievable mistakes if you are socially intelligent. This is the reason why so many mediocre executives survive violent corporate upheavals. Sensitive in their dealings with others, they are genuinely well liked, so when they make mistakes, their supporters help them recover. Social intelligence is often far more important to career success than academic brilliance.

Specific performance mistakes are forgivable—we all make them—

depending on how you handle yourself. People with high social intelligence admit their mistake, alert others in the organization who may be affected by it, take their share of blame, and move on. They do not let their egos and emotions get into the act. As a result we like having them around. He or she "is a pro," we say about such people, not necessarily because they are so talented, but because they are direct, easy, and predictable to deal with. When they make a mistake, it may actually be used to *further* their careers if the boss thinks, That was a really mature and responsible way of handling the situation.

People with poor interpersonal skills have great trouble taking criticism. Often this is the single biggest reason for their failure. Instead of looking at criticism as information, they regard it as a personal attack. When confronted with a performance mistake, they personalize the situation. Their ego and emotions get in the way. They may become moody, volatile, or angry; deny responsibility, or try to pin it on someone else. Instead of dealing with a business problem, they themselves *become* a business problem. They mark themselves as "prickly," "emotional," "temperamental," and then, never realizing their role in the matter, complain that nobody likes them.

Sometimes a failure of interpersonal skills takes the form of arrogance. People believe they are so valuable they can get away with anything. A few years ago one of the rising stars at a Wall Street investment firm, convinced by his own press reports that he was a genius, made a foolish error. Unhappy over an order from his boss to cut down his staff, the man gave a press interview critical of the firm's management. He believed he was invulnerable, a "golden boy," and that the normal rules of corporate life did not apply to him. They did. After his dismissal, which was instant, this man spent the next year relearning humility.

If you have trouble in the area of interpersonal skills, it is important to analyze what specific problems you have. Some people have difficulty dealing with authority but deal effectively with subordinates. Others are brilliant with authority figures but are unpleasant and arrogant to those beneath them. Still others, like Dick Toffler, are so self-centered they are equally insensitive to everyone. The first step in improving your social intelligence quota is to figure out the areas in which you are weak.

It is a good idea to go to a career counselor. He or she will give you a battery of sophisticated tests to pinpoint your areas of weakness. Or you can ask a good friend who knows you well to tell you honestly how he or she perceives your interactions with others. Once you have identified your problem, you have two choices. You may decide to do nothing about it—in which case you should carefully pick a career where these skills are not essential for your success—or you may decide you want to change.

Change is never easy. We all tend to remain locked into behavioral patterns. But the first step is recognition. After that, you may choose to go to a therapist who can help you alter your patterns, or by diligently analyzing your own behavior, you can go a long way toward improving your social intelligence yourself.

In a study done on the differences between successful executives and those who got derailed short of the top, one participant commented that only two really important differences separated the successful from the unsuccessful: successful people had (1) total integrity and (2) an outstanding ability to understand others. Total integrity in this case means not just honesty but predictability, the sense that people can be relied on to be as they have been and to do what they say they will do. Understanding others means sensing what other people truly feel and need, not just what they say—reading the subtext.

We are all undoubtedly born with a basic amount of raw intelligence, sheer "brainpower." But we are not born with social intelligence; it is an acquired skill. The more you practice, the better you get.

It's not easy, but interpersonal skills, like good manners, *can* be learned.

(2) WRONG FIT

You may not have failed at all. You may simply be suffering from a case of "wrong fit." Maximum success requires a matching up of your abilities, personality, style, and values with that of the culture in which you work. Everyone knows some variation of the story of Karen Silvers,* a woman whose Ph.D. thesis, which she had worked on for two years, was not accepted. Her adviser's derisive comment was that her writing was too "flashy." Karen went into a severe depression for several months. Then one day she had another idea. Why not seek out an environment where "flashy" writing would be an asset? "Flashy" is not necessarily bad, she realized—it's just bad in the context of academia.

Karen went on to become a much-sought-after advertising copywriter.

Reasons for failure in one context are often reasons for success in a different context.

You may be experiencing the following kinds of "wrong fit":

- Wrong environment
- Wrong value system
- Wrong co-workers

Wrong Environment

There are several basic kinds of organizational environments: corporate, entrepreneurial, intrapreneurial (independent responsibility within a corporate structure), partnership, or complete autonomy (as in the case of an artist). Sometimes the real you is in the wrong environment.

David Brown, one of the most successful movie producers in America, was fired from three jobs before he realized what the trouble was. His voice is soft, the eyes twinkle, and a kindly smile plays beneath the salt-and-pepper mustache as he says, "I was raised to be a corporate beast, but inside there was an entrepreneur."

In Hollywood he rose to become number two at Twentieth Century-Fox until he said yes to a picture entitled *Cleopatra.* He was fired.

In New York, he became editor of New American Library and thought he was safe. The owners brought in a new man with whom he clashed. He was fired.

Back in California, he was reinstated at Twentieth Century-Fox and was at the top of that corporation for six years. One day the board of directors decided they didn't like some of the pictures he had approved. They locked him out of his offices. Once again, he was fired.

Each time David Brown was stunned. And each time he never stopped to analyze what had caused him to be fired in the first place. Only after the third time did he begin to examine his working behavior. Why was he always running after corporate jobs, he asked himself, when in the end they held neither safety nor any degree of control over his own fate? Why, when he trusted his own instincts and disliked committee-style decisions, did he seek shelter in a corporate niche?

He thought back to his childhood and the messages he had received. His father, struggling through the Depression, had preached the virtue of economic security. And security resided in the safety of the big corporation, not the exposed world of the entrepreneur. Yet surely the way David had behaved in corporations—being outspoken, risk-oriented, eager to move solely on his own instincts—was more the behavior of an owner than an employee. With a start he realized that, contrary to the teachings of his childhood, *he was at heart an entrepreneur.* As he puts it:

I got to the point ultimately of never wanting the guy in the other office to walk up and down and say, "What are we going to do about Brown?"

I was influenced not only by my own firing but by the firing of others I knew who had given long and faithful service to the corporation and who were let go for stupid reasons. That kind of control over the human destiny, the kind of control corporations have, is terrifying. In the end I decided it was more terrifying than doing it on your own.

Analysis of his failure made David Brown go out on his own, "scared but determined, like Willy Loman, sitting outside offices with my sample case in my hand," as he puts it. Freed of corporate constraints, he went on to make *Jaws, Cocoon,* and *The Verdict.*

He wasn't a failed corporate executive; he was a hidden entrepreneur.

Warren Ayres* was the reverse of David Brown. Just as David Brown was an entrepreneur trapped in a corporation, Warren Ayres was a corporate man for whom being on his own was like dangling in the wind. Ayres, fired from a top job at a leading food goods company, decided to become an entrepreneur. Helped by his impressive reputation in the new product development area, he immediately got contracts from major rivals of the company where he had worked.

For the first year his new enterprise seemed to be flourishing, but by the second year Warren Ayres was not sure where his next contract would come from. His wife said it was because he just wasn't hustling enough new business; but it made Warren deeply uncomfortable to "hustle." His accountant said it was because he was sloppy about getting paid on time; but it made Warren even more uncomfortable to have to press for money. In fact, the whole business of being on his own made him wake up sweating at night.

I just am a corporate person. I like not having to worry about notepads and office supplies, knowing there is an in-house research department and other support systems. I hate selling. All that hyperbole I found unpleasant. I disliked always being concerned about where the next dollar was coming from. Even though I was making more than I made at my corporate job, I couldn't get used to the fact that the money was unpredictable. And what a shock it was not to be able to pick up the phone and say, "This is Warren Ayres from _____," a company which was a household name.

This "wrong fit" story has a happy ending. If you wait long enough in most industries, the people who fired you eventually get fired themselves. After the next management shake-up at his old firm, Warren Ayres got a call asking if he would possibly consider giving up his lucrative private business to return to the corporate field. Warren allowed as how he might make that sacrifice.

Have you heard the phrase "the sweet taste of success"? Well, the Monday I returned to the old corporate H.Q., as I was riding up in the elevator, I actually felt my saliva turn sugary. I strode back into my big corporate office, and I knew exactly what "the sweet taste of success" tasted like.

Warren Ayres, failing entrepreneur, became once again Warren Ayres, corporate success. Same person, right fit.

It is important to ask yourself if you are at heart an entrepreneur, a corporate being, an "intrapreneur," a small-business owner, a lonely creative type, or a potential partner. The first kind of "fit" to examine is between yourself and your fundamental working environment.

Wrong Value System

Sometimes you fail because there is a "wrong fit" between your central values and those of the place where you work.

Almost all of us have one core issue that is most important in our work, one value we would not give up under any circumstances and without which we are constantly unhappy. Rarely do we stop to think about what that value is; but if we work in an environment that is at odds with it, we set ourselves up for unhappiness and failure.

Steve Wozniak (known as "Woz"), the young co-founder of Apple Computer, is a classic case. Bearded, comfortable in blue jeans, from childhood a loner, "Woz" found in the early world of computers a perfect work environment. He spent solitary hours in his garage tinkering with circuitry, writing and rewriting codes, dreaming of a new world dominated by something only he and a handful of other people understood, where the thrill of accomplishment was keen and beautiful and lonely. "All my life I have been totally autonomous, but I had to know that what I was working on had value," he explains. Wozniak's core values were autonomy and social benefit.

As Apple Computer grew from a vision in a garage to a billion-dollar company, Steve Wozniak's values collided directly with those of the company he had helped to found. Profit, not social value, was the central motive, and team management, not lonely genius, was the order of the day. "I just wanted to design circuits I could calculate on paper, all by myself," says Wozniak. "Apple was wrong for me and my style. I got hung up there." Today Wozniak runs a company called CL9 Inc. It consists of a few people in separate rooms thinking of new ideas, and everyone wears blue jeans. He is back in synch with his most important values.

For William Ivers, the ex-investment banker we met in an earlier chapter, the core value was morality. Twice he found himself at the top of large corporations that did not share his values, and twice he failed. The first time, the man who had appointed Ivers to his job tried to take over the company Ivers ran. Although he owed his job to this man, Ivers did not hesitate.

I guess I like to tilt at windmills. I have a Don Quixote complex. I thought the people who were trying to take over the company were raping the public, so I stopped it. Of course my "friend" who had appointed me as CEO and who was heading the takeover attempt immediately had me fired.

I was very upset, even though I knew it was coming. But what could I do? In addition to thinking intelligence is important, I was raised to think morality counts. Stupid, I know, but I'm saddled with a certain kind of morality.

Because of his sheer intellectual brilliance, Ivers was then asked to head a large international investment banking firm. Excited by the challenge, he never stopped to consider the values "fit." Two years later, he was displaced as head of the firm, once again because he refused to do something that was "good business" but that he considered unethical.

I seem to be born different from most people, because I do stand up. It probably has to do with not placing a high premium on capital but putting a high premium on feeling that I have behaved "correctly," as I perceive "correctly." I'm kind of a moralist.

If you listen to people's stories of their careers, or if you were to tape your own, you hear key words over and over again. For some people the key value is "risk"; and these people suffer from "wrong fit" in a staid corporate culture. For others the core value is "doing something worthwhile"; and these people are likely to sabotage themselves if they are not in a mission-oriented job.

Here again a good career counselor can give you a battery of tests that will help locate your core value. If it matches up with that of your work culture, you are less likely to fail.

Wrong Co-workers

It *does* happen. Sometimes the chemistry just is not right. You are normally cheerful and self-confident, but there is something about your boss that makes you absolutely tongue-tied. Or the colleague with whom you interact most often at work is so confrontational that you shout even louder to be heard and can't seem to control the way he is making you behave. Or the secretary you have hired is so intense that instead of calming you down, she makes you more frantic. Or the partner with whom you have gone into business hates details even more than you, and you had counted on him to take over in this area. These are all classic cases of personality mismatch, and any one of them can cause you to fail.

You may be able to talk out the situation with your partner, or urge your secretary to calm down, or establish a different technique in dealing with your shouting colleague. But sometimes your best efforts just don't work. He is he, and you are you, oil and water. In this case, it's time to cut your losses and move on. It's another case of "wrong fit."

There is one rather perverse variation of "wrong fit," which we have labeled the "straight hair/curly hair" syndrome. Much the way the woman with beautiful straight hair contemptuously dismisses this feature and longs only for curls, some people refuse to claim success in their strongest area and willfully insist on doing what they *cannot* do well. What they *can* do well seems as common to them as straight hair. Such people don't know success when they see it; they *insist* on putting themselves into "wrong fit."

Peter Sollins,* a naturally talented comedy director, wants to do only serious drama. Though others find it doggedly difficult, comedy comes so easily to Peter that he refuses to grant it value. Instead of doing what he does best, he keeps running up against a brick wall trying to get jobs as a drama director. Eileen Winters,* a truly distinguished and original cook, has tried numerous other professions rather than become the brilliant restaurateur she could be. Susan Weinreb,* one of New York's most successful interior decorators, only wants to do sculpture because decorating is so easy for her she dismisses it as unimportant. Curly hair always looks better when your own hair is straight.

Straight hair/curly hair people have put *themselves* into "wrong fit." They refuse to see the value of their own natural assets.

If you have failed for any of the above causes of "wrong fit," you are in a way fortunate. Professional career counselors can help you find your "right fit." Once you know where the mismatch is, you can take steps to align yourself with a more synchronous work environment.

(3) THE HALFHEARTED EFFORT: LACK OF COMMITMENT

"Commitment is a problem, because you always feel 'What if I make the wrong choice?' " The speaker is Paul Bowers. At thirty-two, he looks like a model for a "dress for success" book. Tall, good-looking, a ready smile on his face, he is at all times affable and at no time intense. A lawyer who has been fired from one firm because he consistently came in late ("I did silent little rebellions, like coming in at nine-thirty instead of nine"), he has not had any other outright failures, but, as he puts it, "I really haven't achieved my expectations." No wonder. Paul cushions himself against failure by never really trying. If he doesn't put himself on the line, if he stays "cool," if his words say he wants something, but his manner says "not really," he can never be accused of failing. He can always tell himself, "I didn't really care about that so much, anyway."

Like many noncommitters, Paul Bowers is one of those brilliant people who surprise their college classmates by somehow not fulfilling their early promise. At Cornell he chose the "college scholar" program because it allowed him to make up his own curriculum without ever specializing. Later he picked law as a field "because it was versatile." At twenty-one his goal was to be a Renaissance man; at thirty-two he says, "I feel like a jack-of-all-trades and master of none."

He graduated from Harvard Law School in the middle of his class—

"it was a big commitment, but I didn't feel it or treat it as such"—then joined a large firm in California, hoping to specialize in the entertainment department. Somehow it never happened. Did he clearly ask to be placed in that department? "Sure I asked," he says, "but sometimes people tell me I don't speak up loudly enough—my voice occasionally is a little soft." When he did not land in the entertainment division, he admits, "I behaved in an in-between fashion, not telling off the senior partners, but not doing a really good job, either."

Paul moved to New York and joined a corporate law firm. Six months later they asked him to leave because he seemed to lack motivation. "I was upset, but it didn't really bother me that much. I didn't like the firm anyway," he says in his usual half-committed fashion. At present he is practicing entertainment law but is forever discontented.

I told my wife, "I'm going to be a partner here, but so what?" I guess you could say I'm a star at this firm, but I've done it without much effort and without really committing myself. Let's face it—this is the minor leagues, not the major leagues.

Another way of describing the "halfhearted commitment" is to say its practitioners suffer from *fear of failure.* The imaginary terrors of failure loom so large that noncommitters try to prevent failure by not involving themselves emotionally and by avoiding risk. Of course what they are doing, by their very halfhearted actions, is *increasing* the likelihood of their own downfall.

These people are often the "hidden failures" we talked about earlier. They have a job but wonder why they aren't doing better. They try to sell an idea but somehow never project enough self-confidence or passionate belief to draw others into their orbit. They may not appear on unemployment lines, but, like Paul Bowers, they have somehow failed their own expectations of themselves.

Underlying the halfhearted commitment and fear of failure is one of the most basic causes of all failure: lack of self-esteem. To be committed—indeed, to be successful at anything—you have to believe you can do it. You must be able to picture yourself as successful. It is that picture, an internal model of success, that allows you to "disturb the universe" to accomplish your goal. Employers search for this, as much as any job skill, in an interview. People with strong self-esteem speak up and project the picture they have inside their heads, convincing others of its reality. People who lack self-esteem, although they may say all the right things, often say them with a question mark in their voices.

It is a vicious circle: failure destroys self-esteem, and lack of self-esteem promotes failure. So what do you do? If you have difficulty committing yourself because you are afraid to fail, because you don't really believe in your heart of hearts you can do the job, you must first recognize the problem. Then you have to take a long hard look at yourself and decide if you want to change.

Whole industries are devoted to helping you improve your sense of self-esteem. That is precisely what therapy, and to a lesser extent career counseling, tries to do.

If you choose not to attack the root problem of low self-esteem and decide instead to focus on its manifestation—lack of commitment—the first thing to do is simply pick any one thing to commit to. It's not important what it is, as long as it is something you truly believe you *can* do—and work on accomplishing it every day. Like an actor in a play, monitor your voice and actions to be sure you are projecting self-esteem. It doesn't even really matter if you don't feel it. Just as lack of self-esteem breeds failure, the projection of self-esteem promotes success. When people react to you positively, you begin to feel more positive about yourself.

(4) THE WILD CARD: BAD LUCK

Sometimes things happen that you just can't help. You are playing with what you thought was a normal deck, and suddenly you pull a wild card.

Wild cards are the uncontrolled events that can trip up the best of us. Thomas Gray, director of the Office of Economic Research and chief economist for the Small Business Administration, started his own business only after the most thorough research and rigorous planning. When he bought a ranch in California and decided to convert it into a vineyard, he used the most sophisticated economic models. Here was a trained economist who had charted the demise of thousands of small businesses and had access to every tool of the planner's art. Gray and his colleagues did their market research, budgeted accurately, staffed properly, focused their energies on the new business, and had enough cash reserve for even so disastrous an event as a 50 percent drop in

American wine market prices. "We didn't make a single mistake," says Gray. "On paper it was perfect." What no one could have predicted was in that year, due to the strength of the dollar, French wines became so inexpensive in the United States the bottom fell out of the American wine market. Thomas Gray was out of business. "The world turned against me," he says philosophically.

For Manny Fernandez, the man who launched the Silicon Valley computer company Gavilan, the wild card came from Tokyo. Fernandez was entirely dependent upon the Japanese to produce a certain-sized floppy disk, which they had contracted to do, when he was informed one day that the Japanese had run into serious technical problems and delivery would be delayed for nine months. Gavilan's engineers frantically sought other suppliers and struggled to redesign, but even as they were doing that, the entire personal computer industry was starting to crumble. Gavilan's product hit the market in February 1983, five months later than scheduled. By then IBM had become the standard for the industry. As Manny Fernandez says, "No company that got started after January of 1983 ever made it in the personal computer business. We were just playing catch-up ball." Unforeseen bad luck.

Sometimes the wild card comes in the form of a person. One day a stranger appears in your boss's office, and you learn that top-management upheavals have occurred. Your boss has been "promoted," and the stranger is now your boss. Of course this stranger—the wild card—really wants his or her own team. You play an uneasy waiting game, but finally, through no fault of your own, you are forced out or fired. This scenario is particularly common in cases of mergers, where the takeover company implants its own key personnel.

What can you do about the wild card phenomenon? Absolutely nothing. But don't blame *yourself* if it happens.

(5) SELF-DESTRUCTIVE BEHAVIOR

Stewart Unger has the distinction of being fired or walking away from the most jobs of anyone interviewed for this book. Twenty-one times Stewart Unger was hired as a salesman, and twenty-one times Stewart Unger managed to pick a fight with the people who hired him. Each time he knew he was right, and each time was like the first time: he never saw the pattern. Like Stewart Unger, many people helplessly repeat behavior that leads to their own demise. At heart, such people are terrified of success.

A secretive man, rather like the Alec Guinness character in *The Man in the White Suit* who tried to invent the perfect fabric without telling anyone what he was doing, Stewart Unger always managed to get hired. A well-educated, affable man with blond muttonchops, he made prospective employers feel confident he would be a star. Once hired, his pattern was always the same: he worked in secret, getting leads for sales and telling no one about them, dreaming up schemes to bring the company millions of dollars but sharing them with no one. He always imagined the sweet moment, the glorious moment, when "yours truly Stewart Unger" (as he refers to himself) would be a hero.

By living in a fantasy world, by setting ludicrous sales goals for himself, he was safe: no one could have succeeded in Stewart Unger's terms. If anybody gave him a suggestion about changing his performance, Stewart viewed it as an intolerable insult. The fight that ensued led either to Stewart's dismissal or his exit in righteous indignation.

He began working for his father at Foremost Soda Fountains, a supplier of restaurant equipment. One day, without telling anyone, he sold a big order that the company could not deliver, and his own father suggested he get out. Undaunted, Stewart found a job as a salesman for Encyclopaedia Britannica. Six months later, when the company's head of sales suggested Stewart learn the product line more thoroughly, Stewart announced his salary was intolerable anyway, and he left. Connolly Rollagrill was his next stop. "Yours truly Stewart Unger" sold frankfurter machines to ball parks and fast-food operations around the country. The pattern was the same:

I was this secretive guy who was running around trying to make deals on the outside and trying to bring glory upon myself. I never told anyone what I was doing because then I might be criticized. By being secretive, if things worked, I could one day take all the credit and be a hero.

In my head I was the supreme being, capable of all kinds of wonderful things. The rest of the world was wrong. I lived in the World According to Yours Truly Stewart Unger.

At Cardinal Electronics, as Stewart was becoming successful, he managed to have a clash with the bookkeeper. She had been there twelve years, he had been there three months, but he knew better. Exit Stewart Unger. The same pattern was repeated at Poll Eyeglasses,

Swift Messenger Service, Adirondack Chairs, and a dozen other employers. Authority was insupportable, criticism was intolerable, and open disclosure was anathema. Better to nurse the fantasy of secret success than to get out there and really try. Ability was not the problem—he managed to get himself hired and to earn a living through all of this—but each time Stewart blindly destroyed his own success.

He only became aware of his self-destructive pattern when a chance incident occurred: at the age of forty, Stewart, who had never had any family concerns, decided to take on the responsibility of fixing his niece's teeth. His sister could not afford braces for her own child, so Stewart, in an uncharacteristic move, announced he would bear the cost. Before, he had always just squeaked by financially; now he would have to come up with several thousand extra dollars a year. When Stewart's boss criticized him a few weeks later, "yours truly Stewart Unger" rose to his feet ready to escalate matters into his usual full-fledged fight. Then he thought of his niece's braces and sat down again. For the first time he kept his job. And since he had to keep his job, he started to *listen* to some of the criticism. More important, he began to come up with solutions instead of walking away.

At the same time, because he needed extra money, he began to risk carrying out one of his secret fantasies. Stewart's real love was antique watches. Over the years he had begun buying them, vainly dreaming of becoming a famous watch dealer one day. Now, in order to make money for the braces, he actually started selling off his watches.

Today, Stewart Unger is the owner of Time Will Tell, a successful antique watch boutique on Madison Avenue. His niece has straight teeth, and Stewart has broken his pattern of self-destructive behavior.

Many people indulge in less obvious forms of self-destructive behavior than Stewart Unger. Like him, they suffer from fear of success.

Martha Simms,* for instance, a woman who now runs her own catering firm, hopes that she has finally broken her self-destructive cycle. In the past, she had abortive starts at several businesses. After numerous failures she forced herself to do a highly useful exercise: she broke down her behavior into its component steps in order to see the pattern. Step one was the start-up, getting a great new idea. Step two: She told the world about it to get approval and encouragement. Step three: She became so overwhelmed by the details involved to get it going, she called in a partner to help her. Step four: She started to fight with the partner, because underneath it all she really did not want to give up control. Step five: She got rid of the partner and reclaimed the idea. Except by now Martha was tired of it. By the end of step five, the business had failed and she was back to where she'd started. That was the Martha Simms pattern. Once she *recognized* the pattern, she could begin to monitor herself to see it was not repeated again.

Actress Barbara Barrie's pattern, which she did not recognize for a long time, was one of frequent clashes with directors. Each time she thought she was justified, and each time she tried not to let it spoil her performance. Rehearsal periods, however, were often a nightmare for her. It wasn't until the opening of *California Suite,* when she experienced a real failure in her own eyes, that she was forced to recognize her pattern.

The director and I didn't get along because I think he was afraid I wouldn't find the character. He didn't understand how I was working—slowly, trusting my craft. The more he was afraid, the more I had difficulty being free in the rehearsal. One day I dissolved into tears and thought, Well, today they'll fire me, and I hope they do. But they didn't.

Opening night I did not give a good performance. What happened was that all my fears took over. I was just flat. It was like the worst dream, in which you're pushed out on the stage and you say, "Just tell me the name of the play and I'll remember my lines." I don't suppose there were more than twenty-five people in that audience who knew I'd failed, but *I* knew.

Barbara Barrie began to look at her behavior and realize that she, like Martha Simms, was really afraid of success.

Success is very difficult to accept. I was saying to the world, "I'm not really ready for this now." I think people have the will to fail, and you have to be very careful that it does not take over.

The incident drove Barbara back into therapy. With the help of an analyst, she realized she had a long-established pattern of picking fights with directors because she was terrified and then becoming even more terrified when they became angry with her. Usually she surmounted her self-destructive tendencies, giving superb performances, but every now and then her pattern would force her to fail.

The key to breaking self-destructive behavior is, first of all, to recognize that you are engaging in it. Most of us never see patterns in what we do. If you have had repeated career problems, try writing down the particular incidents of the last three major setbacks you have had. Each will be different, of course, but if you look beyond the particulars, you may see a common motif.

Once you see the pattern, you can decide if you want to change. Some people manage all their lives to get away with behavior others find most annoying—the tyrannical boss who terrorizes those around him, the person who is impossibly moody but brilliantly creative, the quiet dormouse who never speaks up and then complains no one listens. If you are very attached to your behavior pattern—if you feel you've "gotten away with it" or that it even helps you to be effective— you probably will not change. But by identifying your pattern, by seeing the repetitions in your behavior, you may decide you could be even more effective if you did change. At least, by recognizing what you are doing repeatedly, you will be proceeding from a position of choice.

(6) TOO SCATTERED TO FOCUS

This is the fatal flaw of the "brilliant failure," the person who has a spectacular rise and an equally spectacular descent. Such people do so many things they end up doing none of them well.

Often this flaw is found in "risk junkies"—people who enjoy living on the edge, like Mona Rockwell, the real estate developer in the first chapter, or Nolan Bushnell, the man who founded Atari. When risk junkies are successful, they are the Midases of industry: everything they touch turns to gold. We—and they—believe their success will never end.

The trouble is, when these people fail, they fail big.

Their basic problem is one that applies to many people: *overextension and, as a result, lack of focus.*

Doug Tyson* got to the point where he no longer remembered how many deals he was involved with. Tan, handsome, a champion swimmer, he was a competitor from childhood. "Very early on, you get approval for one of two things," he comments. "You either are what you *are* or are what you *do*. I was always praised for my accomplishments." So Doug's accomplishments kept growing. He started with one building, which led to two buildings, which led to getting more credit and extending himself into yet more businesses.

I was in the construction business, I was in brokerage, I was in management, I took on a hotel, I was converting apartments. I needed to do everything.

It was exciting. I didn't know what I couldn't do, so I was testing the limits of my capabilities. I used to get up in the morning and see my name in the paper, and that made me feel good. And then I would have to see my name in the paper again to make me feel better. It was always "bigger-better-more."

One day the bank called to inform him he was overextended and his credit was ended. They demanded that he pay back his loans. Doug Tyson, boy wonder, had failed.

At first Doug blamed everybody else. It was the fault of the banks, of the economy, of his staff. Finally, he says simply:

I realized I'd blown it—I'd gone too fast, too far. I didn't have a sense of my own limitations. Instead of saying "I don't do those things," I said, "Why not? I'll do anything." I was just too big for my britches.

By trying to do everything, he had lost focus on any one thing. Whatever problem screamed most loudly for his attention that day was the one he would attend to. "I mistook the *urgent* for the *important*," he says. He had failed to set priorities.

The answer was to refocus, to sort out and narrow down to what he did best—real estate development. He went through several lean years, but by narrowing his focus and concentrating, he gradually rebuilt. Today he is once again a successful New York businessman—but with a much clearer sense of his limits. As he puts it:

Now if the thought occurs to me, Wouldn't it be nice to be in the health club business? I stop myself. I say, "Who wants to do that? I make money doing something else—I don't have to do that, too. Let someone else do that."

(7) Sexism, Ageism, Racism

Many times the "isms"—sexism, ageism, racism—are used as excuses for failure. But many more times they are the real reasons.

Take the case of Marcia Cantarella. Hired to coordinate public policy issues for a Fortune 500 company, she was at first exactly what the company wanted, a black and a female. In a job involving community relations and public image, her double minority status was a plus. As long as she was in charge of giving away money, Marcia fared well.

Dutifully she wore pinstriped suits, mid-calf-length skirts, and a smile at all corporate meetings. Educated at the best schools and highly sophisticated, she confidently believed that "if you do a good job, people will respect your talents." However, when Marcia announced she wanted to stop giving away money and move into a line job where she could *make* money—sales—it was a different story. "I began to find where the male chauvinists and racists lurked," she says.

The president of the company assigned Marcia to the sales manager, who said he was establishing a special field orientation program just for her. On her first day as a sales representative, she discovered her "field" was Bedford-Stuyvesant and Harlem. The sales manager seemed genuinely puzzled by her outrage. Why was she not thrilled by this opportunity? Why would she not want to be in charge of opening up black markets? Marcia tried to explain she did not want to be defined or limited in her career by the color of her skin; she preferred to be judged by her abilities and performance.

Eventually Marcia was made so uncomfortable she and the corporation parted ways. Statuesque and self-confident, she is not bitter about her experiences. "I learned two invaluable things from that job," she says. "Because it was a consumer products company, I learned to listen to the customer, and I learned from the women I worked with what a difficult time working mothers had." Today Marcia has started her own company, called Mom's Amazing, a service organization providing complete support systems for working mothers. Unable to change the corporation's views, she took what was valuable and moved on.

The truth is that sexism, racism, and ageism are extremely difficult to combat and even harder to prove. If these are the reasons for your failure, you *can* battle the issues through the courts. It is one choice. If, however, you have neither the will, the money, nor the time, the only other solution is to create an alternative solution.

For some people that means going into a smaller, more personally run business where your age, sex, or color are not held against you. For more and more people, like Marcia Cantarella, it means starting your own business.

This is especially true if your problem is age discrimination. Realistically, a job loss in your mid-fifties or later means you are likely to have a very difficult time getting relocated. But whereas your age may be held against you in the corporate world, when you are your own boss, age spells experience. Instead of endlessly, and often futilely, fighting a gray-haired battle to get back into the corporate world, why not use the opportunity created by your failure to make a real change? Take a look around your community and try to spot an opening in the service sector. What service have you always wished existed?

Career counselor Mortimer Feinberg tells of an unemployed sixty-year-old executive who started a snow-plowing service because he realized how annoyed he had been over the many winters of his life at being unable to get his own driveway plowed. Another man, fired from a job in his late fifties, always had trouble getting his swimming pool cleaned. Seeing in his own irritation a business opportunity, this man hired college kids who were only too happy to defer to his age and experience. Today he runs a small, successful pool-cleaning company.

Service-oriented businesses generally require little start-up money and lots of judgment and experience. Many people have used the defeat handed them by a youth-worshiping society to discover they are late-in-life entrepreneurs.

(8) Poor Management: Over- or Underdelegation

Management itself is a talent. People fail over and over again because they are either not very good at management or cannot adapt their management styles to the needs of a growing company.

The start-up person is a visionary, a charismatic leader who infects others with the strength of his or her dream. This person gets the money for the venture, hires the first few key people, is generally deeply involved in the scut work, and bulldogs his way through the initially difficult time. Then, as the new company teeters on the brink of success, management problems often arise. The very skills that cause something to come into being—creativity, perseverance, intense personal involvement in every aspect of the enterprise—are frequently the opposite of the skills needed to run the venture once it is launched. Where is it written that a visionary is also a manager? Would anyone have expected Einstein to administer his own lab?

Nolan Bushnell is a case in point. The creative genius behind Atari, he went on to start several other companies: Catalyst, a venture capital company; Androbot, which dealt in personal robotics; and Pizza Time, a large food-chain franchise. Full of his own success mythology, Bushnell never stopped to analyze the nature of his particular genius and to recognize his talent was start-up, not management. "Boredom has always been my biggest enemy," he says candidly. He delegated other people to run the companies he had started and went on to less "boring" pastimes.

The only trouble with delegation is in order for it to work, you have to pick good delegates. And you have to monitor them. Nolan Bushnell did neither. He finally started to pay attention to Pizza Time when "the Klaxon horns started to sound," as he puts it. By then it was too late.

We were emaciated managerially. In a food franchise business, managers can move quickly, due to the competition. I simply had not realized how fragile my management was. Often, when I went to make collections, I would find a nineteen-year-old kid in charge of the store. It was really terminal, and I just hadn't paid attention.

Bushnell had overdelegated and had also obviously picked the wrong delegates. The mistake provided him with the first colossal failure in a hitherto colossally successful career.

Underdelegation can be just as much of a problem. Bruce Mannix* lost his job as director of research in an ad agency because he *had* to do everything himself. When the company was small, his "hands-on" approach was an asset. Bruce was the guy who was always there to check his subordinates' data, and if he rewrote their reports, it was because Bruce, a former writer who had moved up to management, was the best. As the company grew, however, and Bruce supervised a staff of thirty, the same "hands-on" compulsion that had earlier been an asset now led to his downfall. Instead of allowing people to do their work in their own style as long as it was consistent with the company's goals, Bruce had to make everything in *his* style. He could not delegate anything. Data or reports from his staff were double-checked and rewritten in his own words. As a result, the company's work backed up, the secretarial overload grew, and employee morale deteriorated. Bruce simply did not have the management skills to run a larger staff, and finally senior management let him go.

Thomas Gray, chief economist for the Small Business Administration, says that forty employees is generally the maximum number at which entrepreneurs can manage a company alone. Beyond that someone else is usually brought in, and if the choice is not a good one, many companies flounder.

If management is your weak area, it's a good idea to recognize it and shore up your weakness. Mortimer Feinberg tells of one executive who was fired because, while he was a superb broad-gauge thinker, he was notoriously poor at follow-up with his subordinates. In his next job, this executive solved the problem by hiring a secretary whose only task was to carry through and double-check the details he so loathed. In his new corporate spot, he was known as a superb manager.

No one can do everything. If your genius is creativity rather than management and you find yourself, willy-nilly, a manager, by all means delegate—but be careful to whom. If it's your store, don't assume the other guy is minding it. If your talent is "hands-on" operations, either refuse that promotion to management—as Bruce Mannix might have done—or consciously change your style and delegate more. People are not born with management skills, but they *can* be acquired.

(9) HANGING ON

There you are. You know it's time to move on, but you cannot. You have learned everything there is to learn, or you see you will not get promoted, or you sense things are deteriorating. Reason dictates you must make a change. *But you cannot move.* Fear keeps you stuck right where you are. You are "hanging on," waiting for you don't quite know what. For the ax to fall? For someone else to offer you a job? For a sudden infusion of inner courage?

You present a picture of success. You go out to dinner and tell people funny office stories, tales of your accomplishments. And all the while you are talking, you hate yourself. *You* know, no matter what *they* know, that you are deeply disappointed in yourself.

Sometimes hanging on too long leads to outright failure. Instead of leaving on your own terms, when you know you should, you "let" yourself get fired. This happened to Hank Horwitt, who watched wave after wave of his co-workers leave in a major cutback at a large conglomerate. Hank *knew* he should leave, but he was scared. It was easier to rationalize: he didn't have any idea of what his next job would be, and besides, maybe he would escape. Hank Horwitt became a "hanger-on." When he was finally fired—which came almost as a relief—it was far harder to get another similar job because the marketplace was by now overcrowded—with Hank Horwitt's very own co-workers.

Usually, however, hanging on does not lead to clear-cut failure; it is more insidious. Hanging on, being stuck, is the leading reason for "hidden failure." The sense that you somehow lack will, that your life is out of control, that you no longer have power over yourself, promotes a deep inner feeling of disappointment. "I shouldn't be this way," you tell yourself. "Why can't I move?" Even though you are not unemployed, you are not living up to your own expectations of yourself.

Mark Ringheiser was one such "hidden failure." Fresh-faced, with a warm, open smile, Mark seemed to be the American success story. Adopted by a wealthy family at the age of two, he displayed an early, strong sense of aesthetics. As he grew older, he discovered what he wanted to do with his life—design buildings. When he graduated from the Harvard School of Architecture, there was no question in his mind about where he wanted to work: if architecture was his religion, I. M. Pei was its high priest.

At Pei's firm, Mark joined the best and brightest of his generation, and for a while he learned and grew. But architects, Mark knew, if they really believe in themselves, must open their own firms and be their own stars. As time went on, Mark felt increasingly trapped by the luster of I. M. Pei. Life there was glamorous, it was easy, it provided him with surrogate success. And he never had to risk failure. The trouble was he was failing himself. He knew it, and the knowledge made him feel desperate.

There are strengths and weaknesses in a star firm like that. The strength is you learn from a master, but the weakness is metaphysical: you aren't strong enough in your own persona to take the gamble, to go out and be yourself. I began to feel like a runner looking over his shoulder instead of focusing on the hurdle ahead. I believed the only way to solve a problem was to go to Pei and have him solve it for me. My fundamental self-confidence was eroding, and it began to affect my home life.

My wife was very perceptive, and she would say, "How can you work for a firm that keeps changing your designs when you're so good? Why aren't you more assertive?" It got to the point where we could not talk about architecture at home.

I had come up against a stone wall. I realized I was going to die emotionally if I didn't leave the firm. They were going to kill me.

When Mark finally did move—a process that was extremely painful and involved the break-up of his marriage as well—he describes telling I. M. Pei:

The day I walked into I. M.'s office and said, "I've leaving," I. M. looked up calmly and said, "Mark, I've been waiting for this for seven years." Then he added, "There are only two people in this firm I thought would be capable of going out and creating major practices, and you're one of them."

Mark realized with surprise that it was not I. M. Pei who had been keeping him a prisoner—Pei could not have been more gracious—it was Mark himself. In all his years with Pei, Mark Ringheiser's most enduring architectural creation was the box in which he had placed himself.

When you stop to think about it, there really is no such thing as "being stuck." There are always options; it is merely a matter of choosing to see them. If we complain about "being stuck," it's usually because we prefer it to the risk of moving on. There is safety in complaining; there is risk in change. We hang on too long because we are unsure what the next move should be; and rather than face "I don't know," we say, "I'm stuck and there's nothing I can do."

In the "hanging on" state, you put the control of your life in the hands of others. The way to get beyond this is to explore your options—indeed, to develop a confident inner belief that you *have* options. Once you sense possibilities for yourself, you have regained control. At that point you will be able to take action.

FACING THE TRUTH

It can be very painful, this business of figuring out what went wrong. It is much easier not to think about it. But if you don't face your past and determine what *really* happened, all your assumptions about the future may be wrong.

Take the case of Ann Sperry, a New York sculptor whose work was shown for years at a prestigious gallery that went out of business when its owner died. A woman in her early forties, Ann found to her astonishment that she was unable to get another gallery. For two years she went from dealer to dealer, using every contact she had, networking among friends, showing slides of her work, sales figures, reviews she had garnered. Still no one would represent her. She could not understand *why*. Sometimes she told herself the work was no good, sometimes she decided her personality must be abrasive, sometimes she felt the world must be punishing her for her early success. She became depressed and unable to work.

One day a dealer who professed to like her work turned to her and said, "Would you like me to tell you the real truth about why I'm not going to show your work?" Ann begged him to do so. He looked at her levelly. "You're too old." Ann, who was then forty-three, could not believe her ears. The dealer went on to explain that gallery owners wanted either a new "hot" artist whose prices were low and who could be "discovered" by critics and thereby make a name for the gallery; or they wanted a highly established "star." Ann was neither. She was a fine middle-priced, middle-aged artist who provided the dealer with neither top sales nor "glamour." At forty-three she was "too old."

Ann Sperry did not like what she heard. But she listened. All of a sudden the other rejections fell into a pattern. She remembered phrases she had heard from other dealers—"mature work," "classical work," "not what's 'in' right now."

Ann Sperry told herself a painful truth: "The chances are I may never have another dealer in New York City." Admitting this enabled her to change her behavior. She stopped pointlessly going from gallery to gallery. If established dealers would not show her work, she would become her own dealer.

Today Ann Sperry plans and publicizes her own shows. She invites people over for wine and cheese to see her work. While she does not like the business side of art, she has learned how to do it. Ironically, she has never been more successful than since she started handling her own career.

The truth may not be pleasant, but it allows you to proceed from correct assumptions.

• • •

For a while after you have had a setback, the past is all there seems to be. You are rooted there. You think constantly about what happened, revising the scenario time after time. Before you can move forward, it seems, you first have to look back and understand. We are all doomed to be our own historians.

The important thing to do when you have a major setback is to be honest with yourself. You cannot integrate the lessons of failure toward future success until you have frankly tackled the question of *why* you failed. The clear-eyed analytical view, not the emotional surge of blame, is what liberates.

Why do smart people fail? They fail for a whole host of reasons, the ones mentioned here and undoubtedly many more. To fail is really not special—the best people do it. To *learn* from failure is what is special.

The distinguishing fact about smart people is this: Smart people learn.

VI _____

Reinterpreting Your Story

One of the most troubling aspects of failure is that you feel *out of control*. Something was done *to* you, something you did not choose. Even if you knew you should leave your job and were planning to do so within a matter of months, if you were fired, you still feel devastated. Why? Because you did not *choose* it; you had no *control*. You feel the same way if a business fails, or if a creative endeavor is badly received: suddenly you are powerless. Forces outside yourself have determined your fate.

That is what it *feels* like. However, that is not the truth.

Failure makes us feel powerless and casts us into the status of victim. But it does not have to.

Reinvention is the process of regaining power, retaking control of your life. You may feel at your lowest—you are unemployed, uncertain where to go next, your money is rapidly dwindling—but you do not have to remain a victim. Although you may not recognize it, you have the most important tool of all for regaining power: *you have your mind*.

We said earlier that *failure is a judgment of events*. Think through the implications. You lose your job, your show closes, you don't pass a crucial test: those are events, facts. Everything after that is a *judgment* about those events. Everything after that is your *interpretation* of those events. You might say, "My boss hated me," "I was no good," "I never liked that job anyway," or even "I'm glad it's over." Whatever you say is a thought, a way of looking at the event that has just happened.

In fact, the term "failure" itself is nothing more than another thought about the event.

But if everything is interpretation, then it is within your power to reinterpret as well.

If failure is a judgment, and if you are the judge, then you also have the power to alter your judgment.

WHY BOTHER TO REINTERPRET?

Max Sommerfield,* a well-known art director, was recently divorced after a twenty-seven-year marriage. Other people regarded that as a "failure." Max says, "I was married for twenty-seven years. It was a success, and then it was over."

Sharon Poindexter owned her own marketing consulting firm, which after several years went out of business. Here is her version of what others regarded as "failure":

I interpret the closing of my business as an event that caused me to experience feelings I had not experienced before, to see things I had not seen before, and out of which I became a more compassionate person and a far more effective consultant.

Both Max Sommerfield and Sharon Poindexter felt pain and sadness at the break-up of a marriage and a business respectively. But their interpretations of what happened to them gave them the power to move on.

Here is why this step in the reinvention process is important.

• The goal is to feel better. Anything you can do to make yourself feel better is perfectly acceptable. You cannot function effectively, much less joyously, unless you regain a sense of success and self-esteem. Therefore, reinterpreting your own past to put it in the most positive light is simply good mental health.

• There is no "objective" truth to what happened. All stories are told through a narrator, and in this case you are both narrator and audience. If as narrator you constantly tell yourself a negative story, you as audience feel sad and powerless. If as narrator you downplay the negative events and emphasize the hero's accomplishments, you as audience are likely to be inspired. The events have not changed, only the narration. A sports coach whose team is losing in the first half could say to his team at halftime, "You guys really messed up in there, and we're in deep trouble"; or the coach could reinterpret the same facts and say, "Even though we are behind, we have plenty of time to catch up and win." One statement emphasizes past defeats; the other acknowledges past defeats but concentrates on future victories.

• The main reason it is important to reinterpret your past in the most positive, empowering way is that *it works.*

As long as you are stuck in a negative interpretation—"I failed at that job," "I don't have the skills I need and they finally found me out," "I'll probably never get another job in this industry"—you are investing a great deal of time worrying. Worrying can become a full-time occupation. It is highly creative, involving great flights of dark imaginings. In fact, worrying is so creative it can sap your best imagination and energy.

Negative interpretations that lead to worrying can cripple you. Positive interpretations give you energy to go on with your life. In other words, reinterpreting your story *is practical.*

LESSONS FROM ATHLETES

No one knows this better than athletes. Daily they must face what the rest of us deal with only occasionally—defeat. Being scarred veterans of the win/lose business, they have a great deal to teach us.

Julie Anthony, a former tennis partner of Billie Jean King and now a sports psychologist, has worked with many top athletes. She explains how Billie Jean and athletes like her constantly use reinterpretation to regain their sense of power.

Losses are somehow stronger in our minds than wins. Any athlete knows that and has to fight it. You may hit nine wonderful shots in tennis, and if you miss the last shot, you don't remember the nine good shots, you remember the one you missed. The more you mentally rehearse the shot you missed, the more you are imprinting it on your mind. All of us do this—we give more weight to the negative than the positive. The trick is to rearrange events in your mind so that you give the positive an equal chance.

Billie Jean once told me that whenever she misses a shot, she never starts the next point until she has mentally corrected what she did wrong on that shot. She goes over the bad stroke in her mind and analyzes what she did wrong and then actually takes the correct swing in the air so that she wipes out the negative imprint and replaces it with a positive one.

Billie Jean King practices instant reinterpretation, stroke by stroke, on the court. But the technique of recasting things in a positive way has become so important to her that, according to Julie Anthony, she is able to reinterpret even her losses in key matches.

I was with Billie Jean once when she got to the finals at Wimbledon. Now Wimbledon is to Billie Jean like no other tournament to no other person. She had been mentally preparing for it for literally twelve months. She went out and played the finals and lost miserably.

I was sitting in the locker room, and I thought she would probably come back and announce she was going into retirement again or planning to commit suicide. Instead she came in and totally surprised me with her attitude. She was hitting the walls and the lockers and slapping her hands and saying, "God, I can't wait till next year, I'm going to do it next year. I know what I did wrong." She was already correcting her mistakes, psyching herself up to keep playing.

I thought the loss was going to be a failure to her. To her, the loss was simply a loss. That's probably why she was a champion and I wasn't. She could take a loss and not let it get her down. She could rebound quicker and get on with the positive. When she came into the locker room she was already thinking about what she had to work on specifically to improve the deficits in her game so she could win the next game.

Almost all athletes are trained to reinterpret events positively. Bob Butera, president of the New Jersey Devils hockey team, says:

What distinguishes winners from losers is their ability to cope with failure and get beyond it. One of the ways they do that is to concentrate at all times on what they *can* do, not on what they *can't* do. If a guy is a great shooter but not a great skater, we tell him to think only about the shot, the shot, the shot, never about some other guy outskating him. The idea is to remember your successes.

Although athletes are trained to reinterpret things on the spot, within seconds putting their defeats in the perspective of past successes, even those of us who are not athletes can do much the same thing; it just may take us longer. In order for us to do what an athlete does almost instinctively, we must (1) analyze what interpretation we are unconsciously giving events so we are aware of how we are thinking about ourselves, and (2) recast those events to put them in a more powerful, enabling perspective.

Two Women: Two Interpretations

Take the strange cases of Alexis Parks and Helene Shaver.* A comparison of these two highly determined women, both professionals in communications, tells us something about the power of interpretation. One woman has chosen a negative interpretation of her failure, and one has reinterpreted her failure in a positive way.

Helene Shaver is a woman in her fifties, attractive, poised, with an air of being at home with the world. The author of a book on communications skills, she teaches those skills to future diplomats, lawyers, and doctors at prestigious graduate schools in the northeast. In addition to teaching, she has a small roster of clients, mostly presidents of large corporations, who pay her handsomely to coach them on dealing with the media. Nationally and internationally known, Helene is making more money today than she ever has in her career. The *events* of her life spell success. But her *interpretation* of those events tells her she has failed.

Ten years ago she was, in her own eyes, a success—in fact, a star of sorts. She pioneered a landmark talk show for women, one that brought important books to their attention, took up controversial issues, and discussed feelings and ideas in a way rarely done on television. Endlessly and passionately, Helene worked on that show. "I felt it was God's work," she says. When the network canceled her contract, replacing her with a younger woman, she felt like a missionary without a mission, a preacher who had been cruelly ripped from the bosom of her flock. Ten years later, emotion fills her voice when she talks about it.

I got a ton of mail that I could not read because it made me weep. The letters were filled with love and sadness at my going, and all I could think was, If I'm so good and these people know I'm so good and they're the audience, why did I get fired? Everywhere I went, people would say, "Helene, we miss you," and I couldn't talk to them. I couldn't stand still.

I was an artist who was removed from her form of self-expression. The injustice of it made me wild. The betrayal! I gave them the best of myself—nobody read every single book, did their own questions, the way I did—and then to be betrayed by people I thought were friends! How could no one have fought for me?

And there was nothing I could do to fix it. It's not just the loss of a job, it's the fact that there is nothing you can do to fix it. I couldn't counterattack. I was paralyzed, wallowing in pain. All I could do was go home and cry in my bed.

How long did I cry? In a way I've never stopped. I've never gotten over it.

Helene held to her first interpretation of events, that what happened to her was an unmitigated disaster. She never allowed herself to get beyond that first interpretation, even as other events filled her life.

In the ensuing years, she got another job as a host on a less prestigious talk show and after a time lost that job, too; then she decided to turn her talents to writing, teaching, and building her own consulting business. Clients came her way easily. Recognition was frequent. People paid her well and thanked her lavishly. Her business was increasing, and by now she was the author of several books, with a growing reputation. How did she interpret her good fortune? "I hated not using my own language," she says. Television was her language, and—in her interpretation—anything that was not television was failure.

I didn't want to let go. It was like a sore tooth you can't stop touching with your tongue. The only thing that would have satisfied me would have been to come back bigger than ever and knock them dead. I would show them how wrong they were and make them feel sorry.

Today Helene Shaver, by anybody else's standards, is a success. She has money, prestige, a growing business, and is doing work she enjoys. That is the reality of the situation. But Helene's *interpretation* is quite different: in her subjective view, the view that governs how she *feels,* success is seen as failure. As a result, even though she is highly effective, she gets less joy from what she does than she would if she interpreted her life differently.

If she had been able to reinterpret her failure, she might have said to herself, "I am a successful businesswoman and writer." Instead she says to herself, "I am a failed television host who managed to start another business." The difference between those two interpretations is the difference between feeling optimistic and feeling deprived, second-rate. Helene might have said to herself, "Losing the pressure of doing a daily talk show will free me to start a new career in writing." Or she might have said, "I now have a wonderful opportunity to influence powerful people in business." Or she might simply have congratulated herself on her ability to adapt and survive. Instead, she remained stuck in her first interpretation of events, stuck, really, in the stage of anger and blame. Her failure continued to be "unfinished business," like some large lump in her throat that forever kept her from enjoying the taste of future success. If Helene had been able to reinterpret, to change the language of her message to herself, she might have been able to see herself differently.

• • •

Alexis Parks, a tall woman with an open, trusting expression, has the opposite view of reality. For years Alexis has met with defeat after defeat. Determined to start a major national magazine supplement focusing on issues of health and environment, she spent all her own savings as well as years of time, only to be met by constant setbacks. Objectively, Alexis Parks has failed. But she does not interpret it that way.

At first Alexis seems like a flower child from some bygone era; then you sense the focus. A free-lance writer from Boulder, Colorado, Alexis believed she had a mission—to launch a socially important magazine—and, inspired by that vision, she and her daughter moved to New York. Her task was formidable: she had to find writers, art directors, advertisers, and money to start a national magazine; and she knew almost no one.

Using the two or three contacts she had, she began networking. One person led her to another, and that person led her to yet another. In need of advertising help, she bought a ticket to an Advertising Council lunch, saw an empty chair at a table near the podium, and reasoning that this table's occupants would be important, sat down there. Her neighbor at lunch turned out to be the head of a major agency, who was at first held captive by and then found himself captivated by Alexis. She had little money, but she did have something rarer to his practiced eye: vision and determination. "It's like walking on a tightrope through a brick wall," Alexis says of her fierce drive. "You just keep going, and either the wall will vanish, or you become a statistic." The advertising executive offered his agency's services free of charge and sent her to other people.

Somehow, after almost a year of work, investing all her hopes and a lot of other people's money, Alexis put out her first prototype issue. It did not sell. The investors and advertisers all concluded it was a failure. Looking at the same facts, Alexis Parks had a different view.

I realized I had been premature. If I had been smarter, I would have done it differently. I absorbed all the information and said to myself, "If I had known more, I could have done it." The outcome of the first issue convinced me that if I could only hold on, I would prevail.

Unlike Helene Shaver, Alexis Parks saw her defeat as an opportunity to learn. She did not dwell on the negative aspects of it—losing her investors' money, having her own hopes dashed—she interpreted these negative events in a completely positive way: here was a chance to learn.

She went back to work, never for a moment stopping to focus on her failure. In fact, "failure" was a word completely alien to her vocabulary. What others saw as failure was to Alexis merely helpful information, a chance to make corrections, a step along the way to success.

Money became a problem. She had gone through her small savings. She and her daughter were forced to move out of their comfortable apartment into a small, drab place in a poorer neighborhood. "I almost don't see my surroundings," was her comment. "All my energy is focused on the magazine." Consciously she surrounded herself only with positive reinforcement, going so far as to put up slogans on her wall like "Go for it," "Don't paddle backwards," "Take action in spite of fear." She would close her eyes for several minutes each morning and visualize her success, imagining a scene in which millions of people were reading her magazine and feeling better for it.

She went back to the money people. Because she was so positive, she convinced others. The investors gave more, and Alexis went back to work, changing art directors, learning from what she regarded as her past mistakes, revamping the format of the magazine.

At the time of her first interview for this book, Alexis was waiting to hear if she would get an additional $5,000, which she desperately needed to stay in business. Without it, she would not be able to hang on long enough to put out another test issue. In other words, without that money, in common parlance, Alexis would fail. Once again, we learned this was not her view. "If you get the money you need, will that be a success for you?" we asked her. "Yes," she readily agreed. "And if you don't get the money and have to go out of business, what will that be?" we asked, pushing her to what we thought was an undeniable admission. She considered this for a few minutes, then looked up, clear-eyed, and replied, "An outcome."

What a remarkable statement. To Alexis Parks, failure is only an outcome; it is not a permanent judgment, as it was to Helene Shaver. There might well be the nonappearance of her magazine, Alexis admitted—she was not blind to reality—but listen to how she regarded it.

The journey was growth, I've met extraordinary people, and I'm offered jobs continuously. I've been on a total high for the last two years despite the fact that I have holes in my shoes. Look at the contacts I've made, the experiences I've had. And by my being persistent and holding on to the dream, people begin to believe in its reality, too.

You know, some people look at zero as being nothing, and some people look at zero as being empty. I look at zero as an empty space, which can be filled. I haven't got the money for my magazine yet, but I consider that merely a lack, a zero, an emptiness to be filled—not a failure.

Some months later we went back to see Alexis. We learned she did get her money and did put out a second issue. Filled with coupon advertising, this issue depended for its success on the buying response of readers. Without strong returns, advertisers would desert. After waiting impatiently for the returns, Alexis discovered that despite all her efforts, the "outcome" was clear: her vision had not worked.

This time it was harder to remain optimistic. Faced with a pile of debts and a child to support, she went through a period of real depression. She felt unable to give up her dream and unable to move on. As she was trying to sort out what to do next, a major newspaper chain approached her and said they would like to consider reviving her idea and financing it in the large-scale way it deserved. Alexis was thrilled. This seemed exactly what she had been waiting for all those years, and she only berated herself for not having found them sooner. For months she waited as the executives of the newspaper chain considered her two prototype issues and met with her repeatedly. At the end of their consideration, the answer was no.

Alexis felt a sudden clarity. Before, she had been uncertain what to do; but this firm turn-down from people she respected made her see it was in fact time to accept defeat and move on.

When that door closed, it was very clean. There was no depression, because I was convinced they were the perfect opportunity, and when it didn't happen, I could no longer hold out hope that in two months or three months or five months my dream would come true.

I did everything I possibly could to make it succeed, and I did not consider it failure at all. In my own mind it felt finished.

It was over. Alexis started writing her resume. Then, in a real O. Henry twist, the newspaper chain that turned down her magazine

concept offered her a job as vice-president of marketing and communications for their entire operation. Enthusiasm and vision like hers were
hard to find, they realized. Though they did not want her magazine,
they wanted her. Alexis Parks will, in effect, be bringing her vision to
bear not on one magazine, but on this company's existing roster of
forty-four magazines.

Does she interpret the two years she spent trying to launch her magazine as failure?

I consider my two years like time an athlete spends training. I became strong
because I refused to see things as barriers—I chose to regard them merely as
hurdles to overcome.
Maintaining the illusion of success when I had no income allowed me to
expand a network of contacts and allowed people to call me. In retrospect,
everything I learned has made me capable of taking this new job.

For two years Alexis Parks met with "negative outcomes," as she
would call them, and for two years she interpreted those "negative
outcomes" as information, "like getting two M.B.A.'s," she says. In her
mind she did not fail because she did not tell herself she failed. "I refused to see things as barriers," she says. "I chose to regard them
merely as hurdles to overcome."

It is easy to accuse Alexis of acting like Candide, stubbornly seeing
only "the best in this best of all possible worlds." *But it worked.* By
acting like a success—even when she was not—she continued to function effectively and actually helped ensure her own "positive outcome." The newspaper chain believed they were hiring a success, not a
failure. And they were. Interpretation governs how we see ourselves.

If you can choose to see things in a way that frees you or in a way
that imprisons you, does it matter what the "truth" is? Why not choose
the empowering view?

ACTING FROM REINTERPRETATION: A CASE STUDY

Once you reinterpret things, you may actually choose to change your
life. Sometimes casting events in a different light causes you to rethink
your values and make major changes. This happened to Bert Salzman.

Bert, a pixieish man in his early fifties with sad eyes, a warm smile,
and a blue beret perched on his head, can be seen today peddling his
bicycle in the tiny village of Pontlevoy, France, in the heart of the

Loire Valley, stopping occasionally to talk with his neighbors about problems with his fig tree or cucumber vine. By most people's standards, Bert doesn't "do" anything: he cares for his garden, talks to close friends in the village, and is writing his memoirs, which he says "no one will read and that's fine." But Bert is a man who notices with joy the smallest signs of the seasons' changes. He didn't before.

Only a few short years ago, this Brooklyn-born man, who now looks as Gallic as his neighbors, was a frantically busy New York film director, driven by the search for success. He seemed to have attained it in 1976 when he won an Oscar for a short film entitled *Angel and Big Joe,* starring Paul Sorvino. Worldwide television covered Bert's acceptance speech. As he held the statue in his hands, Bert was confident this was only the beginning. His goal was to move from short films into feature films. For one year he developed movie ideas and took them from studio to studio, believing his Oscar would be seen by others the way he saw it himself—as an imprimatur of his talent, a mark that he was "hot." Instead, every idea he proposed was rejected. Studio heads did not interpret the award the way he did. To them, Bert had just done a "nice little short film"—there was no reason to sign him up for a big movie. Bert grew increasingly discouraged and unhappy, and finally—in a move that surprised friends and colleagues in the industry—he announced he was retiring to a small house in France. He and his wife had just enough to live on if they were frugal—a little under $20,000 a year—and he intended never to work again.

Why did he do this? Was his move born out of a sense of failure, as most people believed, or was something else going on?

One way of looking at Bert Salzman's choice is to say he failed as a feature film director. In our society, to give up competing is usually considered failure. After all, Bert is sitting in a village in France. He is not making money. He is not making films. He was not successful in Hollywood. The high-powered world in which he once longed to operate barely remembers his name. Those are the facts. But Bert's interpretation is quite different:

I actually consider my failure to become a feature film director as the beginning of what I consider a saner and more successful life. After winning the Oscar in 1976, I had visions of going right to the top, and when I didn't get there immediately, I began to reconsider my life.

Note that the first thing Bert did when he met with a setback was to stop and analyze what was happening. Instead of blindly repeating his behavior—continuously trying and failing to launch a feature film—he used the opportunity provided by his setbacks to appraise his life.

I realized that very rarely did I have any pleasure in working, because right behind the ideal of success was the specter of failure—what if people hated what I did? As I was making a film I was always looking behind me—I had my attention on failure. So I began a kind of soul-searching to see what I was doing with my life, to find out if I could change it so that it was not so filled with anxiety.

Meanwhile my wife and I had bought a little house in France, and we started going there for the summers. I noticed my life was becoming more sane, that I was beginning to see things from a wider point of view. My wife and I would talk more. I would go for bike rides. There was a kind of peaceful feeling inside, a kind of simple joy in daily living.

Bert was *reinterpreting* what success and failure were all about. Making a film was considered a success; yet he realized it filled him with anxiety. Not working, living a peaceful life, was considered a failure; yet he realized it made him feel "sane." Bert's reappraisal led to his developing another option: he could change his life entirely.

A stranger visiting Bert asks, with the prejudices of a success-oriented American, "But what do you *do* all day?"

Bert's answer is simple yet profound. He says with a smile, "My *life* is my career."

Is Bert Salzman a success or a failure? To many people the nonattainment of his goal of becoming a feature film director marks him a failure. In fact, Bert himself, for one desperate year in Hollywood, so judged himself. It was only when he *reinterpreted* the events of his life and acted on it by moving to France that his life felt to him like a success. Instead of saying, "I'm an unsuccessful feature film director," Bert told himself, "I am a successful human being." Today, instead of saying, "I am unemployed," he says, "My life is my career."

Listening to Your Child-Song

All of us think we function in the present. In fact, we are forever listening to melodies from the past. Our interpretation of events does not emerge full blown and logically from the facts of the moment. We see what is happening today through a complex intertwining of experiences, fears, loves, and memories from the past. Of all these influences on our perception, perhaps most important are those messages imprinted upon us in the impressionable years of childhood. Often passed on subliminally, they nevertheless remain forever with us, unconsciously but strongly coloring the present.

They are "child-songs," melodies from the time we were powerless. In failure, when once again we feel powerless, their tune runs through our head. Before you can reinterpret your story, you must be aware of your own child-song, to see what role it is playing in your life.

Patricia Soliman, the former head of a large publishing house, developed violent physical symptoms when she was edged out of her job. Why was she so particularly devastated by failure? What was operating? When she thought about it, Patricia realized that she was perceiving her present experience in the light of her early child-song, and she then began to analyze the melody she was carrying around in her head:

I've always been a compulsive overachiever. I always had to be the best in order to be loved. I was not a boy, therefore I had to do it twice over. When I married, I felt that my husband, like my father, could only handle me when I was a winner, that he couldn't deal with me when I was needy, when I was in trouble.

I understood that the only way you were loved was when you won. You shored up others, you gave to others, but you were only loved when you were a winner. When I lost my job, this song was playing very loud in the wings.

Patricia Soliman's early message, echoing in her ear, gave her an exaggerated perception of the danger she faced. Her message from childhood told her that defeat also meant the loss of love. No wonder she reacted so violently. Once she saw that her child-song was only that, a song from childhood and not a present-day chorus, she could put her setback in proper perspective.

Dorothea Winston, a real estate broker who used to own a design firm, attributes the failure of her previous business to her insufficient knowledge of marketing and finance. Instead of asking for help in those areas, she tried to get by on her instincts. Her reluctance to ask questions was prompted by the fear that she would appear stupid if she didn't have all the answers. So she remained silent, the world thought she was competent, and her business failed. In retrospect, Dorothea realized she, too, had been listening to a child-song.

I was always told, "Children should be seen and not heard," "Look pretty, but don't open your mouth." Implicit in that was, "Otherwise they'll find out you're a dumb broad."

Dorothea misperceived and misinterpreted the business situation because of childhood messages that colored her view.

Doug Tyson, the real estate wizard we met in the last chapter, was unable to get past his failure until he had sorted out his child-song. For him it was simple but controlling: "You're only loved for what you accomplish, not who you are." So Doug built ever bigger buildings and tried to accomplish so much he failed completely. Reinterpreting his life meant first of all recognizing that he was listening to his child-song rather than to his own good sense.

Child-songs never go away. They are part of the psychological baggage you carry with you. But you *can* turn a deaf ear to them.

Ask yourself what messages you received from childhood. Try to see how they influence the way you perceive your situation today. Once you recognize your own child-song, you can begin to look at your behavior with a healthy suspicion and ask: Am I interpreting events accurately, or am I hearing things through the noise of a melody in my head?

REINTERPRETING YOUR OWN STORY

Here is how to reinterpret your own story:

- Write down the barest statement of fact, seven words or less. "I got fired," "The play closed," or "I failed the test" are all examples of simple fact statements.
- Write down, tape-record, or tell someone your version of that event.
- Analyze your version for negative, self-defeating assumptions. What are the hidden messages? Root them out.
- Reinterpret your story—that is, change the language to cast it in a more positive light.

The following story of Charles Gill* will show how the process works. Charles, a man hired as the director of compensation and benefits for a large corporation, had his job cut in half. The company felt he was good only on the benefits side and performed poorly in the area of worker compensation. Although Charles was not fired, he felt humiliated, depressed, and trapped. He was convinced others were laughing at him and he had no options. He felt like a failure. Here are the reinterpretation steps in his case.

Write Down the Factual Event

"My job has been cut in half."

First Interpretation of the Story

Here is Charles Gill's version of his own story:

I got hired to be the director of compensation and benefits for the X Corporation. Here I am, forty years old at the time, and it's a big break for me. Before this, I had been a personnel manager, and these people came to me, I mean they really wanted me. So I do this job, and it was hard—I really worked. Figuring out people's compensation can be tricky. No matter what you do, someone's always angry at you, it seems, but I'm used to that. I think one of the reasons they hired me is that I'm thick-skinned. The benefits side of the job I really liked better—nobody ever got mad at you for that.

Anyway, after I was there only six months, they called me in and told me they were splitting my job in half. They wanted to keep me, and I'd be getting the same salary, but they were giving the compensation part of my job to someone else.

This came out of the blue. No one warned me—I couldn't believe it. When I walked into that office, I couldn't even face my secretary. I could tell everyone was talking about me, making fun of me.

So what the hell can I do? I've got two kids and a mortgage, and I haven't got any choice. I guess I'll have to swallow it, but I feel like a complete failure.

Analyzing the Hidden Assumptions

We then tried to analyze with Charles the hidden assumptions in his story. This is what we picked out:

- I'm lucky to get this job, and what really appealed to me about it was that *they* wanted me.
- I probably don't deserve to get what I want; I have to depend on being lucky rather than on my own ability.
- I'm an insensitive person; I have "thick skin."
- "They" are making fun of me; everyone is looking at me.
- I am stuck because of my two children and the mortgage; I have no options.

We then began, along with Charles, to question these assumptions.

Here is how that process went:

Q. "Was it really 'luck' that got you this job, or was there something in your past performance that led to it?"

A. "Actually, they had heard of me because of my previous work in personnel. I did have a good reputation in that last job."

Q. "Why do you think you don't deserve to get what you want? Did you usually get what you wanted as a child?"

A. "I don't see what that's got to do with it, but in fact my older brother usually got what he wanted, and I had to take what was left."

Q. "Are you really a 'thick-skinned' person? Is that how you perceive yourself?"

A. "No, actually every time I had to give somebody less compensation than they thought they deserved, my stomach would get into knots from it. I didn't show it, though."

Q. "Who is making fun of you and talking about you? Is this real?"

A. "I can't prove it, but that's what I feel. I always used to feel that way as a kid."

Q. "You say you are 'stuck.' What would you really like to do?"

A. "I've always wanted to start my own business, but I can't risk that with two kids to put through school."

Analysis of Charles's hidden assumptions focused on three main areas:

(1) *Separating out his child-song.* As a child Charles had felt he didn't "deserve" things; only his brother did. But as an adult, Charles clearly *did* deserve what he got—it was not a matter of "luck." His selection for this job was based on his own excellent past performance. His sense of failure, of powerlessness, had thrown him back to his childhood patterns, and those hidden patterns were coloring the way he interpreted events. Once he realized that, he was free to rethink his story and to admit he was a worthy person who deserved what he got.

(2) *Reinterpreting the idea of what Charles had "lost."* His assumption was he had lost half his responsibilities, and since we are conditioned to regard "loss" as failure, he was feeling depressed. When Charles was really honest with himself, however, he had to admit he did not like the compensation area—it made his stomach "get into knots"—and he had probably not done a very good job at it. So then what was the loss? Perhaps being rid of the compensation area was a gain. Another way of looking at what had happened to him was that he

was fortunate: he was getting out of something he disliked, for no loss in pay, and was being granted an opportunity to concentrate on what he did enjoy.

(3) *Giving him a sense of control and choice.* Charles Gill had real economic constraints because of his responsibilities for his children's education. This was a serious, not an imaginary, problem. What he would like to do, Charles said, was go into a business of his own one day. However, he was not acting like a man who planned to do that. The dream of being in business for himself was not an empowering dream, because he was doing nothing to make it come true; it was merely tantalizing, taunting him as something he would *never* do. He was giving himself a double message: I would like to go into my own business/I can't move because I dare not risk. Of course he was feeling trapped: he was doing nothing to get himself untrapped.

When Charles analyzed the reality of his situation, figured out his finances, and talked with his wife about their long-range goals, he decided that what he could do was give himself a definite target date to start his own business—the year when his children would be finished with college. He would stay in the present job until then, saving money, learning the skills he would need, and exploring how to start up his business. Suddenly the present job became bearable because it was put into a new long-range perspective.

The Reinterpreted Story

Here, then, in brief form, is how Charles's reinterpreted story would read:

I have always been very strong in the personnel area. In my last job I performed so well that the company I'm now with heard about me and offered me a major job in their personnel department, to be responsible for compensation and benefits.

After being there some time, I realized my real talent was on the benefits side. I did a superb job in that area, and I learned that I did not really enjoy dealing with the frustrations of worker compensation. So the company and I decided to utilize my talents to the maximum by having me do what I do best—benefits. I realized that by getting rid of what I did not particularly enjoy, I gained even more energy to do the part of the job I do enjoy.

My long-range plan is to open my own business. I will to work very hard at this company as long as I am here, but by year X, I intend to be in business for myself, and I am already making plans toward that.

Note that none of the facts have changed, but they have been put into a new light. Once Charles could repeat to himself this reinterpretation of the story—knowing it was even more fully "true" than his earlier version—he regained a great deal of his self-confidence. Reinterpretation of his past gave him a feeling of *control.* He was able to face his co-workers without a defensive, ashamed attitude. He had made up his mind what he would do, and he was proceeding from a sense of power and self-worth.

And the only tool he used was his mind.

• • •

Bob Butera of the New Jersey Devils tells the story of the coach who called his players together when they were trailing badly at the second intermission and said to them, "Men, I don't want you to think of yourselves as losing—I want you to visualize this game as a tie." Fired up with this reinterpretation, the players went back in for the third period and got killed. As they were leaving the field, one of the players put his arm around the coach's shoulder and said, "Don't feel bad, coach—I want you to visualize this game as a win."

Reinterpretation has its limits. But it also has its power. The way you think about events affects the way you behave. If you tell your tale as the story of a loser, you begin to act that way; if you renarrate it as a positive adventure, you begin to behave like a person in control.

Since it is within your power to judge yourself, why be the sternest judge on the bench?

VII ———
Relabeling Yourself

If someone were to ask, "Who are you?" you would undoubtedly answer with a label, maybe with several. The choice and order of them would reveal a great deal about how you see yourself.

"What do you want to be when you grow up?" we ask children, and we do not expect them to say, "A happy human being." We expect them to answer with an occupational label. Almost from the time we talk, the process begins. "I'm a kindergartener," "I'm an eighth-grader," "I'm a fireman," "I'm a Yalie," "I'm a med student," "I'm a lawyer," "I'm a lab technician," "I'm a housewife, "I'm a grandmother." Labels provide a shorthand way of gathering up the disparate parts of ourselves into a convenient name. They make us comfortable. They are a way of packaging ourselves to the outside world.

After you have lost your job, the simple question "What do you do?" feels like an inquisition. In a society that places people according to label, its loss is a profound social embarrassment, leaving you naked, devoid of status. But it is more than that. By losing what you call yourself, you have lost a way of seeing yourself. Labels not only tell others who we are; in a subtle, complicated way, they tell us how to behave. Part of the process of reinvention is examining the label you have been using and deciding if it is still appropriate.

THE POWER OF LABELS

Recently we talked with two young men, both a few years out of college, both talented writers, and both waiting on tables to pay their bills. John, the first young man, described himself by saying, "I'm a waiter." Barney, the second fellow, said, "I'm a writer, working as a waiter."

149

Both were writing, but John labeled himself a waiter; Barney labeled himself a writer. When we asked in some detail what each of them was actually doing, it came as no surprise that John, the "waiter," was writing only a few pages a week, while Barney, the "writer," was working systematically every day. In other words, the self-labeled "writer" was behaving like a writer, and the self-labeled "waiter-who-hoped-to-be-a-writer" was acting exactly like the unclear label he had given himself. "A rose is a rose is a rose," and, like the rose, all of us behave according to what we say we are.

Alcoholics Anonymous is an organization built upon the idea that labels are powerful tools for behavior. The first thing A.A. demands of its members is that they stand up and say, "I am an alcoholic." The label is a recognition tool: by labeling themselves, alcoholics acknowledge who they are and can begin to change.

Tom Jackson, one of the most thoughtful people working in outplacement today, gives the following example of the power of language to influence behavior. Jackson compares two retired people who are asked what they do. One replies, "I am retired." The other says, "Two years ago I retired, and now I'm gardening, playing golf, and seeing my grandchildren." The person who says, "I am retired," is labeling himself in a static way—the very word "retired" implies inactivity. The person who says, "I retired two years ago," is saying, "I got that behind me, and now I am free to do other things." By the choice of language, one person is thinking of himself in an active way and the other is emphasizing passivity.

Labels can empower us to act, or they can keep us stuck.

THE LABEL THAT LIBERATES

Sometimes, if you can just find your label, you know who you are. You may have a whole array of talents you have never been able to put together in any one job—in fact, you never thought they *could* be put together in any one job—and then someone says to you, "Don't you see, you're a _____." A light flashes. "Of course! *That's* what I am," you tell yourself. Someone has repackaged your talents and given them a new label; and the knowledge that all the parts of you can be put together under one name liberates you. The path ahead is suddenly clear.

Gabrielle Dickens,* a bright senior at Smith College, went to her career counselor in considerable confusion. She was certain there was no one career that would combine her talents and interests. Although fascinated by history and economics, she did not want college teaching. She found the life of a writer too solitary, though she was gifted with words. Politics and social issues involved her deeply, but she did not want to become a lawyer. She sat in the placement office at Smith, ran her fingers through her chestnut hair, and confessed she could not think of anything in the world she wanted to be.

A label was what was needed, the career counselor realized, because without that, the young woman was simply stuck. After analyzing Gabrielle's abilities, her adviser looked up at her and said, "I think you should be a public policy planner." It was a profession Gabrielle had never heard of. As she investigated, she realized such a career was a perfect combination of all the things she loved most—history, social issues, writing, and working with people. The career counselor had given her a label, and the label now gave her a clear course of action. She immediately applied to graduate school and tried to get a summer job in Washington in order to meet people in the field. The label had tied up her vague aspirations into a realizable goal. It had launched her.

For Ed Ershow* the label was "organizational development." Ed was one of those people who always had ideas for restructuring the company. He would spend his lunch hours talking to colleagues in different departments of the electronics firm for which he worked, urging them to communicate better with each other, wondering aloud why nobody else saw what he saw so clearly—how things could be better run. Nobody seemed to want to listen. After all, Ed's job was sales. When times grew lean in the electronics field, Ed's boss was blunt. "We don't need amateur psychiatrists, we need salesmen," he informed Ed. "You have two weeks' notice." Ed Ershow had been a salesman ever since he left college—never a world-beater, but always pulling down a steady income—and now, at thirty, he had no idea what else he might do. "I remember looking in the mirror the day after this happened and thinking to myself, I'm an unemployed salesman. It was terrifying."

But even as he was saying that, he now realizes, he didn't quite believe it. He had no other label, but "unemployed salesman" somehow did not seem to fit. He didn't think of himself as a salesman; he was in his own eyes, as we all are to ourselves, a person of many ideas and interests.

One weekend a college friend who remembered that Ed had majored in psychology invited him to come to a weekend seminar on "organizational development." Ed had never heard the term.

It was a conversion experience. I didn't know people did this for a living. People got paid to interview people inside the company and then to diagnose what the psychological and sociological issues were, and then they worked together for change. And this was called organizational development. I became absolutely clear that this was what I had to do with my life.

Ed went back to school, got a degree in organizational development, and today is a highly regarded professional in the field.

Deborah Darnall was a product of the sixties, still a flower child after the flowers had faded. As the sixties turned into the seventies, Deborah wandered around the country, occasionally doing murals and house repairs to make a little money. She knew she loved art and was good with her hands, but she never thought of this combination of painting and traveling as a career.

One day Deborah stumbled across a description in an art book of a man named Rufus Porter, who, almost a century ago, traveled around the country much as she did, stopping from town to town and offering his services to people who wanted their houses beautified. Wherever he went, he distributed calling cards. On them were his name and the phrase "itinerant artist." Click. Someone with Deborah's eclectic set of interests had actually given those interests a name, and even though it was in a historical book, the name sounded like a career. Suddenly Deborah had a way to think about herself. Like the character in the book, Deborah had cards printed up and began to seek business aggressively. Today she travels around the country painting colorful murals on houses, enjoying the serendipitous nature of her life, and announcing proudly in each town in which she arrives that she is "Deborah Darnall, itinerant artist."

If you think there is no label for your particular set of talents, it is probably no more true than it was for Deborah Darnall, Ed Ershow, or Gabrielle Dickens. To try to find that liberating label, you can look at the *Dictionary of Occupational Titles,* put out by the Department of Labor; you can go to a career counselor; or you can talk to friends who know you well. A label can serve as an effective organizer, pulling together your various talents into a name. Once you have a name, you have a direction.

THE LABEL THAT CONFINES

Like the child who has been growing invisibly in his sleep night after night, then puts on his good pants one holiday only to discover they are too short, we sometimes try to stuff ourselves into our old labels without stopping to examine if we have outgrown them. Labels can be liberating; but occasionally, without our even realizing it, they can be confining.

Andrew Bliss* is a man in his late forties who stumbled into his first job as a wine salesman by accident and, not knowing what else to do, labeled himself forever more "a wine person." His first chance job, working for a family friend selling wine, led to a better one, still selling wine, and to yet a bigger job working for a wine importer. Eventually Andrew and two partners opened up their own importing business, not out of any passion, but because, as Andrew puts it, "Why not? That's what I was, I was a wine person."

For two years the business went steadily downhill, and for two years Andrew Bliss clung to it tenaciously. He had gotten into the wine business because, as he says, "I didn't know what else to do," and once in it, the business had become his label. Being "a wine person," how could Andrew Bliss become anything else? Change terrified him. He began to fight with his partners, claiming they were not pulling their weight. He quarreled with his accountant, accusing him of mismanagement of funds. He held on to his dying company until it was a corpse.

And then one day Andrew Bliss took a course that made him see things differently. Entitled "Entrepreneurship," it was intended to teach people how to start their own businesses, but Andrew drew from it a different message. As he participated in a series of workshops with his fellow students—bankers and artists and housewives and garage mechanics—Andrew realized these people regarded him not as "a wine person" but merely as "a talented person." The other students saw him as multifaceted, and their view of him enabled him to discard his old label.

Some time during this course I realized I did not *have* to be in the wine business anymore. My life had been ruled by the need to save the business. Day after day was desperate activity. Now it hit me as a reality that I did not have to do this, that I could do something else.

Andrew consciously gave himself another label, a purposely temporary one. The label was "dreamer." His wife was working, and with the money he had saved up, Andrew Bliss figured he could function as a dreamer for about six months. During this time, he began to explore other businesses, take courses, examine what he really wanted to do.

He concluded he would enjoy working with his wife because they had complementary talents—"She's a great opener, I'm a great closer." Today the two of them operate a small suburban partnership, and Andrew Bliss has a new label: real estate broker.

Many people, like Andrew Bliss, confine themselves by their label. A literary agent we know, whose business was failing, would not even go for an interview to be a museum administrator, though his administrative talent was clear to all who knew him. "I'm a word person," he announced, and that was that. This man was not unlike Anthony Abruzzi, the New York cabbie we met earlier who labeled himself "a $40,000-a-year purchasing agent" and preferred to drive a cab rather than change his label.

CHANGING YOUR LABEL

Consider just one powerful statistic: Most Americans switch their *careers*—not just their jobs, but their *careers*—three times in the course of a working life. Although we rarely think about it, the first step in any such move is *changing your language*. Before you can change careers, you must first believe that you *are* that new career. You must first *change your label*. This does not mean, for example, that if you are a lab technician, merely by saying "I am a dancer" you will become a dancer. But it does mean the language you use to describe yourself *to* yourself becomes a powerful inner reality.

Tom Jackson, the outplacement counselor, says that when he is hired by a company that is laying off a large number of workers, his first job is to get these workers to *change their language about themselves*. This may sound rarefied—why does the language he uses about himself matter to an unemployed steel worker, for instance? Tom Jackson sums it up:

When a steel mill is forced to shut down, think what happens to the worker who has spent his whole life at that plant. The chances are he looks at himself in the mirror every morning and says, "I am an unemployed steel worker." Just by the name he calls himself, he is telling himself he is a failure, and how do failures operate? By failing.

If I can get him to look in the mirror and say, "I'm not an unemployed steel worker—*I'm a human being with options,*" then I have set him free in a powerful way.

An "unemployed steel worker" who keeps repeating that phrase to himself acts according to that label: he is, first of all, "unemployed," a word that means "idle"; second, he is a "steel worker," and if that is what he is, how can he be anything else? He is likely to keep looking for a job as a steel worker and just as likely to run into a dead end.

On the other hand, a person who repeats to himself that he is "a human being with options" reminds himself first of all that he is a human being—not just a worker, but a *human* person with other parts of his life to sustain him—and second that he has options. Perhaps he can do other factory work. Perhaps he is good with his hands and can open a small repairs business. Perhaps he has always wanted to move to a different part of the country, and being laid off from the steel mill has given him the push to relocate. As long as he thinks of himself as "an unemployed steel worker," he will never see these possibilities; once he relabels himself "a human being with options," he can look around.

There is nothing more liberating, nothing more conducive to optimism, than a sense of choice. As Tom Jackson says, "Operating optionally allows you to operate optimally."

A FALLBACK LABEL

Without knowing it, all of us have a fallback label. This is the job we can do when all else fails.

We tend to haul out our fallback label at parties when we announce, "Well, if worse came to worst, I could always be a _____." Paul Gottlieb, the six-foot-five-inch president of an art book publishing house, says that his fallback label is "doorman—it helps to be tall." Almost all actors have the fallback label of "waiter" or "bartender." Many female executives, who worked their way up from the secretarial pool, have the fallback label "secretary." A novelist we know who writes his books on a computer calls himself a "word programmer."

These labels, often spoken in jest, are actually worst-case-scenario occupations. They can offer comfort in a time when you need it.

Walter Cronkite, one of the most successful newscasters in television, has a standby label that he finds liberating. Cronkite used to work as a writer for the wire services when he was young, and to this day, he says:

I always feel that television is a dream world, and that underneath I'm really a writer with a desk at United Press. I could always end up back there, I tell myself. It hasn't happened for thirty-six years, and I don't suppose it will, but that's what I tell myself.

Cronkite's sense of having a fallback occupation helped him when he was dismissed by CBS as anchorman of the Democratic convention in 1964. Though personally "shocked and angry," he recognized "it was their candy store," and they had the right to do what they did. Cronkite contained his anger and managed to put his disappointment behind him. With the press, he was extremely discreet. Since he had never embarrassed the network publicly, CBS felt quite comfortable later reinstating Cronkite as convention anchorman.

"Being able to shrug one's shoulders is one of the most important attributes we have," Cronkite comments. And then, as if to explain his lack of bitterness, he adds, "I always felt I had a fallback position."

"I'M AN EXPLORER"

What, then, do you call yourself when you are "between engagements"? How *do* you answer that persistent question "What do you do?"

If you have decided what you want to be, grab hold of your new label and stick it onto yourself with confidence. The very act of using it reinforces your own and other people's perceptions of you in that career. When you say, "I've switched from _____ to _____, and I am very excited by the possibilities before me," you are declaring yourself affirmatively and forcing the world—and yourself—to take you seriously.

If you have not decided what to be and are scared and uncertain and searching about, or trying to make a living doing twenty different things, or frantically waiting for rejection letters in the mail, or hating to go out to dinner because of your terror at having to answer the dreaded question "What do you do?" try an interim answer that has proved helpful to many people. Say with a confident smile on your face, "I am an explorer."

In fact, you are an explorer. You are on an exciting, and at times terrifying, search for what you will do next. By giving yourself a title, "explorer," you have dignified your confusion, legitimized it, even given it a noble sound. This is important not only for others—it is important for you. You *can* be an explorer. It is a valid occupation. It is perfectly legitimate not to know what you will be and to take the time to explore.

Think about the difference in the way you and others see yourself if instead of saying, "I'm looking into a bank job and doing a little writing, and waiting to hear about a few other things, and I'm not quite sure what I'll be doing next," you say, "I'm an explorer." By changing your language, you have given a positive label to an otherwise negative-sounding state of confusion. You have become your own validator. The very act of relabeling yourself has created positive energy for you to act.

• • •

Labels are useful in making you feel more comfortable with yourself and in giving others a way to see you. If your old label is no longer appropriate, defeat gives you an excellent opportunity to shed it and put on a new one. By changing your *language,* you are changing your self-perception, and by changing your self-perception, you inevitably change your behavior.

Most of us never stop to examine the way we talk to ourselves about ourselves. But the tool of language—especially when the listener is ourselves—is one of the most potent weapons we have.

Think of the story of the umpire at the baseball game. Asked if a particular pitch was a ball or a strike, he looked his questioner in the eye and said, "It ain't nuthin' until I say what it is." Now there is a man who understands the power of language.

VIII

Expanding Your Choices: Getting "Unstuck"

When *you* can decide what you want to do, rather than be the person *to whom* things are done, you have moved from being victim to being in charge. This feeling of control comes from a sense of choice.

Most of us think we have no choices, or at best very few. We continue to see ourselves as what we were, unable to imagine what we might be. It is not that we do not want to change, but rather that *we cannot think what to change to*. Over and over people say, "I have no idea what to do next," "I can't think of a single viable alternative," or, "This is the only thing I know how to do."

It simply is not true.

There is no one reading this book who does not have options. It is only a matter of seeing them.

If you have come to a turning point in your working life—because you failed, because you feel you are failing, or because you have decided what you do is no longer right for you—your task is to figure out what to do next. As long as you look at the future with thinking from the past, the task can seem overwhelming. What is needed to explore the unknown is fresh thinking. Your goal, by thinking in new ways, is to develop a set of options.

SETTING UP GUIDELINES

Theoretically, anything is possible if you are willing to go after it. How, then, do you decide what to eliminate and what to pursue?

You have to know yourself.

Take a good, hard, honest look and ask yourself what you absolutely *must* have in any working situation. Not what you think you *should* have, or what other people *tell* you is important, but what you yourself, deep down, really need in order to feel happy and productive. These basic conditions, called "career anchors" by some placement specialists and "core values" by others, are really old-fashioned "guidelines." Guidelines are not specific career choices; they are simply reminders of the basic set-up you need in *any* career choice.

One of the best ways to get guidelines is to see what has and has not worked for you in the past.

Perhaps you get your best ideas only when you "spark" off another person. That tells you to avoid autonomous situations and maybe look for a partnership.

Perhaps you are unhappy in your highly paid job because you feel it is not socially important. That tells you to look for a "mission"-oriented job.

Perhaps you got pushed into management and discover you miss the satisfaction of hands-on work. That tells you you require a technical, nonmanagerial spot in the future.

In setting up guidelines, be sure to analyze your failures. Generally they tell you more about what you really need than your successes.

Milton Glaser, art director of *New York* magazine, is a well-known designer who is offered many free-lance projects. To evaluate them, he has set up the following guidelines for himself. Any job he takes must (1) evoke an initial intuitive, passionate response, and (2) if it is a partnership, be done with an equal-weight partner. This latter guideline grew out of a failure. Someone brought Glaser an idea to which he had a passionate, intuitive response (his first guideline), but the originator of the idea was a weak man with a questionable reputation. Believing he could help rehabilitate this man, Milton Glaser entered into a business that proved to be not only a financial disaster, but a personal nightmare. He learned from his failure to set up his second guideline.

Marion Maged, a woman whose dress company was forced out of business because of undercapitalization, developed new guidelines after that experience. She realized she disliked two things about her business: the stress of supervising many employees, and the relentless pressure of finishing one line and always having to design the next. These dislikes helped her form guidelines for the future. Any new endeavor for Marion must (1) involve only herself or one other partner, and (2) be a finite project with a clear beginning, middle, and end.

Guidelines are only general. They provide an important framework by which to judge possibilities. But how do you get possibilities?

What follows are some ways we and other people have gotten past feeling "stuck." These are methods of examining your life and analyzing opportunities that can enlarge your sense of choice. The goal is to move from a position of "I have no options" to a position of "I can choose."

WAYS TO EXPAND YOUR CHOICES

(1) Recycle Your Talents

One job equals three skills. That is the first rule of recycling.

Most of us think of what we do as a fixed, nontransportable thing, like a massive piece of furniture that cannot be moved. Therefore if we lose our job, it means leaving the furniture behind. But if we think of our job as three separate skills, losing a job is not a total loss. Like modular furniture, the parts can be reassembled elsewhere.

One job equals three skills is a formula for power. It enables you to recycle the usable parts of your job and create something new.

When Lyle Keston* lost his New York job as a movie producer for Twentieth Century-Fox, he was convinced it was the end of his career. Having produced films for two decades, he believed this was the only job he could do, yet every New York studio office was cutting back, and he did not want to move to California. Incapable of imagining himself doing anything else, Lyle saw his job as an immovable piece of furniture with a firmly attached label, "movie producer."

Sometimes it takes others to see us differently. One day Lyle accidentally ran into an ex-Fox colleague who had since left the studio. When Lyle lamented his plight, the friend looked at him with surprise. As Lyle recalls the conversation:

He said to me, "What are you worried about—you have lots of skills." I was so depressed I remember saying, "I do? What are they?" He said to me, "You're a great salesman. Don't you realize all those years you were always selling movie ideas to the guys in the head office? Hell, if you could sell to those sharks, you could sell anything to anybody."

Then he said, "Besides, you're a great writer—you always wrote the best ad copy for your own movies, so in a crunch you could always go into promotional writing." Then he just threw in the last little bit, "And of course you're the best people putter-together around—that's what a producer does. So you could probably open up your own casting agency and make a fortune. The way I see it you've got a lot of choices."

He punched me on the shoulder and we said good-bye, but I must have stood on that street corner another twenty minutes. Those few remarks changed my life.

Today Lyle is a highly paid free-lance promotional writer, specializing in the movie industry. It did not happen overnight. But that conversation with his friend enabled Lyle to look at himself differently. Breaking down his one job into three skills enabled him to see himself as a person with options, and once he sensed his options, he was free to move.

The former head of a landmarks preservation commission who lost her position used the "one job equals three skills" approach. Instead of looking for another hard-to-find spot heading a commission or foundation, she analyzed the component parts of her job to see how they could be recycled. Running a landmarks preservation commission, she reasoned, required a *trained eye* to spot what buildings were historically important, *political savvy* in getting zoned variances, and *managerial skills* in running an office. The job might be gone, but its component parts could be transferred and used for her own gain.

The real estate development company that this woman set up specializes in converting overlooked landmark-status buildings into usable office spaces. She uses her *eye* to spot underappreciated buildings, her *political clout* to get zoning variances to convert the buildings, and her *management skills* to run her own business.

Breaking down your job into skills immediately enlarges your choices. By getting rid of your general job label and relabeling yourself according to your skills, you begin to see new directions. In the case of Lyle Keston, for instance, instead of saying "I'm a movie producer" (which meant implicitly "I'm stuck"), he would say, "I'm an experienced salesman," "I'm a promotion writer," "I'm a people manager." He could then take any one of those skills and look for specific jobs where such skills were needed, whereas if he had continued to see himself only as his general job label, he would have concluded he had no options.

• • •

The second principle of recycling is that *no experience you ever have is wasted.* In looking for your next career direction, think what you can retrieve from the past. We are all amalgams of everything we have ever done, and we never know which of our past experiences will be useful.

Tim Marx studied geology and environmental sciences in college, a field he thought would prove extraneous when he decided to become a film production manager. One of his first major interviews was for a worldwide documentary requiring all outdoor shooting. The producers hired Tim because they felt his knowledge of the environment gave him an edge.

In thinking through your past, it is important to remember that nothing any of us ever does is wasted; it can all be recycled into new opportunities.

(2) Make Your Avocation Your Vocation

Imagine what would happen if you really *enjoyed* what you did—enjoyed it like play. In considering options, one of the sources we tend to ignore is the area of pleasures, hobbies, pastimes. Work should be serious, we tell ourselves, the opposite of play.

Turn that idea around. Work should be creative fun; and if the place where you feel most creative is in your hobbies or at play, why not see if those areas can provide an inspiration for work?

Career counselor Mort Feinberg tells the story of an executive fired in his late fifties who found himself virtually unemployable in the traditional corporate world. When Feinberg asked him about his hobbies, the man answered with some annoyance that golf and gardening were his passions, but he did not see the relevance of this question to the pressing problem of finding a job. Feinberg convinced his client to take a few courses in professional gardening, and the ex–corporate executive has now set up a groundskeeping business for golf courses. He has a contract with two of the large clubs where he used to play during his corporate days. He confesses the job "doesn't feel like work."

Alan Winetsky,* the young son of an architect father and interior designer mother, left college in his sophomore year feeling like a total failure. In the world of his peers, academic achievement was the gold ring, and Alan, who detested school, had gotten off the merry-go-round. Though talented as an artist, he balked at going in the career direction of his parents. He had no interest in the corporate world; he was too free-spirited for that. Going back to school for any retraining was unthinkable. As far as Alan could see, he had no marketable skills nor any choices.

Ever since he was a child Alan had loved to cook. Other kids would get together and order pizza, but Alan Winetsky's dinners for his teen-aged friends started with celery rémoulade. In addition to a good palate, he had the eye of an artist, fussing lovingly over the "presentation" of his dishes. He brought a passion and discipline to cooking quite lacking in his studies. This was understandable: cooking was pleasure; school was work.

It was a family friend who suggested one day that Alan become a chef. At first he dismissed it ("straight hair/curly hair"—how could anything he did *naturally* be worth doing?), but then he began to consider the idea. Could he see himself in a white hat? No, he told himself, no serious person from an intellectual family had ever become a chef. The family friend, realizing Alan needed a role model, knew a young restaurateur who had just opened one of the city's hottest new restaurants. This young man, like Alan, had been an undistinguished student from a high-achieving family, drifting from business to business until he landed a sous-chef job in Paris and discovered his métier. After spending an afternoon with the young restaurateur and visiting his gleaming kitchens, Alan had found his role model.

The former college dropout is now opening oysters and trimming green beans in the very kitchen he admired, working his way up toward becoming a chef in the time-honored European apprentice system.

Many successful people have found their careers by turning to their hobbies. For years Nancy Denburg was a housewife raising money for the Cancer Society, the League of Women Voters, and other charities. In casting about for a career she could start in her forties, she realized her avocation, fund-raising, could also become her vocation. The New Jersey Heart Association hired her as a paid fund-raiser, based on her volunteer track record.

Paul Sperry quit the corporate world after getting his Harvard Business School M.B.A. to pursue a career of concert singing, an activity he had always loved but had been afraid to treat seriously.

Many of the antique stores and boutiques in this country represent hobbies, personal passions that people have turned into careers.

Play, in other words, can be a source of ideas for work.

(3) Start Your Own Business: Look for What's Missing

At some time in their lives almost all people toy with the notion of starting their own business. Maybe this is the time for you to do it.

Entrepreneurs are not necessarily solitary geniuses who tinker in garages until they come up with a brilliant notion; more often they are people who have looked around them and noticed something is missing. The man who got tired of having his paper bookmarks slip out of his hymnal at choir practice invented the removable peel-off yellow stickers that 3M now produces. He looked at something that annoyed him and saw in it an opportunity. Of such stuff are entrepreneurs born.

A surburban woman we know had so much difficulty finding a decorator with whom she shared similar tastes that she started her own service business matching clients and decorators.

Another young man who had lost his job in video production got the inspiration for his next career when he noticed his father falling asleep while reading corporate annual reports. The young man realized his father was simply bored with the same trite presentation of data. Of course, he thought. Who wants to read endless printed columns? Today this young man is the boss of his own firm specializing in videotaped annual reports for Fortune 500 companies.

When you read about successes like those mentioned above, it all sounds easy, but sometimes entrepreneurs are born reluctantly, kicking and screaming all the way. Larry Atlas is one such case. An intense, dark-eyed man in his mid-thirties, no one is more surprised by his success as a businessman than he.

Early in his life, Larry Atlas determined he would never be in business like his father. His would be a more "creative" life, and so he became an actor and a playwright. Author of a play called *Total Abandon*, Larry was assured by everyone that he was the next Tennessee Williams. At thirty-two, with his play about to be produced on Broadway, he almost believed it himself. *Total Abandon* received wonderful reviews from every critic except one, Frank Rich of the *New York Times*. That was the one that counted. The play closed after one night. "I felt like I was watching a child die," he says.

For six months Larry drank, took drugs, and could not write a word. Nothing lifted his depression. "It did not escape me that playwrights in similar positions had simply died," he says. At times he felt close to death. He considered suicide more than once. Then, he says:

I began to feel challenged to survive. I sensed that I had a choice. I could let the *New York Times* kill me, or I could fight back. The only idea I held on to was that I would not let people see me beaten. And I would not behave in a dishonorable way. I wouldn't even let myself say, "It's Frank Rich's fault." This seemed to me to be dishonorable. And it also seemed dishonorable to say, "I agree with what the world thinks about me, that I'm no good." Honor dictates that even if you are alone in your interpretation of events, you don't surrender it. Honor became all-important to me. I clung to my own judgment of myself and determined to move on.

Larry got through the first negative stages of failure, but then found himself "stuck," staring over and over at a list he was making of his choices. Here is how Larry's initial list of choices read:

- Teacher (no money)
- Study acting seriously (no money)
- Get shack in woods and live in poverty
- Become an army mercenary
- Technical writing (no training)
- Business??

For some years Larry had been harboring an idea for a business but, like many of us, thought, The idea of starting a business is too demanding, too scary—*it's the sort of thing other people do.* Now, after his failure, given a choice between being an entrepreneur or living in poverty in a shack in the woods, he decided business didn't look so bad.

From his days as an actor Larry had always been frustrated at the random way casting directors chose actors for parts. Casting directors relied on their memories, which were faulty, or on often out-of-date pictures and resumés. They were unlikely to know specialized information, for instance, like who could do a sky-diving stunt for a commercial. Since Larry Atlas was an actor who could actually perform a sky-dive but had never gotten called for one, he was particularly frustrated. Out of his frustration he saw a clear, simple idea for a new business: he would store information about actors on computers and sell the service to casting directors. Actors would pay a small annual fee to be on his constantly up-to-date registry, and casting directors and producers would pay to subscribe.

Ideas are easy to hatch; the question is, who has the drive to carry them out? Larry Atlas was not yet ready to be an entrepreneur because he could not *think* of himself as an entrepreneur. It took another person to see him that way. In talking to people about his idea, he met a man in the computer business. Immediately this man offered to go into partnership with Larry. Suddenly Larry saw himself differently. He still thought of himself as an actor and a writer, but now he could see that being a businessman was possible, too. He could add a label and still keep the other two. It was the other man's enthusiastic belief in him and his concept that gave Larry the drive to become "unstuck."

Ironically, or perhaps predictably, once he committed himself to the business, the other parts of his career blossomed as well:

As soon as I started pursuing the business, acting jobs started to come along like crazy. Having my own business began to take the pressure off. When the acting didn't matter so much, I was more relaxed, and when people sense you don't need them so much, they want you more. I also began writing again, which I had not done for a very long time. So I was able to keep all three things going.

Recently Larry Atlas's picture appeared in the *New York Times,* this time triumphantly, though not on the page he would have liked. The *Times* praised him not for his playwriting, but for the ingenuity of his new company, RoleCall. Willy-nilly, the man who had said starting your own company was "something other people did" was being lauded for starting his own.

Instead of waiting for an incredible idea to spring full-blown into your mind, try looking around you to see what is missing. What have you always wished you could get done more easily? What kind of product or service do you personally find lacking?

Before you dismiss the idea of being in business for yourself, remember none of the people described here thought they were entrepreneurs, either.

(4) Learn Something New

If you stay in a room, nothing happens. If you talk to the same people you have always known, something may happen, but probably nothing all that surprising. However, if you force yourself every day to do something *new,* if you consciously expose yourself to experiences you have not had before, you dramatically increase the probability that "something will turn up."

One of the best ways of enlarging your choices is to *learn something new*. This can take the form of career-related information—which you can get from books, pamphlets, weekend seminars, or courses—or it need not be specifically related to your career. Simply by learning anything new, you are broadening yourself, tweaking your mind, stimulating yourself to think in different ways, *refreshing yourself*. This often has important benefits.

An executive dismissed from a Fortune 500 company last year enrolled in a ten-week orientation course given by the New York Citizens Committee for Children, designed to expose people to the city's social problems as they affect children. Each week participants visited a different facility, from drug abuse centers to foster homes, and heard from experts in the field. The course had nothing to do with this man's job search, he thought. He enrolled because some part of him felt cramped and hungry; he yearned for a sense of perspective on his corporate-centered life.

The course gave him that and more. Not only did it take him to places he had never been—homes for unwed mothers, juvenile detention centers, mental hospitals—but the pictures imprinted on his mind burst forth into his conversation. He found himself talking more animatedly with other people. Though unemployed, he sensed himself filled now with interesting observations, excited by the way his mind was expanding in new directions. His sense of his own humanity was reawakened. He even found himself exploring the idea of moving into the nonprofit world. Though in the end he did not do so, the very act of taking this course provided him with intangible but very real benefits.

At the very least, learning something new replaces the loss of failure with a positive gain. It's like giving yourself a present after others have taken something away from you. The act of learning quickens your sense of self. It reminds you that you are smart and able.

Taking a course can also lead directly and specifically to your next career. The best example of this comes from the story of Alice Heyman, who started the First Women's Bank. Alice changed her entire life and career direction because of one course she happened to take.

For eight years Alice Heyman worked in her family's prosperous jewelry business and would probably have continued in it had her beloved father not died. But when he passed away, Alice, the only girl in the family, found herself orphaned and also suddenly pitted against all the men in her family. Her uncles were trying to devalue her father's estate for tax and inheritance purposes. Giving her no satisfactory explanation, they put papers before her and asked her to sign. Alice, who had always thought of herself as Oscar Heyman's daughter, would have had difficulty fighting for herself, but in the name of her father she now took her uncles to court.

For two years, her family hired top law firms to defeat her. Every family relationship she had was severed. She turned for comfort to her religion. Her intensely spiritual sense fueled her desire to fight and sustained her through that struggle. As she puts it:

I would scream with outrage, "How can my uncles do this? They, too, were brought up as religious Jews with an internal sense of ethics. How could they violate their sense of ethics?"

I realized I was born into a religion of a group of people who are survivors. I am not very different from my ancestors, who went through the Inquisition, or my father, who emigrated from Russia to America. Judaism gave me a sense of continuity.

Two years after she had begun her fight, the court ruled. *Heyman* v. *Heyman* was a landmark decision, championing the rights of people in Alice's position, beneficiaries of an estate. Alice Heyman had won.

But had she? Bereft of her family, uncertain what to do next, she was adrift. The court ruling felt more like a defeat than a victory. The bitterness of the lawsuit coupled with her uncles' powerful connections meant the jewelry business was closed to her. She thought about doing something in business or politics, but the thoughts refused to take specific form. She considered becoming a therapist, but that meant long years of school.

Unsure which way to turn, Alice decided to expose herself to as many new opportunities as possible. Among them was a course that dealt with discrimination against women, given by Betty Friedan at the New School for Social Research. One session focused on finance. Alice listened keenly as speakers discussed women's difficulties getting credit and being financially independent. These were issues she understood. Without her family business or the support of her relatives, she'd had no one to count on but herself. Hearing that other women had been just as afraid of financial independence suddenly gave her a direction.

In that course, I saw what was missing was a women's bank. It was an idea whose time had come. I raised my hand and said to Leigh Miller, the deputy superintendent of banks, "If we women get it together, will you charter us a bank?" And he said, "Yes." I ran down to Carol Bellamy and said, "Carol, I'm serious. We really have to do this." That was the start of the First Women's Bank.

For Alice, taking that course, exposing herself to new ideas, changed her life. As she sums it up:

People use the expression "breakdowns lead to breakthroughs." I had a lot of breakdowns—my relationship with my family broke down, my job broke down, and I was personally feeling broken down. But out of those breakdowns I had a breakthrough—namely, the creation of the First Women's Bank. In the process I created my own identity, too. I stopped being Oscar Heyman's daughter. Finally I became Alice Heyman.

(5) Think Whom to Work with, Not What to Do

This is another way of attacking the problem. If you have been unable to come up with a clear idea of *what* you want to do next, try framing your future in terms of *whom* you want to work with. This can give you another set of options. Is there someone you admire so greatly that that specific *person* is more important than any specific *job?*

This person might be a "great figure," a superstar of enormous charisma around whom you are happy to float as an acolyte and learn. Or it might be a peer. In either case, by looking for an opportunity through looking at a person, you are putting the *people factor* high on your guidelines. Some people care more about *what* they do than with *whom* they do it. For them, the process of their own work is paramount, and the surroundings are less important. But for others, the personalities of the people with whom they work are crucial

People are a resource that can provide you with ideas. You can expose yourself to key people even without having a definite idea in mind. Begin with specific people in the hopes that discussion with them will lead you to a specific business. Many new enterprises are formed this way. People within companies spot key people with whom they enjoy working, and by getting together and brainstorming, they decide to form something new.

Sometimes the person you would like to work with is someone you admire but do not know well—perhaps in a field you would like to break into, but for which you do not have all the qualifications. If you can identify a "great figure" from whom you think you can learn, try writing that person a letter and offering your services free on a limited time basis. Basically, you are "making someone an offer he can't refuse." The very boldness of this approach says you believe in yourself so strongly you are willing to work for nothing because you know you will show this person you belong in his or her organization. Clearly not everyone can afford to work for nothing, but sometimes this is a daring way to gain an apprenticeship. It has the element of surprise, charm, and flattery: who can resist someone who has enough confidence in himself to offer his services and enough taste to admire the "great figure" receiving the letter?

Almost none of us are able to reinvent ourselves alone. Sometimes we make the mistake of thinking we have to have everything figured out before we approach others. But it need not be such a lonely struggle. By turning to others for inspiration and ideas, by regarding them as *starting points,* we gain another source of options.

(6) Looking in the Newspaper

This sounds so obvious as to be foolish. But smart people often do the obvious thing. Newspapers can give you ideas in two ways: by providing stories of people doing things you may not have thought of, and more specifically, through the want ads.

No less illustrious a figure than John Brademas, president of New York University, got his job through the *New York Times.* Brademas had been a member of Congress for most of his adult life. During the time he was fighting the campaign that finally unseated him, part of his mind was seeking what he might do next.

In 1980 all the negative forces came at the same time and were too many to overcome. They all fused, and that's when you lose an election. Intellectually I understood what was happening. I didn't like it but I understood it. If you understand with your mind, you become more able emotionally to deal with failure.

There is a period when you ask yourself, "What am I going to do?"

Being pretty sure I was going to lose the election and as a faithful reader of the *New York Times,* I'd noticed in the *Times* the Sunday before the election, in the ads for academic and medical positions, one that said, "Wanted: President of New York University." I filed that away in my head, and on

Wednesday morning, the day after the election, I called Mayor Koch, my old colleague in Congress, who said, "John, I'm sorry."

I replied, "Ed, that's the way it is."

He asked, "What are you going to do now?"

I said, "Ed, I want to be president of NYU."

Koch immediately replied, "If Mondale doesn't want it, I'm for you!"

When in February 1981 the *New York Times* reported that I had been chosen the new president of New York University, Mondale called me to say, "John, I'm glad at least *one* of us won a presidency!"

Whether it's a college presidency or an administrative assistant job, sometimes the simplest options are right in front of you, in the pages of your morning newspaper.

(7) Wild Ideas: Grabbing On to "Why Not?"

Sometimes when nothing else works, when you are at the very end, when you haven't got an idea in the world, something crazy happens. Call it luck, call it a fluke, call it divine intervention, but something presents itself. If you are receptive, you look to the heavens and say, "Why not?"

Nowhere is this better illustrated than in the story of Nick and Liz Thomas.

Nick Thomas started his career as an air force jet fighter pilot. The son of Rumanian immigrants who worked double shifts to send him to college, Nick was a believer in institutions. God, family, and career, in that order, were his priorities. Liz was the picture of every air force pilot's girl back home. A strawberry blonde with a perfect complexion, a throaty singing voice, and a laugh that always managed to cheer him, Liz came from a down-at-the-heels Philadelphia Main Line family. When they married, she converted to Catholicism and settled down to be an air force wife. For five years it worked. Only when Nick was ordered to the Aleutian Islands—wife and infant baby to stay home, please—did the fighter pilot quit. Family, after all, came ahead of career.

They moved to suburban Philadelphia, where Nick went into the insurance business. Three more children arrived. Liz took care of them full-time and for recreation sang in the local Gilbert and Sullivan company. "He brought home the bread—my job was to butter it," she says. The two were very close. Nick Thomas was never out to beat the world; he just wanted to make a decent living and enjoy his family.

At New York Life Insurance Company, where he worked, the slogan among the guys was "Mother NYLIC never screws you." But at the end of eight years there, it looked very much as if Mother NYLIC was doing just that. The long-promised promotion to manager never materialized, and now they told him if he wanted to get ahead, he would have to move to the head office in New York. Nick had no desire to compete in this high-powered world. He quit.

His next job was regional manager for a smaller insurance company. After nine years, just short of being vested in the pension plan, he was fired. Once again, he left empty-handed.

For a time he tried his own financial consulting business, but it was undercapitalized and soon failed. By now Nick Thomas had a wife and four children, a house with a mortgage, and absolutely no idea what to do next. He had gotten to the point of the other people in this chapter—stuck.

NICK: I was very embarrassed. Here I was, forty-seven, with enormous financial pressure and no place to go. The only thing I could think of was to try to refinance the house. You sit there and you wonder how, with education, drive, and desire, you've seen nothing come to fruition. I had always had a positive attitude, and here I was going deeper and deeper into depression. I felt I was a failure.

LIZ: I consider failure something that happens in a person's personality, not in what he's paid, so I didn't consider Nick a failure, but I was frightened. An inertia seemed to overtake him. He just didn't know what to do, and Nick had never not known what to do before.

Liz took a part-time job in a doctor's office. They swallowed their pride and asked her mother to meet the mortgage payments. There was no one else to borrow from. The more they thought rationally about their problems, the more insoluble they seemed. The Thomases were down to their last two hundred dollars.

Liz Thomas started going to church. She found in the daily mass a quiet time, a respite from her worries. Within her was a deep desire to abandon the lonely struggle of trying to figure it all out herself. She turned to prayer, and with that admission of the need for help, with that loosening of control, a truly remarkable event occurred.

LIZ: Nick's mother had passed away the year before, and I was very close to her. The day before she died she insisted on sitting with Nick, without the oxygen, and she wanted to hold his hand. During that time Nick said to her, "You know, Mom, I've really had a lot of struggles. I know you're going to see the Lord soon, so when you do, will you please put in a good word for me because I really need some help." She looked at him and said, "I will, honey." That was the last thing she ever said to him.

Every morning I would be in church praying for something to happen, and one morning—and I know this sounds unbelievable, but it really happened—I kept hearing three words over and over again. I felt Nick's mother was trying to tell me something. The three words were "Make the mustard."

"Make the mustard"—what on earth did that mean? Liz's family had been in possession of a mustard recipe since 1917, the year her aunt had run off to New York to become a ballet dancer, enrolled in the respected Chalif School of Ballet, and, to her family's horror, married seventeen-year-old Edward Chalif. A Jew, an immigrant, and a dancer, Chalif brought little to the union besides his ballet slippers and a recipe for mustard that his family had taken with them out of Russia. The marriage lasted fifty-four years.

LIZ: I went home and said to Nick I thought his mother was trying to tell us it was time to give up fighting so hard at the same old thing and to try something completely new. For years we had made this family mustard for friends at Christmas, and they always told us we were sitting on a gold mine. I began to think maybe the opportunity we needed was sitting right here in front of us and we were overlooking it.

Nick Thomas thought his wife was mad. On the other hand, two hundred dollars was not enough to pay any other major bill, and at least this was a new idea. He turned to Liz. "I can't fight you *and* my mother," he said. "Let's go ahead."

One thing Nick Thomas knew how to do was sell. Mustard, he figured, couldn't be harder than insurance. He would recycle his talents. He called on the local cheese shop. The man gave Nick ten objections, then tasted the mustard and ordered the Thomases' entire inventory. Not only that, he paid cash. Nick realized he had been wrong: selling mustard was *easier* than selling insurance.

The turning point in Chalif's growth came when the Thomases decided to tackle New York's most famous food store, Zabar's. Friends had convinced them that if the mustard was to go national, it first had to move off the shelves of this revered West Side establishment. Liz and Nick Thomas drove to New York, mustard in the trunk of their car, prepared to do battle with one of Zabar's owners, the redoubtable Murray Klein.

Short, balding, and eternally harassed, Murray Klein controls a powerful empire built on smoked salmon and pastrami. Intruders from Pennsylvania he didn't need. "You'll leave the mustard," he intoned over the noise of frantic crowds packing the store. "The tasting committee will let you know." And with that Murray Klein turned back to the crowds at the fish counter. The interview was over.

But Nick Thomas had been a life insurance salesman, and rejection was his middle name. For three months he pestered Murray Klein. He called him, wrote to him, visited him. It was David and Goliath, only this time David was a tall, blond Catholic and Goliath was a short, bald Jew. After three months of badgering, Murray Klein finally agreed to an in-store tasting demonstration. "What you sell you sell," he announced. "If it doesn't sell, that's it for Zabar's. You have till two o'clock."

It was pouring rain the day of the tasting. Discouraged, the Thomases drove to the city, figuring no one would be in Zabar's. They didn't know New Yorkers. When it rains in Manhattan, *everyone* is in Zabar's. As the rain teemed outside, Liz Thomas's wonderful throaty voice, which long ago had charmed her husband and more recently had sung Gilbert and Sullivan in Bala Cynwyd, floated over the crowds at Zabar's, hawking mustard. In five hours thirty cases disappeared.

At exactly two o'clock the floor manager came over to Nick. "Mr. Klein said I should make room on the shelves," he announced.

Nick wondered if his mother was listening.

Chance, accident, the hunch, or a voice from your dead mother—who's to say where ideas come from? Nolan Bushnell said that if he had to choose between being smart and being lucky, he would choose being lucky. Luck, he pointed out, always involves good judgment in that you have to be smart enough to take advantage of it. Only when Nick and Liz Thomas were willing to say, "Why not?" did they see the luck in front of them. As Nick puts it, "You have to be afraid to the point of desperation before you can abandon control."

When nothing else works, all of us can turn to faith, luck, chance.

We can listen to our inner voices. Somewhere in there, or somewhere out there, an idea may be lurking.

   •   •   •

What we are talking about here is not what you *do,* but how you *think.* In a way, getting a job is the easy part; getting your thinking straight is the work. Reinventing yourself is first and foremost a conversation with yourself.

Jobs may come and go, and the direction you set out in even after you examine yourself may change yet again. But if you can learn how to *think* clearly about failure, if you can recapture your sense of yourself, if you can learn that you are a person who *always* has choices—as we all always do—you will have acquired an invaluable lesson for the rest of your life.

IX ————

The Transitional Steps

First you turn inward and clarify the way you've been thinking about yourself. Then, when you are sufficiently focused and self-confident, there comes a moment when it's time to turn outward again.

Between the stages of thinking and doing, there are certain transitional steps that are generally overlooked. But not if you're smart. Like a good painter who spends more time preparing the wall than painting it, because he understands that careful attention to the base surface makes the final paint job easier, successful failures take the time to go through these transitional steps.

What are they?

- Getting rid of past debris that clutters your mind.
- Grappling with the practical issue of money.
- Establishing a support group.
- Learning the best way to ask for help.
- Pampering yourself.
- Crediting yourself for every small success you have achieved.

SAYING GOOD-BYE TO THE PAST

There is a reason for ritual. Ceremonies mark transitions in our lives. Birthdays, coming-of-age rites, weddings, even divorce papers serve as notices that one stage has ended and another is about to begin. But failure has no clear ceremony about it. If we are lucky, its effects fade away; they don't, by themselves, *end* on a certain date.

And yet an ending ceremony is exactly what is needed, because failure is untidy. Having our former security ripped away leaves rough edges, jagged pieces of the past that can get in the way of the future. Unless we clean them up, this debris can clutter the new landscape. If we have not dealt with our feelings about the people associated with our setback, if we have not confronted or forgiven them—in short, if we have not completed our past business—any reminder in the future, even seeing former co-workers, makes the adrenaline rise in much the same way it does when seeing an old lover after an unpleasant parting. There is still "unfinished business."

A further reason to confront the past and mark an end to it is to be able to retrieve from it what is useful. On a purely practical basis, it is helpful to tap your past contacts; and if even touching on your old life is too painful, you will be unable to take advantage of what is rightfully yours.

Philip Locke,* an ex-actor, is an example of a person who never confronted his past. Some years ago he had a disastrous encounter with a well-known director for whom he taught an actors' workshop. Though Philip worshiped the man, one day he and the director had a dispute that resulted in Philip's dismissal. Shocked and angry at the time, he is still haunted by the incident years later. Time has passed, but he finds the event almost as painful as when it happened. The reason is clear: Philip was never able to confront the director, air his grievances, and put an end to the experience. In the intervening years, he has not found a job that satisfies him, in part due to his inability to call a single person he knew from those workshop days and ask for help. Because he has not confronted his past, it remains land-mined territory.

If Philip Locke could write a letter to the director, explaining his feelings, if he could, with a new sense of perspective, even wish him well, he would be making a major advance in his own recovery.

Successful failures all seem to take this step instinctively. The ending ritual can assume many different forms. Several people forced themselves to revisit the place where they had failed. They walked through familiar rooms or offices so that they could finally say good-bye.

Some exorcisms were more bizarre. One young woman, consumed with anger at her ex-boss, wrote his name on a piece of paper, placed it in the freezer, carefully closed the door, and for the first time in months was able to smile. The act of "freezing" her anger, shutting the door on it, was so therapeutic she confesses to never even bothering to "thaw" her boss out.

Often the ending ritual takes the form of a letter. One woman, fired abruptly by her mentor after a long association, wrote him the following note:

Dear _____,

I know the events of the past weeks have been painful for you, as they have been for me. I trust and hope that after the bitterness has receded, we can both remember the good times we shared—for there were many—and the support we gave each other. I cannot forget how much I gained from my work in this company. I shall always value it.

Since this is the Easter season, I wish for you, as I wish for myself, peace.

The result of the letter was, as she puts it:

I could look him in the eye again. I was never afraid of meeting him in the elevator or at a party. I felt I had behaved honorably, even charitably. In a curious way I felt I had gained the upper hand. And I knew, when I mailed that letter, it was over, once and for all.

Another way of saying good-bye to the past is to retrieve part of it in your present.

Maggie Rogers* taught English at a top Ivy League university for ten years. She did everything she thought was required to get tenure. She published, won prizes for teaching, and worked long hours with her students. The one thing she refused to do was socialize with other members of her department unless they were close friends. Maggie believed tenure depended on the quality of her work rather than whose friend she was or how well the chairman of the department liked her. Being smart was enough, she thought.

After a decade at the university, she was passed over for tenure, a decision that, she was told, was "purely social." Her work had been fine. When she heard the news, Maggie retreated to her large office with a fireplace—a room that had become a sanctuary, "the place where an academic would dream of growing old"—sat in her favorite chair, and wept.

Eventually Maggie Rogers got a job at another university. But even though she had another position, she still had not come to terms with how to relate to the people she had known in her beloved first university. She couldn't pretend those years did not exist. How should she deal with them when she felt so hurt?

Her solution was instinctive and effective. Informally she assumed the role of mentor to several junior English faculty members at her first institution. Maggie began to interact with her former colleagues almost more than she had done while she was there. She focused on the junior people, telling them what she had learned from her failure: that being smart was only part of what was required, that promotion also depended on making contact with department members on a social basis.

Becoming a mentor to these junior people empowered me in some way. I knew it was the right thing to do. As a result, I am even now the person many of them still turn to. It makes me feel I am still in human contact with people I knew there. It makes me know I haven't lost that whole period of my life.

At her new academic home, Maggie determined not to make the same mistake she had made before. This time, as she puts it:

I made the right social contacts. I did everything I didn't do earlier. I went out of my way to be gracious and charming and to listen to my colleagues attentively. I didn't try to show how bright I was—they could read my books. As a result, when it came time to decide on my getting tenure, the department made its first unanimous recommendation in ten years. I had learned.

Letter writing, calmly conducted meetings with people from your past, even a mild voodoo ritual—all these can be therapeutic. They serve as catharses for emotions. In the absence of socially existing ceremonies, they become self-styled exorcisms. And of course they have the added benefit of enabling you afterward to walk back into your past and retrieve the pieces you want.

DEALING WITH THE MONEY ISSUE

There is probably no more touchy subject in our lives than money. It is not just the stuff that enables us to buy what we need or want; it has become society's report card. For many people, how much money they have tells them how successful they are.

Because money means so many things to us, it is usually what we focus on first when we fail. Its deprivation elicits our most primitive fears—not only loss of income, but loss of security, power, the predictability of our lives, the world's approval, even our ability to be loved.

Because money is so important, both in real and symbolic terms, part of reinventing yourself involves clarifying your attitude toward it.

The best way to quiet your panic about money is to make yourself sit down calmly and assess your financial reality. If your income has been cut off, what other assets do you have? Savings? Life insurance? A house you can mortgage or sell? Are you eligible for unemployment insurance? What are your options?

People we interviewed dealt with the money issue in several different ways.

Some lived off their savings, like Jane Seely, who was fired from her television job.

I was damned if I was going to lower my standard of living one bit. I figured, The minute I start thinking poor, I'll end up poor. This was the rainy day I'd been saving for, and it was time to get out the umbrella.

In the ensuing months, Jane never skipped an exercise class, a massage, or an evening at the theater. Six months later, when she finally landed a new job, she had gone through every dollar she'd saved. But no one had ever looked better while unemployed.

It is a matter of values. For Jane Seely, "appearance" was paramount. Style formed a large part of her life. She was willing to use up her life's security rather than appear down at the heels. Was she anxious about her finances? "Sure," she reports, "but living off my savings was almost like a vote of confidence in myself. I figured I'd find another job when I really had to."

Jane Seely went through every penny she had and never felt poor. Others find the idea of withdrawing principal unbearable. People feel "poor" at different levels.

Living off your savings rather than taking a part-time job is at best an optimistic view, and at worst foolhardy.

Some people took part-time work. Jonathan Rossner* is an architect married to a highly successful advertising executive. When his firm failed a few years ago, Jonathan at first devoted his full-time efforts to finding another job as an architect. But almost all architectural firms were laying people off; and as the months wore on and he had to keep asking his wife for money, he decided "something was better than nothing." He resorted to his "fallback label."

All my life I've loved drawing and painting. I would spend ridiculous sums of money buying the best pens, a special brush, a new set of charcoals—it was like an addiction. When my wife and I got married, I used to say to her that if all else failed, I could get a job selling art supplies. One day, after I'd been out of work for longer than I like to remember, I went into my favorite art supply store and asked them for a part-time job.

Two days a week for almost a year, as his wife commuted to her high-powered New York job, Jonathan Rossner rode his bicycle to his "office," the local art supply store, where he worked as a sales clerk. He earned barely more than the minimum wage, but, as he put it, "I felt I was paying my way."

Jane Seely would have felt a loss of pride taking a "low-level" job like sales clerk. Jonathan Rossner's pride insisted he be financially independent and not invade the money he and his wife had saved. To him, earning *some* money at *some* job was more important than the nature of the job. He would have labeled Jane Seely's attitude "false pride." At the end of a year the economy had improved, and he was able to find work again as an architect.

Work, any sort of work, seemed healthy to people who took part-time jobs while continuing to search for what they really wanted. Earning money, however little, not only paid part of the bills, it made them feel like active, contributing people. The part-time activities they chose ranged from consulting jobs to bartending.

Some went into debt. They borrowed from friends and relatives, either because they were forced by circumstances or because, having made a decision to change careers, they needed money to retrain themselves.

There is nothing wrong with going into debt. Sometimes it is the smartest thing to do. When Andrew Bliss's wine importing business collapsed and he had no idea what to do next, he borrowed money from his family in order to take courses to find a new career—his own real estate agency. Borrowing money for a clearly defined goal can be the best possible financial decision.

Some changed their living standards drastically and made do with less. When you think of it, there is no law that promises upward mobility. When William L. Shirer, author of *The Rise and Fall of the Third Reich,* was fired from his first job as a correspondent on the *Chicago Tribune,* he decided to see how long he could live on his meager savings. He moved to Spain, one of the cheapest countries in Europe, and survived for a year on a thousand dollars. By the end of that year, he was offered another job. Lowering his living standard had bought him time. Later, when he was fired by CBS, he again discovered he could live on considerably less than he thought. In fact, Shirer found, simpler living did not even make him terribly unhappy. For him, the important thing was his inner life, and that was impervious to money.

It all depends on what is more important to you: where you live or how you live.

The period of reinvention is the perfect time to consider the role money has played in your life and the role you want it to play. How important is it to you and why? Do you accept money as the basis for others to judge your success? Is it the basis for your own self-assessment? Will more money really change your life significantly? Where, on your scale of values, does it rank in relationship to the nature of the work itself and your pleasure in it?

Not everyone can decide that money is unimportant and, like Bert Salzman, live in a village in France on a fraction of what he used to make. But few of us even consider it. We are so caught up in society's attitudes, so convinced we must always have more money, that we rarely stop to consider *why.*

Perhaps the question to ask is not "How can I make more money?" but "Will more money make me more satisfied?"

ESTABLISHING A SUPPORT SYSTEM

No one can do it alone. No one should have to. This is the time to gather support troops. Sometimes support comes in the form of friends, those reliable "loved ones" who will not walk out of the room when, like the ancient mariner, you endlessly repeat your tale. Friends and loved ones can help you exorcise your demons simply by listening or, in some cases, by reinterpreting your story and keeping you focused on the future.

Lisa Monroe,* an independent television producer who has frequent ups and downs in her profession, has devised an effective way of countering the downs. When she feels herself becoming discouraged (for her the telltale signs are sleeping late, forgetting to manicure her nails, and generally letting her appearance go downhill), she calls a friend. Alan is her prearranged support partner, and she performs the same function for him when he is discouraged. She describes the following sample conversation they might have:

LISA: I'm really discouraged about the business.

ALAN: What exactly is the problem?

LISA: I'm always short of money. I have a lot of things in the works, but nothing is set. And I can't seem to get the energy to do anything about it.

ALAN: Why not?

LISA: I'm just scared, I guess. I'm afraid I'm a failure.

ALAN: What have you failed at? As far as I know you've done _____, _____, _____, [Alan reminds her of her successes]. Now, are those the accomplishments of a failure?

LISA: Of course not. No.

ALAN: So you're not a failure. The way I see it, you've just got a cash flow problem. Now, what options do you have?

LISA: Well, I could get some development deals, or I could assist some other people on a part-time basis, or I could look for full-time work.

ALAN: Okay, that's good. Which option is the most realistic? Which can occur the fastest?

LISA: A development deal. I have one already in progress with _____.

ALAN: What would it take to clinch it?

LISA: A few phone calls and maybe another meeting or two.

ALAN: Okay, put that down on your list, and I'm calling you tomorrow to see if you've done it.

Alan's support, in the form of a daily phone call when Lisa needs it, performs several important functions. It gives Lisa an independent judge of her actions who reinterprets her problem in a more positive light. What Lisa labeled as failure, Alan saw as a temporary cash flow squeeze. When Lisa focused on her setbacks, her friend reminded her of her successes. And perhaps most important of all, having a support partner made Lisa feel accountable to someone else—she *had* to take action, or Alan would be disappointed when he phoned the next day.

Sometimes support comes in the form of an organized group. When Mark Ringheiser, the talented young architect who finally left I. M. Pei's company to start his own firm, was having business difficulties, he and two close friends banded together to form a highly effective support group. Jack Weber* and Ralph Richmond* were roughly the same age as Mark, also architects working on their own, and, like Mark, tired of feeling isolated with their career problems. All three had gone through broken marriages and were determined to help each other avoid the pain of yet another defeat. The formal rules of the group were few: they would exchange information about one success and one setback at each meeting. The informal understanding was more important: each man would be completely open with the others about his feelings.

MARK: I really felt beat up. I would come to these guys totally emotionally exhausted. I would be within two weeks of bankruptcy, but both of them had been there and fought their way out. They weren't going to let me drown. They were going to hold me up by my collar as I was going down for the third time.

JACK: I'd say to Mark, "Hell, just a year ago I was out there and I had used up all my credit cards, living on my friends. You'll make it."

RALPH: At those meetings, each of us had to tell one problem and one thing that was going well. I remember a whole year in there where I didn't have much to say about "well."

MARK: What you discover is that there are always good things going on, but you become obsessive about your failures and forget to notice the good things. When Jack would say, "Mark, it's your turn to say something good," I'd think, Boy, he has no idea how bad it is. Then I'd think, Wait a minute, we did get published in a place I didn't expect, and I'd tell them about it and I'd feel a little bit better. Or I'd describe a clause I had put in a contract which had really helped me, and one of the other guys would say, "That's a really good idea—can I borrow it?"

RALPH: At every single meeting I felt I got more from the group than I gave to it.

Mark Ringheiser's support group formed the emotional center of his life for a crucial period of time. It was the mechanism that enabled him to turn his career around, regain his self-confidence, and have the courage to continue in what eventually became a successful architectural practice.

Support can come from loved ones, from friends, from formally established groups, or from professional counselors or therapists. Who the support is does not matter; what matters is to rely upon the people you choose. Having a defined support system in which you can safely and repeatedly ventilate your problems prevents you from talking randomly in places where it might hurt you—in the job marketplace, for instance. It gives you emotional strength when you need it most. And it reminds you that you are not alone.

ASKING FOR HELP

To reach out and seek help from others is neither weak nor shameful; it is part of being human. But most of us have great difficulty. We hate to "bother" people. We are afraid of "being a nuisance." Or we say to ourselves, "They'll think I'm stupid." In reality we fear that seeking help shows our weakness.

If we do manage to ask for help, generally we don't do it well. So afraid are we of having the door slammed in our faces we virtually assure our own rejection by the way we ask. "You wouldn't know of any jobs in sales?" says a nervous voice on the end of the phone to someone who might help him. The negative phrasing of the question and the generally tentative tone invite a "No, I'm afraid not." The questioner hangs up, victim of his own self-fulfilling prophecy: it's just as he thought—he was a bother and a nuisance.

If you have trouble asking friends and acquaintances for help, there are professional places to which you can turn. Career counseling services exist throughout the country. Another source of help is your own college or university. Its placement office usually helps alumni as well as new graduates. And you can take courses on career planning or on specific careers at almost every local college and university.

But it is also extremely useful to learn the art of effectively asking help from friends and acquaintances.

After you have reminded yourself that everyone needs help at some point and that you have the *right* to ask a fellow human being for assistance, these few specific guidelines may be of use:

Be specific about what you want. If you say to someone, "I have no idea what to do next, and I want to come talk to you," you are presenting that person with a large, multifaceted problem. If they say yes, suddenly there you'll be, in *their* living room or office, dumping out your woes on *their* floor, asking them to solve *your* life. Their instinctive reaction will be to recoil.

But if you can present what you need as a limited, clear request, you have a much better chance of getting what you want. If, for instance, you say, "I've been exploring your field of _____, and I've already talked to many people. I would appreciate a half hour of your time so I could narrow down what area of the field I would be best suited for," you have given someone a limited task. They are willing to help because you have thought through your part and are not expecting them to do all the work.

Other examples of carefully focused requests for help would be: "Do you know any job openings in _____? If you can just tell me the name of the company where there is an opening, I can take care of getting an interview." Or: "I understand there is an opening at _____; would you feel comfortable calling on my behalf?" In both these cases, you have narrowed down what *you* want from the other person—you have not dropped an ill-defined problem in their lap.

Be as positive and self-confident as possible. Instead of "I've been out of work for six months now, and I thought maybe you had some ideas," try: "What I learned from my last job was that I'm a better hands-on person than a manager, so I've decided to get back to that. I'm exploring several options now, and one of them is in your field. Would you have a half hour for a drink?" You really *do* have options—we all do—and that is what you are reminding the other person as well as yourself. Nobody wants to feel you are clinging to them like a life preserver.

In your choice of language, make the exchange as equal as possible. Instead of, "Could you give me some ideas?" try: "I'd like to brainstorm with you." "Brainstorm" involves an *exchange;* it is a two-way process. The very use of the word puts you on a more even footing. Or: "I have several interesting ideas about what I want to do next, and I'd love to get your feedback." Even if what you really want are specific leads on jobs, presenting your request in a way that emphasizes equality makes both people feel more comfortable.

Flatter the other person. The reason you want their advice is because you respect their thinking, their accomplishments, their judgment; you truly value what they have to say. Usually the flattery is genuine, but often we forget to voice it. Most people love to give advice if they are asked in a way that makes them feel good about themselves.

Always follow up any meeting, drink, or even a helpful telephone call with a short note of appreciation. There is probably no more important way to gain an ally for the future than this, yet it is astonishing how few people do it.

If someone has spent time with you, in a way, they have invested in your life, and most people like to follow their investments. They are probably genuinely interested in what happened to the leads they gave you. Did you follow their advice, or did you go in a different direction? If you have "hooked" them on your story, they will want to hear the end of it. You may feel you don't wish to be a further burden, but the truth is *by continuing to keep them posted of your progress, you are making them feel good about themselves.* How thoughtful that this person has kept me informed, thinks the recipient of a note. By engaging in the simple courtesy of communication, you have allowed the person who gave you guidance to feel wonderful about himself and kindly toward you.

PAMPERING YOURSELF

When you have failed at something in our success-oriented culture, most people expect you to let your hair get dirty, pull a blanket over your head, and hide. But reinvention is doing the unexpected.

This is exactly the time to treat yourself well. First of all, this means taking good care of your body. Stress makes all of us more susceptible to illness and injury. The doctor who treats the New Jersey Devils hockey team reports that when the Devils are on a losing streak there is inevitably a dramatic rise in the incidence of injuries and accidents to players. A sense of failure seems to make people more susceptible to bodily harm. Instead of neglecting your body, therefore, this is the time to take especially good care of yourself. Proper nutrition and exercise are more, not less, important than usual.

It is a time to be good to yourself. Even though you cannot afford it, this may be exactly the time to treat yourself to a massage, go to a new hairdresser and tell him to surprise you, or buy yourself an item of clothing you always wanted. You have had a massive blow to your ego; you are entitled to a little soothing.

When Patricia Soliman was maneuvered out of her job as head of a publishing house, she pampered herself with a vengeance. After getting through what she terms her "near death experience," she looked hard at herself in the mirror. What she saw was a woman who had gained almost one hundred extra pounds over the years. "I had betrayed myself," she admits, "but I was determined I would love myself again one day." Patricia set out on a rigorous self-improvement program. She embarked on a diet that continued for almost a year ("only protein—chicken, fish, and veal—vitamins and two Stoli martinis per diem"), hired an exercise trainer twice a week ("my only previous activity had been fluttering the fan"), and put herself in the hands of one of New York's top hairdressers, who remarked as he restyled her hair, "I see some fucking phoenix rising from the ashes." Patricia smiled for the first time in weeks.

One thing I never underestimated during this period was the value of shopping. It was almost symbolic. In my earlier life I had been a devotee of the silk caftan. I had enough silk caftans to outfit a small third-world country. I threw them all out and headed for Armani. I, who had sneered at cosmetic ads, now hired a makeup artist to show me how to redo my face. And as the pounds came off, and my body was pummeled into shape, and the boxes of clothes arrived from the department store, I did not even mind the bills, which were of course also coming in, because I looked at myself in the mirror and loved myself again.

The new Patricia Soliman landed a job as vice-president and associate publisher in a larger and more powerful company than the one she had left and never regretted indulging herself during this time of transition. "Out of this cosmic kick in the ass," she remarks with typical wit, "I turned back into the great beauty I was."

CREDITING YOURSELF FOR SUCCESS

Part of reinvention is reminding yourself of your successes. The strong emotions generated by failure tend to crowd out the memory of success. It's like playing a great game of golf and then missing one key putt: what you remember is not all the good strokes but the one missed putt. Therefore, a necessary recovery step involves retrieving memories of your past successes, then reinforcing the pattern by creating new successes, no matter how small.

How do you do this? First you look back at your own history and extract from it all the successes you had, those experiences that, in the miasma of failure, you forgot. Before you failed at whatever you did, you undoubtedly succeeded, too. Dust off those memories and dwell on them. Give them at least equal time with your failures. Some people we talked to made lists of their successes, useful reminders to themselves when they were feeling discouraged. Psychiatrist Yvette Obadia calls this "making your own success chain."

Then turn to the present. The idea is to focus on one success, any success you have each day. You are edging your way back into life, gaining strength as you go, taking small steps. Learning that you can successfully take small steps gives you the confidence to take bigger ones.

Your daily success need not be spectacular. Quite the reverse. In this transitional period, the idea is *to credit yourself for any task you set out to do and actually complete.* The nature of the task does not matter. It could be jogging for a mile, writing a letter requesting an interview, painting the room you've been meaning to paint for a year, losing five pounds, finding out what courses exist in a field of interest, teaching your child to ride a bike, or making an appointment to see someone. *What* the goal is hardly matters; *accomplishing it* is the point. You are reimprinting yourself, reminding yourself that you are a person who can accomplish what you set out to do.

When Harold Jacobs* lost his job as a museum director and was unemployed for a long while, he gave himself the task of building a rather elaborate treehouse on his property.

After the first story was on, I realized it was mine—complete with ladder that lifted up and trapdoors and cranks for wine and cheese. Building the treehouse absorbed me in something. I became quite compulsive, almost demented about it. I remember my wife and I were going out to a big party, and I rushed out in my jacket and tie to put in a few more boards. I was consumed with it. It was so wonderful! Something I had built with my own hands that wasn't going to fall down!

It could have been anything—a small boat or a stone wall, something that was going to last, that was tangible, a product! It helped greatly, that treehouse. It made me say, "Okay, stop feeling sorry for yourself, wallowing in self-pity, and get on with it."

By not aiming for big successes, you take the pressure off. Elaina Zucker is an organizational development specialist who must sell her services to large corporations. When she was first starting out, this seemed a formidable task, especially since her previous dismissal from an advertising job had shaken her confidence. Instinctively Elaina understood the idea of focusing on small successes instead of pressuring herself to attain large ones. Rather than walk in cold and try to clinch a sale, she gave herself the task of making "research calls" only, forays to find out a company's needs. Because her goal was only a research call, she was relaxed and confident. She had a narrowly defined objective and was able to accomplish it easily and feel pleased with herself. Not surprisingly, probably just because she relaxed and sensed she was succeeding, she also picked up several clients in the process.

• • •

When you fail once, you feel vulnerable. Perhaps you will fail again. On the other hand, if you succeed once, no matter how small the task, perhaps you will succeed again. Just as all of us are overly harsh with ourselves for our failures, most of us forget to credit ourselves for deeds well done.

The most important part of reinvention involves thinking. Figuring out why you failed, reinterpreting your own story, relabeling yourself, expanding your options—all these are processes of thought. But between the thinking and actually going out into the world with a sense of re-creation, there is a period of transition.

The steps outlined here are really safety measures, practical things you can do to give yourself the best chance of future success. You are clearing away obstacles. Some come from unfinished business in the past, and some come from a form of self-sabotage in the present.

What you want to do is to give yourself the cleanest possible new start.

X ⸺

The Reinvented Person: Two Stories

Some people are strengthened by failure, and others are defeated by it. Who survives and who does not has little to do with money or advantage; it depends more on inner strength of character, a primitive toughness that protects the self and will not let mere external events destroy it. This kernel of survival is a precious possession, and discovering it is one of the very real rewards of failure. It is a profound and powerful kind of self-knowledge.

The two people whose stories follow are both innate survivors. One comes from a well-to-do background, and one was born into poverty, but both became the person he or she wanted to be only after surviving failure. Their stories do not follow the step-by-step program for reinventing yourself outlined in this book, because real life is rarely as neat and predictable as the structure of a book. But each of them instinctively stumbled onto parts of the process. Intuitively and successfully, they "reinvented" themselves, without ever hearing the phrase.

FACING UP TO YOUR MISTAKES—JEWELLE BICKFORD

Jewelle Bickford is the newest senior vice-president of one of New York's most prestigious investment banking firms. In her early forties, dressed in a Valentino suit, silk shirt, and Cartier gold earrings, she exudes confidence. But behind the eyes, breaking through the veneer and humanizing the perfect exterior, is a hint of vulnerability. When she looks at you, she seems to be saying, "Isn't this wonderful?" and you feel she will add in the next breath, "Isn't it silly, too?"

What gives Jewelle Bickford perspective and makes her a survivor is her honesty with herself. When the future of her career was at stake, when she could have turned away in defeat, she was able to face herself in a way most of us cannot. She forced herself to "figure out" her failure. Once she understood the truth of it, she was able to reinvent herself and become the person she wanted to be.

If ever there was a "late bloomer," it was Jewelle Bickford. For the first thirty-seven years of her life she was someone's daughter, someone's wife, someone's mother. She identified herself through the strongest nearby object, and no wonder. Her father was an old-fashioned business rogue, whose fortunes appeared and disappeared as magically as the rabbits pulled out of hats at the birthday parties he arranged for her in his flush days. Unscrupulous as he was charming, he announced to his wife and teenaged daughter one day that the bank was taking over their twenty-room Tudor mansion on the Hudson and he didn't quite know where they could go. Born into luxury, Jewelle never got accustomed to the near poverty and constant upheaval caused by her father's recklessness. "I became this odd combination," she says of herself, "on the one hand absolutely fearless—what can you do to me? I've had my home taken away—on the other hand deeply insecure."

At nineteen she dropped out of college to marry a young lawyer who was as steady and solid as her father was not. A career was the last thing on her mind—security was what she craved. She had two children in short order and vowed to give them the stability she never had. To be the world's best wife and mother was her goal; she stilled her other drives.

But as the years went by, those drives resurfaced. When her daughters became teenagers, she went back to college and at thirty-six finished her long-abandoned degree. Politics lured her. Fearless from childhood, she believed in "the democratic cause" (with both a little and a big "D") and knew how to use her considerable charm and intelligence to get what she wanted. In short, she was a natural fundraiser. She first contributed her money-raising skills to a brash congressman named Ed Koch. When he became mayor of New York, Koch did not forget Jewelle's efforts on his behalf: he named her deputy director of the Community Board Assistance Unit, her first paid position. Her job was to help implement revisions to the city charter. Within a year she was director.

It was as if all those quiet years at home with the children had been waiting time, and now she was ready to sprint. Jewelle developed a style that even she characterizes as "hard-charging." She drove herself mercilessly and those around her only slightly less so. Koch had given her a job to do—God knew she was starting it late in life—and she was determined to succeed. In a way, she did, if you judge by a *New York Times* editorial that praised her department's performance. However, along the way she also managed to offend people, and in politics that can be a grave error. If one of the people you offend is the Brooklyn borough president, who has the mayor's ear, it can be fatal.

Politics is the game of double-speak, so nobody ever told Jewelle directly she had failed; the mayor's deputies merely announced that His Honor had decided to close her department. Koch officially blamed it on New York's fiscal crisis. Others said she had done such an excellent job she had rendered her own department obsolete. No one said anything about her offending important people, and Jewelle, like all of us, tried to believe she was blameless. Stunned at the news, she told herself her unit was never intended to be permanent, that she had been given a limited job to do and had done it. "One day I said it was the Brooklyn borough president who hated me; one day I said I had completed my mandate, so it was time I left; one day I said it was politics and had nothing to do with me specifically." No matter what she told herself, it felt like failure.

At this point Jewelle made the mistake most of us make: she did not take the time to stop and figure out what went wrong. She tried to deny the pain, gloss over the defeat. The only answer was to move fast, she told herself, to get another job immediately so no one would ever think she had been fired.

After the rebuff from Koch, politics seemed closed to her, and she had no real business experience anywhere else. She was in her late thirties, lacked any specific training, and had just lost her only paid job. But she was instinctively a survivor, and she displayed the survivor's gift of adaptive thinking. Intuitively she understood one of the key concepts of reinvention: break down your job label and recycle the component skills. Instead of saying to herself "I am an unemployed director of a city agency," she said, "City agency directors have political savvy and drive; those skills will be usable elsewhere." Jewelle could walk the no-man's-land between two hostile groups and somehow end up with a deal. The hard-core realities of politics, the give-and-take among constituencies, were by now second nature. Rather than dismiss her natural talents, she labeled them as viable skills. The goal was to find a field in which they would be useful.

Banking was an industry that had constant interaction with government. Jewelle packed up her office at City Hall and set out to woo Wall Street.

She had done her homework and knew the governmental needs of various banks. Instead of looking for a vacancy that existed, she went into Citibank and told them what she thought she could do for them. In a sense she invented her own job; within weeks they offered her a vice-presidency. Her task was to draw in other constituencies to work alongside Citibank in an effort to change New York State's usury laws. It was the kind of job she had performed both for the mayor and as a volunteer. Jewelle bought a navy-blue pin-striped suit, had new cards printed, and put her failure at City Hall behind her. "I felt vindicated by getting this new job for much more money," she says, "so I was able to do what a lot of people do—not think about my role in the firing and just move on."

She was riding high. Three years ago she'd been a housewife making breakfast for her children; now her own secretary made her coffee in the morning. Having given little thought to her mistakes in the previous job, she dove into her work and—predictably—made the same mistakes again.

Underneath the façade, I felt insecure. I felt I needed to promote myself and my abilities to anyone who would listen. I was very vocal and I undoubtedly moved too quickly. It wasn't that I couldn't do the job—I was doing the job brilliantly—but the way I did it heightened the anxieties of everyone around me. Some were envious of my job, and some were afraid of me. The combination of their anxiety and my lack of corporate savvy was a disaster.

Within eight months Jewelle Bickford was fired. This time the dismissal hit her with devastating force. She went through the classic stages of failure she had managed to avoid before.

I knew for certain it was my fault. I knew I had really failed, and I wasn't sure I could rebound. My reputation was dreadful. I felt desperate. I thought I might never be able to get a job again, that I might have to be only a volunteer. And I felt very bitter. I felt like I used to feel as a child—sort of an overall gloom.

No one said she had done "too good" a job. There was no Brooklyn borough president to blame. Nothing her husband or children said seemed to help. Jewelle had failed. Worst of all, through the shock, the panic, the anger, and the depression, there was somehow a familiar ring, a sense of déjà vu. Citibank felt like city government revisited. She had an uncomfortable feeling there was a pattern to her defeat, though she could not give it a name.

Then a remarkable thing happened, a stroke of luck that changed her career. She met a person who reinterpreted her failure.

David Switkin was a small, bouncy man in charge of outplacement in Citibank. His was the door they sent you in just before they showed you out the front door of the bank. If the meeting with Mr. Switkin gave you new direction, fine; in any case, it eased the corporation's guilt. Jewelle went to Mr. Switkin's office, sat down, and told him in a dead, flat voice that she knew her career was over. Everyone hated her; her boss had made this explicitly clear when he fired her. Other people found her energy abrasive, her intelligence threatening, her urgency wearing. She had failed, truly and totally. Mr. Switkin just listened. He gave her three long tests to fill out, then asked her to return the next day. As she got up to leave, he said, "By the way, not everyone thinks you're terrible. I made a few phone calls. There's a small, highly placed group of people around here who think you're rather brilliant."

When Jewelle returned the next day, Mr. Switkin didn't even bother to say hello. Holding her test results in his hands, he greeted her with "Why in the world did you go into banking?" Before she could get her coat off, he added, "Traditional banking is much too slow and conservative for you, Jewelle. You don't know it, but you're an *investment* banker." As she was taking this in, he uttered the kindest sentence of all. "You haven't failed," he told her, "you've just been in the wrong environment."

I felt as if someone had thrown me a lifeline. It was as if I had been drowning and David Switkin showed me a way back to shore. When I left his office I knew I was going to make it. I had been given a second chance.

Just because she had failed at banking and city government, the outplacement counselor pointed out, did not mean she herself was a failure. What were liabilities in those jobs—her maverick way of thinking, her intense drive to "close" things quickly, her high personal ambition—would be assets somewhere else. Jewelle was suffering from "wrong fit."

. . .

Sometimes in our lives, if we're lucky, as Gertrude Stein said, there is a person who says "yes." That one "yes" can validate us for the rest of our lives. For Jewelle Bickford, David Switkin was that person.

Armed with Mr. Switkin's relabeling, she might have gone on and found another job in investment banking; but if she had not taken the step she next took, she would surely not have become the success she is today.

Usually we fail for a combination of factors, and Jewelle decided she had to look more closely at herself.

I knew I had to do some serious thinking about my behavior. Mr. Switkin had shown me what I could become; now it was up to me to "clean up my act" so I could become that.

What responsibility did she have in her own downfall? she asked herself. Was it simply that she was the right person for the wrong job and therefore completely blameless? Or was there more to it? Jewelle began a tough review of her behavior. She realized she was deeply insecure about her abilities. She had no real understanding of how corporations worked, nor any in-depth knowledge of banking.

In a way, I had come in under false pretenses. I wasn't as good as I sounded, and if I had realized this, I probably would have gone backward before I went forward—I would have come in as an assistant vice-president, then slowly moved up. On a technical level, there was an enormous amount I simply didn't know.

On a personal level, too, I was lacking. To cover up my insecurity I had tried to promote myself quickly and vocally. I had to succeed in a hurry, and I made the mistake of driving everyone else by my timetable. Inwardly I was terrified, but to the outside world I seemed abrasive. It was clear to me I had to learn patience.

Jewelle was now doing the essential task of reinvention: figuring out why she had failed. This was the step she had omitted in rushing into the Citibank job, and its omission had made her blindly repeat her earlier pattern. Yes, she was suffering from "wrong fit," she told herself; but she also needed to improve her interpersonal skills. That, in the end, was what had closed her department in city government; that, in the end, was what had caused her downfall at Citibank.

The truth can be painful, but it can also be liberating. Jewelle now set about changing herself as purposefully and diligently as a runner would train for a marathon. First of all she needed time and a safe place. Through Mr. Switkin's efforts, she managed to get hired by the investment banking side of Citibank.

It wasn't the ideal place for me, but it was convenient, and it would give me a chance to repair the damages. I made a vow to myself at that time: I decided I would not leave this institution where I could safely hide out until I had thoroughly learned my profession, until I knew I could work in a corporation of any size, and until I was certain I would never make the same mistakes again.

Typical of Jewelle's maverick way of thinking was her first practical act. She needed to know more about economics, and business school seemed too long a route to take. She decided to hire a personal tutor. She asked business friends for suggestions, but none of the people she met seemed right. Trusting her instincts, she waited. On an airplane enroute to a business meeting in Phoenix, one of her colleagues introduced her to a fellow investment banker. "This guy," he said, punching him in the shoulder, "is the best numbers jock in the business." Jewelle smiled and bought him a drink. By the time they landed in Arizona, the numbers jock was her once-a-week tutor.

She worked with him for two years. By the end of that time Jewelle Bickford knew her profession.

At work, she forced herself to go slower, to be calmer, to listen harder.

I stayed at Citibank four long and difficult years, but when I left there I understood timing and balance. I learned to get along with people, even if their pace and style were different from mine. Once I did that, I realized the people I worked with were not evil or horrible or necessarily wrong; it was just that we were incompatible. I was simply more risk-oriented than they. There was no anger. I felt I had grown up, and now it was truly time for me to get out.

Instinctively, Jewelle was performing a necessary step in the reinvention process: she was saying good-bye to her past. As long as she railed against the people at Citibank for their mistreatment, she was spending part of her energy concentrating on the past. Once she could look at them with dispassion, with forgiveness, with the knowledge that she had completed this part of her life, she was truly energized for the future.

In her new senior vice-president's office at the investment banking firm where she works, Jewelle runs her fingers through her chestnut hair and looks out the window thoughtfully. "I never thought about it this way before," she says, "but I guess I wouldn't be where I am today if I hadn't failed."

USING WHAT YOU'VE GOT: BILL TATUM

Bill Tatum is the chairman of the board and editor-in-chief of the *Amsterdam News,* America's oldest black newspaper. The rich and powerful of the city court his favor. He goes downtown to lunch, swills wine, and plays power games with the best of them. On his way back uptown after lunch, he frequently laughs: Tatum has seen a few things in his lifetime; he's hard to fool.

Bill Tatum had none of Jewelle Bickford's advantages. Jewelle was white, privileged, raised in a mansion on the Hudson River. Bill Tatum was black, one of thirteen children, and never saw indoor plumbing until he went to grade school. Bill Tatum got where he is by his own wits and because he had a powerful dream. From the time he won the Scholastic Press Award in 1951 in his North Carolina high school—or maybe even before that, from the time he read the works of his hero, Thomas Wolfe—Tatum knew he would go to New York and become a writer.

At twenty-one Tatum came to New York, holding the hopes of his family and his small town, a black kid who against the odds was voted "most likely to succeed" and had graduated from college. He applied for jobs in publishing, on newspapers, at magazines; no one even interviewed him. Eventually he lowered his sights to waiting tables. Still he could find no work. He moved out of the YMCA and into flophouses on the Bowery. He would take any job at all, he decided— dishwashing, emptying garbage, anything. Still he could find nothing. He began sleeping in doorways. Ruefully he thought of Thomas Wolfe: like Wolfe, Tatum could not go home again.

He started stealing food to survive. He started hating himself. One day as he was pocketing a piece of fruit from a grocery store on Second Avenue, he felt a hand grab him on the collar. As he was being hauled inside the store, he began screaming, "You want to arrest me? Go ahead! I'm a thief—that's right, I'm a thief!" Morris Moskowitz, the grocery store owner, deposited Tatum in a chair in his office and answered in a mild voice, "On Tuesday you stole a banana and a roll, on Wednesday you stole a package of bologna, today it's a piece of fruit."

He looked at a scrap of paper as he spoke; obviously he had been keeping notes. "You're not a thief, you need a job." Moskowitz told Tatum to write up an inventory of the store's merchandise, stood up, tossed him the keys, and told him to lock up when he had finished.

Bill Tatum stayed up all night working. The next day Morris Moskowitz gave him fifty dollars. "Get some clothes and a place to stay," he told him, "and forgive me for saying so, but you could use a bath."

We become what we are largely because the world agrees with what we say we are. But sometimes the world contradicts us. When Bill Tatum said he was a thief, Morris Moskowitz said no. This was a primitive kind of relabeling, one that freed Tatum from the way he had begun to think of himself and left him open to new possibilities.

Bill then began a time of his life that he now regards as his "hidden failure" period. He continued working at the grocery store, became head of the Cooper Square Committee, a community protest group formed to stop developers from tearing down his bargain apartment, and with the dawn of the sixties drifted into the civil rights movement. He joined every protest march he could find, as if by protesting loudly enough he could force other people to listen to his most basic protest: Why can I not realize my dream of becoming a writer? It was this that gnawed away at him. In everyone else's eyes, Bill Tatum was a success. (Or, as they would have said, "For a black man from a poor family in the south, he's a success.") But Bill Tatum considered himself a failure.

I was an abject failure in terms of what I wished to be and lying about it, not only to myself but to everyone else. I would write a few paragraphs and read them to the Harlem Writers Guild and pretend they were notes on a novel. All the while I was working in the grocery store, as a postal worker, as a snow shoveler, as a clerk typist, I would make excuses to relatives, family, and friends, saying, "I'm really not those things you see me being, I'm really different, I'm talented, I'm a writer." And all the while I hated myself.

The collapse of the civil rights movement, coupled with his personal sense of defeat, provoked a rage in him that finally exploded. On a New York City bus one day, Bill thought he heard a man call him a "nigger." Something snapped. He put his hands around the man's throat and almost killed him. Only some primitive survival instinct made him loosen his grip. Shaken, Bill Tatum got off the bus and decided to leave America.

He bought a one-way ticket for the whitest country in the world, Sweden. To this day he is not sure why he chose Sweden, except that he had been given the name of a young Swedish writer, and that was one name more than he had in New York.

To reinvent ourselves we need validation from the outside world. As we try our new selves out, we need someone who says, "Yes, you are that person, I know you are." Jewelle Bickford was able to stay at Citibank and reinvent herself there. Without physically changing locales, she made other people see her in a new way. In order to reinvent himself, Bill Tatum had to move to a different continent. In New York, he was another black man with dreams; when he arrived penniless in Sweden and announced that he was a writer, people took him seriously.

He stayed there for two years, establishing his credentials as a journalist, doing long newspaper articles about America. After a while an important change occurred: he began to think of himself as a writer. But he was still an expatriate writer. The news of President Kennedy's assassination was the electric jolt that broke through his expatriate identity and reminded him he was an American. Maybe, he thought, maybe you *can* go home again. He decided to try.

Back in New York, even with his clippings from Sweden, he could not get a job as a writer. He buried the dream. Perhaps, he thought, that's what growing up is, making compromises.

In 1966 he was offered a job with the Lindsay administration. For the next thirteen years Bill Tatum worked in city government. He might have been content, swallowing his disappointments and settling for what he had achieved, were it not for the election of Ed Koch as mayor of New York. By sheer coincidence, the man who closed Jewelle Bickford's department and set in motion her reappraisal of her life would do the same thing for Bill Tatum. Koch took office in November, and on Christmas Eve Tatum, an avowed Koch opponent, was told to pack up his things and get out.

Not being a writer was a hidden failure, but being fired from city government was public and visible. Panicked by his defeat and by pressing debts, Tatum decided it was time to call on the many people for whom he had done favors over the years. He set up meetings. The pattern was always the same. They would take him to expensive lunches, order a bottle of the best wine, urge him to "keep in touch," but never hire him. In the end, Bill Tatum realized, it was like being a poor black boy in North Carolina—you could only count on yourself.

There was one other person Bill Tatum could count on—his wife. In 1966, despite the violent objections of her family, Bill had married a white woman named Susan, who was to provide him with the support and validation he needed to reinvent himself. Out of love she did for Bill Tatum what David Switkin had done for Jewelle Bickford out of professionalism: she reinterpreted her husband's failure. She was that person who says "yes." When Bill Tatum talked shyly of being a writer, Susan said, "Why not?" When he talked about building up savings, amassing what he called "fuck-you money," Susan never pointed out that they could not even pay existing bills. When he dreamed of becoming an important voice in black America, she regarded that as a career option, not a fantasy. And because of her belief in him, he began to see himself differently.

After you analyze why you have failed—in this case, Tatum had drawn a "wild card" in the person of Ed Koch—the crucial step in reinvention is *being able to see yourself differently.* That is what reinterpreting your story helps you do. It is what changing your label is all about. It is what has to happen before you can expand your options. Some people can see themselves anew all by themselves, but most of us need a guide. Susan Tatum was that guide for Bill. As he describes her:

Before real belief comes, there is bravado. What you are doing is laying out in your own mind who you are. Very often we are not strong enough individually to carry it off, but if there is one other person in the world who buys our scenario, it is a support mechanism which allows us to move forward.

I blue-skied constantly. I talked about a world out there that was so far from the possible only a demented person would have believed it, and Susan believed it. In order for a dream to become real, there has to be reinforcement, and Susan represented that reinforcement. In terms of attempting anything, she never said no. She was my drum major, and you don't have to have a whole cheering section if you just have a drum major.

With Susan in his corner, and having nothing to lose, Bill decided his defeat marked the perfect time to clarify his goals. As long as he was dreaming, he decided to dream big: he wanted a platform for his writing, one that would also provide a power base so no one could dismiss him ever again. At the time, Bill Tatum owned a part interest in the *Amsterdam News,* which he had bought for a small investment some years ago. His dream now was to take over the paper.

There were built-in problems. Not only did he lack the capital to buy more shares; even if he raised the money, the paper was not profitable. It all boiled down to money. Bill and Susan Tatum needed money, all sorts of it—money to live on for the moment, money to buy more shares in the *Amsterdam News,* money to live on in the future if he was successful in taking control of an unprofitable paper. His *identity* and power base would come from the newspaper, he decided, but his *money* would have to come from someplace else.

On the face of it, the task seemed impossible. Bill Tatum was unemployed, had no immediate prospects, and was entertaining wild dreams of taking over a newspaper. But he did not tell himself it was impossible. On the contrary, in his own head he relabeled himself "newspaper publisher." Once he made that shift in his thinking, he asked himself the practical questions—How was he going to get there? What did he have to build on? What were his assets?

Outplacement counselor Tom Jackson tells a story of taking a train to an important sales meeting in November wearing only a lightweight summer suit. The weather changed suddenly to snow, and when he got off the train he had no raincoat, no umbrella, there were no taxis, and the nearby phone was broken. Standing shivering in the snow, all Tom Jackson wanted to do was cry. Then he reasoned that fate had dealt him this hand, that this hand was all there was, and he had better figure out a way to play it. He got on the next train that came in, took it one stop farther, called for a cab which he asked to wait while he bought an umbrella, and went on to the meeting. "You've only got the cards you've got," Jackson points out, "but you've got a variety of interpretations of the situation and a variety of actions. Instead of bemoaning your fate, the thing to do is identify which actions and which interpretations will produce what you want to produce."

Without ever meeting Tom Jackson, Bill Tatum understood the idea of using what you've got and only what you've got. Tom Jackson arrived at that idea through his intellect; Bill Tatum knew it in his gut. He was born into poverty, lived by his wits, and, in a queer way, was almost relieved when everyone except Susan let him down—as if by shedding false baggage he could move faster.

Bill and Susan took an inventory of their assets. They had a run-down house they had bought some years ago on New York's Lower

East Side and rebuilt with their own hands, and they had a small ramshackle cottage up in Canada. If that was all they had, that was what they would use. "I learned long ago," says Bill, "that as long as you could use your hands and were in relatively good health, you could survive."

They would use their assets—their houses and their hands—to create the money they needed to fulfill their dream. First Bill mortgaged his house and used that money to buy another house in Staten Island. Then he took off his tie and jacket, put on overalls, and started to work. With his own hands he fixed up the Staten Island house and made it rentable. Susan, who had been a designer and understood blueprints, went up to Canada and, working alongside cheap local laborers, built an addition to the cottage, which they then also rented. They continued mortgaging properties, using the money to buy other properties, pouring in their own labor and building up their equity. Along the way Bill took a part-time job as a public relations person for a health insurance plan. The goal was first of all to survive, then to create enough assets from the real estate business to buy up shares in the *Amsterdam News*. Bill Tatum would use what he had to create the result he wanted.

As a boy growing up in North Carolina, Bill Tatum formed his first ideas of black history by reading the pages of the *Amsterdam News*. Today he runs it. His editorials give the paper its tone, and the very people who a few short years ago would not give him a job now call to say, "Let's have lunch—it's been too long." Bill laughs and names the most expensive restaurant he can think of. Somewhere around dessert, as they are getting past the small talk and around to asking for a favor, Tatum, a bulldog of a man, leans over, grabs them by the collar, and says, "Where were you when I needed you, you _____." Then he settles back into his seat, finishes his wine, and feels ever so much better.

• • •

Reinvention looks simple to the outside world, which sees only the final result—Jewelle Bickford, investment banker; Bill Tatum, publisher of the *Amsterdam News*. The process, however, is complex and largely internal. Some people, like Jewelle Bickford, reinvent themselves neatly and only once. Hers is a classic case: she figured out what she did wrong, reinterpreted her past failure, relabeled herself, said good-bye to the past, and moved on. Others, like Bill Tatum, fumble around and fail a few times, searching intermittently for who they are and who they wish to become. Tatum reinvented himself once in a grocery store on Second Avenue, once in the civil rights movement, once as far away as Sweden, and finally in the city of his dreams, New York.

Jewelle was fortunate enough to find everything she wanted in one convenient new label—investment banker. Her career gives her both money and a sense of identity. Tatum's solution was different. He separated his livelihood—the money he got from his public relations job and his real estate holdings—from his identity, publisher of the *Amsterdam News.* Jewelle has an all-in-one identity; for Tatum, the parts add up to a satisfactory whole.

But what they have in common is more important than what differentiates them. They share the hallmarks of all successful failures: the ability to adapt to changing circumstances, the willingness to take responsibility for their own mistakes, the refusal to be a victim.

An earlier successful failure, Winston Churchill, summed it up: "Success," he said, "is going from failure to failure without loss of enthusiasm."

PART THREE
Toward Real Success

A fisherman was lying along the banks of a river in Maine one day, lazily casting his line into the water. Every so often, just frequently enough to punctuate the long, sun-filled hours, he caught a silvery salmon. That plus a six-pack of beer and some homemade sandwiches made for a thoroughly agreeable day. As he was hauling in a fish, a prosperously dressed businessman from a nearby town strolled over. "Don't you realize," he asked the fisherman, "that you could catch many more fish if you put several lines into the water at the same time?"

"Why would I want more fish?" asked the fisherman.

"Well, if you had more fish, you would have more to sell, and you would make more money," the industrialist replied. "And if you made more money, you could buy a big fishing boat. Then you could open up a store and sell your fish to the whole town. After you opened one store, you could open a second, and then a third. You would have many people working for you. Eventually you could open a large wholesale fish market, shipping fish all over America." The sun made little reflections on the water as the industrialist continued to spin his dream of success. "You could become a very rich man," he concluded triumphantly.

The fisherman took a swig of beer and looked unconvinced. "And then what would I do?" he asked the industrialist.

"Why, then you would be successful, and you'd have all the time in the world to do whatever you most enjoyed doing. You could just lie on your back, relax, and go fishing!"

The fisherman looked up at him and smiled. "But that's what I'm doing now!"

A few years ago a powerful movie stars' agent went to a glamorous New Year's Eve party in New York, at the home of Woody Allen. A woman in her early thirties, born into a poor family in Brooklyn, she had managed through hard work, talent, and drive to represent film stars whose names were household words. This New Year's Eve she arrived in a limousine, wearing a long gold lamé dress, escorted by an actor who had just been nominated for an Academy Award. Everyone in the room greeted her warmly. The thought flashed through her head as she made her way among the guests, I have everything I always wanted.

Just before midnight she excused herself to go to the ladies' room. She was feeling the effects of too much champagne, and as the sounds of the party echoed through the wall, she suddenly caught sight of herself in the full-length mirror on the bathroom wall and inexplicably began to sob. This isn't it, this isn't completing me, she thought to herself. Something is very wrong. Never was she more aware of her loneliness than at this moment when she had everything she thought she ever wanted.

Years later, when she had changed jobs, moved to another city, and begun a long reexamination of her life, she said of that incident, "I believed that if I wore a gold lamé dress and walked down a staircase to adoring glances, somehow I would be filled up, content. I thought success would make me lovable."

•   •   •

The apocryphal fisherman from Maine knew what the talent agent from New York learned: it is not the outward trappings of success that satisfy us; it is a sense of our inner selves being at peace, a day-to-day, minute-by-minute joy we take in what we do. The fisherman understood his success was measured not by flotillas of boats, but by a feeling of contentment he already had. Similarly, the talent agent who had all the outer trappings of success learned that these things were empty without a sense of worth, a core understanding of who she was.

It is possible to go through your whole life never confronting this sense of self. It is particularly possible if you are very successful. Not everyone looks in the mirror and begins to weep. Most people rush to fill the void with more possessions, more stimuli, more toys, more escape.

But failure brings you up short. It cuts away all the trappings, forcing you to confront your inner self. It throws you off balance, makes you examine who you are without the accolades and possessions and social status. Failure makes you look at yourself in the bathroom mirror at midnight.

True success can be built only upon a solid sense of self. It comes from striking a balance between who you are and what you do; establishing an inner sense of values so that you yourself, and not others, judge your work and worth; learning to take joy in the process of what you do rather than its outcome.

True success, then, may involve a fundamental reappraisal of self, a reshuffling of the pieces, a painful look inside.

What makes us undertake such a difficult endeavor? Generally only a setback such as failure. Only when we are literally "set back"—rocked on our heels—do we reexamine ourselves. By making us take a long overdue inner journey, our defeats hold the potential for becoming shortcuts to true success.

The real successes, in other words, are often people who have learned the lessons of failure.

XI _____
The Inner Journey

Freud said that man's two great drives are work and love. For most of us, balancing these sources of identity is fraught with difficulty. If we love too much, expending the bulk of our energies on our emotional lives, our appetite for work is often dulled. Conversely, if we invest as fully in work as American culture seems to demand, what is left for our inner selves?

Balancing these two drives is essential. If we ignore our interior life at the expense of the success ethic, then when work crumbles beneath us, we stand in danger of losing our very selves. To strike the balance between love and work, all of us must ask at some point: Who are we without our work?

Failure prods us to ask this question. It shatters the carefully constructed balance of our lives and forces us to examine by day what most of us look at only fleetingly in the dark of night—our own values. For some people, the readjustment after a career setback can be as simple and superficial as finding a new job. But for the real explorers, for those who derive the most benefit from failure, it can be as profound and important as examining one's inner landscape.

The two stories that follow are of people who took that inner journey and who, by looking within, finally found a balance between who they are and what they do.

ROB COHEN'S JOURNEY

When you grow up in the movie business in California, the last piece of advice anyone gives you is to look inward. "Eyes forward" is the conventional wisdom—focus on your next job, your next film, your

210

next success; or "eyes to the rear"—someone may be nipping at your heels. For a long time Rob Cohen never worried about the people in back of him; he was too busy moving steadily ahead. It took failure to make him change his gaze, to look neither ahead nor behind him, but to stop and look within.

Now in his mid-thirties, with intense blue eyes and a receding hairline, Rob Cohen no longer has the appearance of a boy genius, but for many years, when his hair was fuller and his eyes less vulnerable, he not only looked like one, but was widely hailed as the latest of that breed in a town that hothouses geniuses only to toss them aside when they wilt. Rob seemed to hit L.A. out of nowhere. Born in New York, he graduated from Harvard with a major in anthropology, then went to "the coast" with a desire to get into the film business somehow. Berry Gordy, the charismatic entrepreneur who founded Motown Records, thought he recognized a kindred soul in Rob, and Gordy is a man who plays his hunches. He hired Cohen.

From that moment on, Rob Cohen had, even by California standards, a meteoric rise. Two years later, at the age of twenty-four, he was running Motown. He was, as he puts it, "the youngest head of anything in this town, which has been used to seeing a lot of young people." At an age when his fellow classmates from Harvard wore three-piece suits and took the subway to management training programs, Rob Cohen slipped into his blue jeans and drove his Porsche to the set of the first feature film he produced. It was called *Mahogany,* and, defying the odds of Hollywood, it became a hit. In a town where people struggle for years to get a film produced, Rob Cohen produced ten movies in the next six years. In 1977 alone he had three films in production, including the most ambitious one he had ever undertaken, *The Wiz.* At Beverly Hills watering spots so chic that only the powerful knew their unlisted phone numbers, agents slipped Rob scripts and told him he was "fabulous." His success eclipsed the fevered dreams of his cramped dormitory rooms at Harvard.

When you are on the upward path, it's very easy to convince yourself it can never be any other way but this. You tell yourself you are always going to be successful—and it's because you're smarter than anyone else, you're more crafty, you're more talented, you're more deserving. Your fantasies about yourself are of course inspired by your true fears, but it's very easy to forget that. When you're successful, you lose the ability to distinguish between those two things. You think your success will never end.

Rob Cohen's success might never have ended, had he been content to continue as a producer. Underneath, however, he thought he was more "creative" than that. In Hollywood the producer puts the deal together, but the real power and glory belong to the director. Rob Cohen left Motown, determined to direct.

He managed to direct one picture, *Small Circle of Friends,* which opened to mixed reviews and poor box-office business. And suddenly his luck seemed to change. The man who had been accustomed to getting more money, more power, more accolades as quickly as he could amass them now struggled for years to get his second picture going. Rob Cohen, director, was not as desirable as Rob Cohen, producer.

Confidence, always a fragile commodity, is ultimately what Hollywood is based on. It takes an aura of confidence for people to give you millions to direct a movie. And it takes self-confidence to put your own vision on the screen. As time went on, in Rob Cohen's case, both kinds of confidence eroded. Two other projects he wanted to do fell apart, one with Richard Gere and one with Michael Douglas, as studios began to question their faith in Rob as a director. The process of waiting and trying and hoping to get these movies going had also shaken Cohen's confidence in himself. Finally he managed to direct a picture with Robert Hayes and John Gielgud. It proved nothing short of a disaster.

Rob Cohen's whole life now began to disintegrate. It was as if whatever charmed power had guided him so surely on the way up was now pushing him precipitously downward. In one year his movie failed, his friends deserted him, and his marriage fell apart. He fled California and sought the anonymity of New York. Desperate to sink new roots, he bought an apartment that used up every cent he had and plunged him into a debt level he could not sustain. He was acting from panic. "I was overwhelmed," he says.

As he sat in New York, contemplating the wreckage all around him, faced with failure in both his personal and his professional lives, he realized there was nothing to do but stop running. There was no place left to run, nothing more he could do to change his luck or to shape events. A sense of quiet enveloped him.

The Chinese word for "crisis" is the same as the word for "opportunity"—a rather brilliant linguistic marriage. I began to regard my crisis as just that, an opportunity. It was like a shakedown of everything that was wrong. It was almost as if I needed this crisis to see things clearly.

Rob Cohen realized that for him, as for so many high achievers, the key issue was control. He *had* to be in control, and what was most shattering to him about failure was that he was no longer in control. But as he looked within, he began to wonder. Maybe he did not *have* to be in control. Maybe he could change. Maybe he would even be happier if he changed.

I was a control freak. I had life by the throat, and I was saying, "You're going to give me what I want," and it wasn't. When you exercise every ounce of control in your human capability, when you will things to happen and you force them to happen and you fight for them to happen and they do not happen, you have only two choices—you can go insane, or you can relax your death grip on life.

I think there is a random set of forces at work in any career or life which are uncontrollable, not discernible or understandable in any way. There are times when you're rolling sevens with the dice, and there are times when you're rolling snake eyes, and when you inevitably roll snake eyes, it's not because the dice hate you or you're no longer the smart one—that's just your luck and you have to accept it.

What I learned is that there is a combination of acceptance and fierce fighting back which you have to do. If you only fiercely fight back, you find the mountain is somewhat immovable—you'll roll that rock up to the top, and it will roll right back down again. And if you passively accept failure, you'll never get off the floor. You have to pick yourself up calmly, knowing you're fighting back, but knowing this is a period of resistance. You have to be like the reed of grass in the Chinese proverb, which survives the strong wind, unlike the mighty oak, which gets blown over. You have to bend and yield to a kind of karmic force.

What he had to do became clear: Rob had to return to Los Angeles, the scene of his failure. Armed with a newfound humility, he had to start over again. But he was not really starting over again; he was operating from a radically different sense of himself, and it was this inner knowledge that sustained him.

I realized I had to come back to Los Angeles, the place where my defeat would be most keenly understood, the place where I had been a wunderkind. I had to reassess myself. I would go back to being what the world always thought I was, a producer. I didn't like producing, but I was going back to it. And I was determined to turn it into a positive experience for myself. The name of the game was "You don't have power now, don't pretend you do, and don't be ashamed that you don't."

I learned there were many people who were happy I was down and felt I had gotten too much. There were many people, the vast majority, who were totally indifferent to me. There were the few true, honest friends who would put their names behind mine and say, "I want this man set up again at your studio." And then there were people who made you feel like dirt for asking a favor, and I knew when I left their offices they had no intention of ever helping. But that was fine. I just put it away in terms of knowledge of the situation, not for revenge or vindictiveness, but basically because I now knew where they stood.

And I began to realize that this was the value of this period—this clarity. Not the confusion I felt, but the clarity.

Everyone was declaring themselves, whether they knew it or not, and I really saw the world with eyes I had never had before.

Using every favor he could muster, Rob Cohen managed to get himself an office on a studio lot—no salary, but an office, a place to look for opportunities, a start. One day his attorney phoned and inquired, with some embarrassment, if Rob would consider taking a job as a producer-for-hire on a feature film to be directed by someone else. Rob Cohen, who a few years ago had put together a twenty-three-million-dollar picture called *The Wiz*, didn't ask his lawyer too many questions and didn't argue about the salary. Gratefully he said yes. "I knew what I was doing," he comments. "I had to go backward three steps to go forward four. The backward steps were very painful but had to be taken."

Eventually Rob Cohen did climb back to the top in Hollywood, not as a director or even as a producer, but as a movie company executive. Today he runs a medium-sized film company and once again has a large office in Century City. Once again the phone rings with invitations to lunch from the same agents who romanced him when he was formerly powerful and dropped him when he was down. He has seen it all and bears no rancor.

Rob Cohen knows he is a survivor. He knows *what he does* is not really *who he is.* He has learned.

The real lesson is a newfound appreciation of anything good that happens. I realize it is not my due, that I am not owed this as my lot in life. When anything good happens now, I cherish it and feel grateful.

Here I am ten years later running another movie company. On the surface I am doing what I did before, but internally I feel quite different. If you can view what seems to be a period of disintegration not as a stripping away and loss, but rather as a shakedown of all that is useless, phony, and false, then it is not a loss. Life could be a two-mile sprint, and at the one-mile point you're lucky to get a chance to shed all the extra weight you've been carrying so you can run the second mile light.

Rob Cohen is running light. His values are clear. He may have more reverses in his career—in the movie business they are almost expected—but he will never be destroyed by them again. In his own eyes, success came not from climbing back to becoming head of a motion picture company, but rather from the process of examining his life. He regards this inner journey as his most important accomplishment.

MONA ROCKWELL'S JOURNEY

Though she has never met Rob Cohen, and though the specifics of their stories are quite different, Mona Rockwell went on a similar voyage of self-exploration.

The attractive Chicago-based "Robin Hood of real estate" whom we met in the first chapter of this book experienced one of the most spectacular rises and falls of anyone we interviewed. But even before she failed so dazzlingly in real estate, Mona Rockwell had hints her life was out of balance. One occurred long before her business collapsed.

Part of a high-powered social set, Mona was supposed to go to dinner and the ballet one evening with the photographer Richard Avedon and another friend, the chairman of Macy's. An avowed workaholic, she had been looking forward to a rare night out. But as she sat in her office that day, dressed in a clingy black dinner dress for the evening and working on yet another real estate deal, she knew she could not go to the ballet. How could she leave her staff working? Suppose something went wrong? And—though she did not admit this to herself—how could the ballet be as exciting as the deal she was working on? Leaving her papers on her desk, she told her staff she would be back shortly and drove over to the restaurant, where Richard Avedon and the chairman of Macy's were waiting.

Mona did not even park her car; she just tipped the attendant and told him to wait with it until she returned in a few moments. In the restaurant, using all her considerable charm, she told the two men she was sure they would understand, but she simply had to go back to her office and work. She describes the reaction of the chairman of Macy's:

He literally screamed at me, screamed like a lover might scream, "You can't do this to yourself, you can't work like this, it's crazy." His reaction shocked me. It scared me. I didn't change my plans, but I did take note. I saw I was so narrowly focused I could not see outside my own focus. I didn't have strong feelings about loved ones. I just thought everyone would understand that I was so focused. I didn't think they would care. I thought I wasn't very meaningful to them, since they weren't very meaningful to me. I didn't think I had a choice—I had to continue on my path to success.

Eventually people stopped asking Mona Rockwell to dinner, and, as she put it, "my horizons got narrower." Like a mole, she burrowed ever deeper into her work.

It was only when her business world collapsed—when the banks called her lines of credit, when she was forced to sell her house, move into a small apartment, and take in boarders to get money for food— that she faced herself. Only then did she feel all the emotion she had been refusing to feel for years. She went through a long dark period of despair.

I was emotionally leaky. You'd touch me and I'd cry. I'd go to the bank and beg them to just lay off for a while so I could get my act together, and I would be weeping. This was totally unlike me. I had no emotional stamina at all. I felt I was a complete failure, that all the dreams of ten years were crashing around me.

I went to a man who had been my boss earlier and said to him, "I need you to do me a favor. I have a feeling everything that happened to me was pure luck, that I have no talent. The biggest favor you can do is to tell me this is true." I wanted confirmation of my nothingness so I could fall fully into the chasm of failure. This man was aghast. I was just a lump, begging for someone to give me fifty more lashes. My former boss did me a great favor. He told me to take a look at what was going on with *me* the person and not to worry about the business for a while.

As long as Mona Rockwell's method of dealing with the world was working, she felt invulnerable. With the myopia of the fortunate, she thought her good luck would last forever. Success rarely demands that we face ourselves; failure dislodges our worldview.

I realized the system was bigger than me. My ego had said to me, "You can beat it, you can manipulate things." But now I saw I was really a very small piece of a big machine, and no matter how smart I thought I was, I could not stop the acceleration of that machine when it started to go downhill. I understood my vulnerability, my fragility, and I accepted it instead of trying to think, You can beat it. I accepted my humanity. I acquiesced to the fact that I could not make it anymore.

•   •   •

Humility. Vulnerability. Admitting "I don't know." The erosion of certainties. These are the first painful steps that prepare us to look within.

For Mona Rockwell, the look was terrifying. What she saw when she examined herself was emptiness at the very core.

At that nadir I had nothing left. I had been stripped of all my pretensions— stripped of my house, stripped of my cars, stripped of my business, stripped of everything. *And what was utterly terrifying was that I realized there was nothing there.* What I had done to myself, through my intense focusing, was let the other parts of my personality go. Without my business I had no idea who I was.

She had gotten to the point of zero. She could either have given up, overwhelmed by her financial and spiritual poverty, or gone on and tried to rebuild.

In any case, she knew she needed help. Mona was fortunate enough to find a psychiatrist who would treat her for no money because he believed she would recover and repay him. The process of therapy, coupled with her own need to be ascetic—not only for financial reasons, but in order to see better who she really was—set her on a long and difficult path.

I could not borrow any more. I had barely enough to live on. I did not have my teeth taken care of or go to a doctor for a year. I learned what survival was. And eventually I learned I was a survivor. But first I had to figure out who I was.

I did it by dissecting the parts of myself. I tried to analyze my roles, so that by seeing the parts separately I could put them back together and see the whole. I said to myself, "Mona is a woman, she is a businesswoman, she is interested in psychology, she plays tennis, she is a lover, she is confident, she is terrified, she is overreaching, she is vulnerable." I started separating the parts out. What had happened in the past was that Mona the businesswoman had so expanded she took over all the other parts. I had become totally at the mercy of that businesswoman and lost contact with myself.

I said to my doctor, "You know, if I had a best friend whom I had treated as badly as I've treated myself, the best friend would have walked away."

In the meantime, many of Mona Rockwell's former friends, like Rob Cohen's friends, did walk away. Once, she recalls, two women she had known from her earlier life took her to Trader Vic's and said without thinking, "Let's split the bill." Too proud to protest, she paid her share, twenty-one dollars, then ate potato chips for the next few days. No longer economic bedfellows, they never saw each other again.

Yet the asceticism was not uninteresting. It was as if the trappings of her old life had somehow gotten in her way, clouded her vision, confused her. Stripping them away, she found herself not only more self-aware, but more keenly sensitized to other people. Layers between her and the outer world had been removed, and sensations now bombarded her directly. One day on an impulse she postponed her own rent payment and bought circus tickets for some impoverished neighborhood children. "I gave away more money when I was poor than I ever did when I was rich," she says. For the first time she felt other people's pain. And their pleasure as well.

Over and over again she replayed the scenario of her downfall, punishing herself endlessly for not seeing her own demise. One day she took a course in business management, in which she was asked to write down her successes and failures. The exercise proved a turning point for her. As she described her failures to the class, she realized that while all of them had seemed monumental to her when they'd occurred, over the years her perspective on them had changed. What was overwhelming at the time receded in importance with more time. Somehow she had survived.

After Mona had finished, a young man in the class stood up to speak. Mona's story, he said, made him realize his own reluctance to take risks. From listening to her, he saw that his unblemished record of success was in itself a failure—that he had always chosen to play it safe. He turned to Mona and said, with genuine admiration in his voice, "I wish I could be more like you."

Hearing him, I felt as if the sun had begun to shine. Sure I had failed, but I had never been afraid to take risks. I saw that my ambition had clouded my assessment of risk, but I also saw that at least I had been a player. I think it was at that moment that I began to forgive myself.

Mona Rockwell forgave herself. And she filed for bankruptcy. Those two steps marked her completion with the past. She could now get on with her inner rebuilding.

Recalling past survivals encouraged her future survival. She felt "vaccinated" by her past defeats, armed by the antibodies her spirit had produced long ago to fight failure. They were deep within her, these survival antibodies, and now that she needed them, she could summon them again for another fight. Surviving failure once gave her the confidence to survive it again.

She began reading Eastern philosophy, looking for principles of guidance, seeking some way to balance the disparate parts of herself more harmoniously. From months of reading and from her therapy, she developed a notion around which she organized her life.

I developed a sense of a "higher self." I called this sense my "witness." It is almost a Buddhist or Zen idea, a part of me which functions to watch over me. If I get scared or too competitive, for instance, this "witness" self will say, "Mona, look at what you are doing: that's only a part of you functioning that way and taking over all of you." This sense of my "witness" self helps me to control the myopia which used to dominate me.

When you are a high-energy person, it's like a locomotive coming down a mountain—you can't stop. But now I feel I can get on or off the train. Before I *was* the force, I was *in* it, I could never step out of it. I have a greater sense of choice now.

It's like being in the trenches when you're fighting a war. You don't even realize you are in the trenches sometimes. Then your "witness" self wakes you up, taps you on the shoulder, and says, "You're in the trenches. Get up and take a look at what's going on and make a choice of where you want to be."

When you are in a failure mode, a negative state, you tend to see everything that way. That's why the "witness" idea is so important. That's the voice that tells you, "Let's remember the part of you that does make money, that has been closing deals; let's focus on that part of you, also."

All the major material changes in Mona Rockwell's life were minor compared to her inner, spiritual changes. Failure forced her to reexamine the most basic human question: What was she doing with her time on this earth?

As she looked inward, she began to wonder if she had ever been a success. Certainly the world had judged her so as it watched her put together high-flying deals and acquire more and more possessions; but now, from the vantage point of failure, Mona Rockwell herself was not so sure. "I thought I could fill myself up with money," she says of herself in those earlier years, "but I was never an integrated human being."

Slowly Mona started her career again. She stayed in real estate, carefully beginning to put deals together again, humbler now and unafraid to think small. Her career didn't change, but her approach to it did.

I make different choices about who I want to do business with. I used to do business with anyone who had money. I'm now aware I prefer to deal with people who have a sense of decency about them. I distrust people who operate solely from greed. I prefer people who seem multidimensional. For me the central questions are how to make money and still live comfortably with myself, how to make moral business decisions. I find most of the clients I enjoy working with are asking the same questions—without having gone through failure. I have better eyesight now.

The end of Mona Rockwell's inner journey was a radically new definition of success. The woman who once measured herself by the number of fur coats and stretch limos she could afford now says, "Success is being in touch with that higher self, feeling integrated, being fully able to express all the parts of me, living a balanced, whole life."

•   •   •

If you were to meet Rob Cohen or Mona Rockwell today, you would be struck by something about them. It is not their impressive offices or even their air of confidence, because both had those attributes before they failed. Rather, it is an intangible quality they both project: a sense of being "centered." There is about both of them a kind of quiet sureness, a feeling, when they talk, that they are proceeding from some inner core rather than saying what they think others want to hear. Along with their drive comes a curious aura of calm. Even in the midst of the frenzy of their work, you sense that both know this isn't all there is. Both have a sense of balance.

The inner journey Mona Rockwell, Rob Cohen, and others made after defeat is one of the most important journeys of a lifetime. If you have the courage for the trip, it puts you in touch with yourself in a way different from any you have known. You come out of it with an armor of self-knowledge that makes you invincible. Difficult, painful, exhilarating, this final journey after failure is the one that makes you truly victorious.

XII ———

Changing the Measurement

Visible accomplishment, winning, money, validation by others—these are the hallmarks of success American style. It is success by results, measuring the game by the score rather than the quality of the play.

The trouble is that true success, in our view, involves almost the exact opposite. True success includes knowing and liking your inner self regardless of visible accomplishments. It is not measured by money, but rather by satisfaction. It is judged by you yourself and not others. And above all, it derives from enjoying the game—what you do—for its own sake, concentrating on process, not results.

The people who coped best with failure, who were able to internalize its lessons and use them for greater success, *who in fact did not regard what had happened to them as failure,* all had one thing in common: they concentrated on the *process* of what they did, not the results.

These are the "fireproof" people, who kept their center no matter what, who were able to pick themselves up and keep going after what others considered a defeat. Certainly they wanted to "succeed" in the eyes of the world, but these fireproof people, these "successful failures," were their own most important judges. For them the real joy, the real "high," was the work itself, the minute-by-minute, day-to-day quality of what they did—the *process* of work, not its end results.

If you can learn to think this way, to approach work for the pleasure of process, not the measurement of results, failure will not hold the same terror for you. In fact, with this attitude, failure, or success, are almost beside the point.

Is Winning Everything?

Take the story of Kevin O'Connell, a lawyer who by any objective standards suffered one of the most crushing professional defeats imaginable. For seven years Kevin O'Connell fought the biggest banks in his state in the name of trust holders who in his view were being cheated by the banks. And after seven years he lost.

A short, neatly dressed man with salt-and-pepper hair, Kevin O'Connell looks like an aging preppy and indeed started out believing in the traditional preppy idea of American success. He was a "fast tracker" before the phrase came into fashion. A graduate of Harvard Law School and member of the *Harvard Law Review,* he worked for a while as a federal prosecutor, then became a partner in several big firms. He had everything they teach you to want at law school—money, prestige, profitable cases. Except that he was, in his own words, "thirsty all the time." He chased everything—women, business, possessions—and the thirst was never satisfied.

It seemed to me life had to be more significant than spending an entire career taking positions that maybe you didn't believe in. The more reading I was doing, the more unsuited I was becoming to being a straight advocate, that is, only arguing the client's interest. I started to have terrible problems. I no longer believed in the positions I was taking. I felt I was not dealing with significant issues. And it got worse rather than better.

Kevin O'Connell was successful in a results-oriented way. He won his cases. He made money. He was promoted. But like the talent agent who looked at herself in the mirror and wept, Kevin felt empty inside, "thirsty all the time." The *process* of what he did—the day-to-day activities he was involved in—seemed vapid to him; therefore no amount of success could satisfy him. What he sought was a fundamental change in his attitude to work, an involvement with the *work itself,* regardless of results.

When the case of *Van de Kamp* v. *Bank of America* was presented to his law firm, no one wanted to touch it. Banking and law interact constantly and complicatedly, but almost always on the same side. Banks hire lawyers; they don't expect to get sued by them. No prominent lawyer wanted to stand up against the power of the banks.

To Kevin O'Connell the issues were clear. Banks were loaning out millions of dollars of trust funds at high income levels and often crediting the trust holders with far lower savings account interest rates. Why, O'Connell reasoned, should the banks enrich themselves instead of the holders of the trusts to whom the income money rightfully belonged? He took on the case, which quickly became one of the most celebrated and controversial in the state.

Why did he do it? He asked himself that question many times. Certainly it was not for the money. Fees in cases like these are paid on a contingency basis. Kevin was gambling seven years of his life on the verdict of one judge, and though he might make a great deal of money if he won the case, he might also lose and get nothing. During the seven years he fought, the salary he drew from his law firm was less than that of a starting lawyer, and he had a wife and children to support. Did he have the right to risk so much? Why, he kept asking himself, was he doing this?

The answer was that Kevin O'Connell, despite his appearance of success, had been feeling like a hidden failure. No matter how much money or praise people receive, they always feel like hidden failures if they are not happy with the simple, day-to-day business of the work itself. To Kevin O'Connell, that work no longer mattered. In *Van de Kamp* v. *Bank of America,* not only did he believe the issues were important, but he saw in the case a chance to reorganize the very *way* he worked.

He had to; it was impossible to put together the kind of team that would normally tackle such a case, because no one wanted to get within miles of it. Twenty-two law firms turned him down when he approached them for help. Some said the contingency fee structure was too risky. Others candidly admitted they did not want to offend the banks. To fight the case, Kevin would have to invent a new process, create a different kind of team.

His eighty-two-year-old mother gave him the way to think about it. She pointed out to her son that he was approaching the problem too traditionally in looking for young, successful lawyers. They had a great deal to lose. Why not go for someone retired, she suggested, with an under-utilized passion for work, no cash flow problems, and no future to worry about? The first member of Kevin's team was a seventy-six-year-old retired lawyer who was thrilled to be asked.

Imbued with his new way of looking at things, when Kevin needed an investigative lawyer to ferret out information, he turned to a disillusioned private investigator. This former F.B.I. agent, like O'Connell, felt he had not been doing anything that "mattered" since his days with the bureau. He loved the challenge of being on the side of "right." By chance, the private investigator's son was a lawyer, and his firm came in on the case. Another key person was a divinity student who took a year off from his studies to work as a paralegal.

They became a close-knit team. For all of them, the work itself and their belief in its importance were the sustaining factors. Financial and emotional sacrifices were great. As the case lumbered through the courts of California, Kevin O'Connell's wife developed cancer. He felt burdened by his inability to pay bills, guilt-ridden by his difficulty in giving his wife and children the comforts he felt they deserved.

As he was battling all this, the bank made a settlement offer, under the terms of which the lawyers' bills would have been paid but the plaintiffs given nothing. Though the temptation to settle was strong, Kevin felt he could not, with honor, pay himself and get nothing for the people in whose name he was fighting the case. He refused the settlement.

January 23, 1985, seven years after he had started the case, two months after he had made his last summation and left the court completely confident of victory, Kevin O'Connell heard the judge's verdict: he had lost on all counts.

Numb, shocked, overwhelmed, Kevin faced the press. All he could think was that he had to be a "good loser." He talked about appealing the case (which indeed he is now doing), and he spoke about the important issues that had been raised. But defeat is defeat, and at the moment it occurs, it shocks and hurts. Nothing shields us from that, no amount of involvement in work, no comforting knowledge of our inner selves. Shock is the stage everyone goes through after failure, and Kevin was not immune.

But—and this is the point—because of his orientation toward his work and because of his knowledge of himself, Kevin O'Connell never felt he was a failure. He looked at the event—the loss of a case about which he cared deeply—and after the shock wore off, he was able to say to himself, "I do not regret it. I had to do it. I would not do it differently." The validity of the work itself sustained him.

The case was very satisfying. It dealt with important issues. Lincoln commented when he lost to Douglas that he had a chance to address some significant issues. Robert Penn Warren says you have to be "brave in your own time." Plato says it's not life that counts, it's the *good* life. Who am I to say that just because I spent seven years on something I am entitled to success? Did I do it for the success, or did I do it because I thought the effort itself was valid?

If winning is the only thing, then if you've lost, you've lost everything.

According to the traditional definition of success, winning *is* everything. In that case, failure is akin to death. If Kevin O'Connell had subscribed to that notion, he surely could not have gone on. But if *how* you play and *what* you play are more important than the results of the game, defeat can only shock you temporarily; it cannot possibly destroy you. Your satisfaction comes from an almost daily sense of joy in the work and your relationship to it.

SUSTAINED BY WORK: WILLIAM L. SHIRER

Years before Kevin O'Connell, William L. Shirer, author of the bestselling *Rise and Fall of the Third Reich,* had a similarly long bout with defeat.

Shirer, now eighty-two, is adapting one volume of his memoirs for television, writing a play, and learning Russian, "just to get the cobwebs out of my brain." Easily recognized by his beard and wild white hair escaping from his blue beret, he is often seen hurrying to the library along the main street of Lenox, Massachusetts.

Work remains his passion. What sustained him through two major defeats was his writing.

At the age of twenty-eight, Shirer was in charge of the Vienna bureau for the *Chicago Tribune.* Fluent in several languages, he had covered Europe, India, and Afghanistan for the paper and was known as a star foreign correspondent. But Colonel McCormick, owner of the paper, became angry with Shirer over some story he had written and in 1933, at the height of the Depression, fired him.

I was deeply resentful. I'd risked my neck getting them some major stories in Asia, particularly in Afghanistan, which was a rather dangerous country, and I thought, What a fine way to repay me! Of course years later I realized that that's what you do when you're a foreign correspondent—you risk your neck—and that McCormick didn't owe me anything special for it.

Shirer and his wife went to Spain, where they lived in a fishing village on their meager savings for a year. In 1937, when the news service Shirer was working for in Berlin folded, he met Edward R. Murrow, who was looking for an experienced correspondent to help him launch CBS's radio coverage of Europe. Over dinner at the Adlon hotel Murrow hired Shirer.

Excited by the prospect of developing radio as a major medium of reporting the news, Shirer and Murrow became close personal friends. Bill Paley, owner of the network, seemed highly pleased with the two young men as they rapidly put CBS first in covering the growing Hitler-inspired crisis in Europe. Fortune seemed to be favoring Shirer: he had good friends, a fascinating job, and, after the war, when he returned home after twenty years abroad, the highest-rated Sunday daytime broadcast on the network.

But then came the days of the Cold War. The sponsor of the show dropped him—Shirer believes because he was too liberal. In what he terms "a poisonous affair," Shirer watched his "friends" Edward R. Murrow and Bill Paley dump him out in the cold.

Not long afterward, Shirer, with 150 others, was listed in *Red Channels* as a possible Communist sympathizer. Nearly everyone on the list became blacklisted on radio. Bill Shirer now found himself unemployable. His income dropped from $2,000 a week to about $50. Occasionally he lectured. Friends on magazines would accept an occasional article, which they would not publish because of Shirer's supposedly leftist views. Paying the grocery bills became an arduous task. By any of society's judgments, William Shirer was facing defeat.

There were days when I just didn't know what to do. Nothing worked. I would write memos to myself: "Don't give up." "The world's a tough place for everybody, but particularly for writers." I did a lot of reading of history, which helped. A number of people inspired me: Gandhi had a great many setbacks in his life, and Benjamin Franklin. And Plutarch, who writes so eloquently of the adversities of men. You begin to see you're not the first person to have suffered.

Shirer's dark period lasted for twelve years—from 1947, when he was fired by CBS, until 1959 with the publication of *The Rise and Fall of the Third Reich.* During those years he had difficulty feeding his family; his books barely sold. How was he able to go on and work when nothing in the outer world told him he was successful?

In the final analysis it has to do with what your values are. I was never ambitious to be vice-president in charge of news or the number-one person in status or pay. I was not ambitious to be more than a good journalist and a good writer. My inner life was the most important thing for me. That, and the value of the work itself. The main thing is living with yourself.

In the end getting fired from CBS was a blessing, which I did not appreciate for a long time. What it set me to doing was what I had always wanted to do, which was to write books. When you're working for a big paper or a big network and you're making a lot of money, you keep putting off the time you are going to write that big book.

Everybody told me—my agent, my publisher, my editor, my friends, people like the daily book critic of the *Herald Tribune*—*The Rise and Fall of the Third Reich* "is a fine book, but how are you going to support your family on it?" Everybody in the world said it wouldn't sell. It was 1,200 pages long, and its price of ten dollars made it the most expensive book on the market. After nearly ten years of work, during which I had completely exhausted our savings and borrowed as much as I could, to be told by everybody concerned that the book wouldn't sell was very discouraging.

One day my English publisher was in New York and asked to come over to lunch. We knew he liked martinis, which we could not afford, but we bought a bottle of red wine for a dollar and scraped together a makeshift meal. At lunch he told me they were not going to print the book in England despite the low printing costs; instead they were buying 7,500 copies from Simon and Schuster. I pointed out that Simon and Schuster was only printing 20,000 copies of the book. He said, "I know, and I'm buying 7,500 copies of them." I almost threw him out of the apartment, I was so angry and discouraged. This left only 12,500 copies of the book for America—that's all the confidence the publisher had.

I don't think there was a single person involved with that book who believed in it except me.

In the end, Shirer proved them all wrong. *The Rise and Fall of the Third Reich* made publishing history. Its 12,500 copies were sold out of every bookstore the first day. Critics praised the writing. Foreign sales were strong. A quarter of a century later, it remains the all-time biggest seller in the history of the Book-of-the-Month-Club.

FOCUSING ON PROCESS

Involvement with process is the key to combating failure for many people in such high-risk occupations as acting. An actor's ego is always on the line. Whether on stage, in front of the camera, or simply auditioning for a part, actors face rejection more often than almost any other professional group.

The most successful ones—those who remain integrated, self-confident human beings even if they don't get the part—have found exactly the same way of remaining steady as Kevin O'Connell: They focus intensely on the *process* of their work rather than on the results. Barbara Babcock, who won an Emmy for *Hill Street Blues,* never had public accolades or even a steady livelihood until she was over forty. But all through the lean years, she was able to keep going because of the way she looked at her work.

For me the most important part of my career is the process, not the result. The most satisfying stage is generally the rehearsal, working on a role rather than performing it. That is one of the ways I have coped with the concept of failure. I think failure is always goal-oriented—what has happened as a result, and not the process of getting there. I measure myself against the process—did I do the scene well? Did I find out something interesting about the character? Did the moment feel alive for me? These are the satisfactions that sustain me.

Excellence of craft is the issue, not reviews or medals.

Playing Your Own Game

Can this attitude work even in the most competitive fields, such as sports? The answer seems to be yes.

There is probably no arena in which winning and losing, succeeding and failing, become the two poles of existence more clearly than in professional sports. If actors face the sting of rejection and bad reviews, at least those defeats can be viewed as subjective judgments by others. Athletes, however, either win or lose, and everybody's scoreboard is the same.

Or is it? That is the question Julie Anthony, a former tennis pro, had to face in her own career. When she herself was a professional tennis player, success and failure were uppermost on her mind. As she traveled the tournament circuit, which consisted of sixty-four players, she knew that every week, in the value system of that world, there would be sixty-three losers. It was not enough to be number sixteen; being number one was everything.

Sports was, in effect, a heightened version of big business. Like big business, it was built on competition and judged people by results. No one in the world of sports questioned this value system. Not only was it obviously correct—who could dispute that there are winners and losers?—but it was also extremely effective in making athletes play better. The more athletes told themselves they were losers if they were less than number one, the more they would "psych" themselves up to win.

As time went on, Julie Anthony began to question that.

Even though I was sixteenth in the world, the more I played professional tennis, the less of a success I felt. When you're in that tennis world, the only thing you know is trying to be number one. So every week, as long as I used that model, I felt like a loser.

That was supposed to motivate me by putting pressure on me to do better. But as I looked at myself, I was not sure that it did. I think that believing "number one is the one thing" actually resulted in my playing worse. And certainly the pressure itself was not enjoyable.

Kevin O'Connell had concluded, "If winning is the only thing, then if you lose, you lose everything." Julie Anthony was coming to the same realization. Furthermore, Julie saw that the emphasis on winning and losing created a psychological catch-22: To feel good you had to be a winner, but nobody could stay a winner forever, so everyone was destined to feel bad a lot of the time.

Eventually Julie Anthony quit the world of professional tennis and made the transition to sports psychologist. As an adviser to athletes, even more than in her own career as a professional player, she continued to question attitudes toward winning and losing. If athletes daily judged themselves success or failure, how could they withstand the strain of defeat? And did their harsh self-judgment in fact really help them to win? In addition to the toll on mental health, Julie began to wonder seriously if the success/failure ethic really *worked*.

Her conclusion was that it did not. The win/lose ethic, she felt, promoted neither victory nor psychological well-being. There had to be another way of approaching even the ultimate win/lose arena of sports. Her answer, like that of Kevin O'Connell, William L. Shirer, and Barbara Babcock, was to focus on process. Greater attention to the pleasure of the game itself would make a player more relaxed, she felt, and this greater sense of relaxation would actually promote winning.

If I were to do it again, with more maturity—and this is what I advise athletes today—I would focus on my individual potential and my individual fulfillment, not on outside competition. What is relevant is how gratifying playing the game is. The more enjoyment I can attain from the game, the more likely I am to play well and probably do better.

Julie Anthony now advises athletes to make their own rules for the game they are playing, to create their own goals for what they want to accomplish. By "playing your own game," you are setting your own standards for success or failure.

If people see me with a racket in my hand and a round ball, they think I'm playing tennis; but I may be playing a totally different game than they think. That day I may be playing not to win or lose, but merely to hit a great cross-court forehand. If I hit a few good ones that day, I'm going to be happy with myself, because that's the game I'm playing.

Outside measures may not measure the game I'm playing, and therefore other people's ideas of my success and failure may not be correct. You have to play your own game and not let other people's measures be the barometer of your success or failure.

There is a kind of Oriental philosophical balance which I urge athletes to try to achieve. When you go on the court, you want to play as if it were a life-or-death situation because that's the kind of effort you want to put out there. But then there's the part of yourself that has to know it's not life or death, that it's just a game, and it's okay if you lose. And those two things are going on at the same time.

Even in sports, it's a matter of balance, of perspective. The striving for success, the fierce desire to win, have to coexist with a larger sense of self, an acceptance of the possibility of loss, an understanding that neither winning nor losing are the real measures of ourselves.

THE BEST STREET CLEANER AT MGM

Actress Nancy Walker, of *Rhoda* fame, tells the story of one of the most successful people she knows, an old man who cleans the streets of the Metro Goldwyn Mayer studio lot.

This gentleman is one of the best and happiest human beings. To me he is the best because he does his job fully and brilliantly. Every day he gets to the studio early, immaculately dressed. He makes it his business to know everybody on the lot. He has eagle eyes looking around for any debris that would clutter up his workplace, and when you see him at the end of the day surveying the grounds, you know he feels he's done a good job. That street cleaner knows MGM is *his* studio as much as anyone else's, and he is proud to be able to keep its streets clean. In my view he is far more successful than many of the actors, who think success means having your own makeup man. The street cleaner believes what I have always believed: it comes from the work itself.

Being the best you can be at what you do has nothing to do with the status of your occupation. It has to do with your attitude toward work. According to this criterion for success, the street cleaner at MGM is as successful as Nancy Walker. Both put themselves fully into what they do. Both take pride in the process. Both feel pleased with themselves at the end of the day.

Years after his defeat by Richard Nixon, George McGovern does not consider himself a failure. He lost an election—that is the objective fact. But McGovern understands what the MGM street cleaner and Bill Shirer and Kevin O'Connell and Barbara Babcock and Julie Anthony all learned: If you are fully involved with what you do and feel that you have done it as well as you can, there can be no lasting feeling of failure. "I would rather be George McGovern, loser, than Richard Nixon, winner," he says. The win/lose, results-oriented attitude produces Richard Nixon, a man willing to do anything to stay on top. Caring about the process of what you do produces a man like George McGovern, who is able to withstand the loss of an election and not feel like a failure.

You cannot prevent failure because you cannot control results. But you can control process. You can learn to become involved in what you do in a different way, so that your emphasis is on the pride and pleasure you take in the work rather than on the results.

In doing that, you will have changed the basis for measuring your own success and failure.

XIII _____

Learners

Benjamin Barber teaches political science at Rutgers University. He also writes novels, composes music, choreographs, lectures all over the world, and thinks deeply about things that interest him. Recently we asked Professor Barber his opinion of the prevailing division of people into successes and failures. He sprawled back in the chair in his study and considered the question. While any division of people into two opposites was arbitrary, said Barber, there was one division he thought interesting and possibly accurate.

I don't divide the world into the weak and the strong, or the successes and the failures, those who make it or those who don't. I don't even divide the world into the extroverted and the introverted, or those who hear the inner voice or the outer voice, because we all hear some of both.

I divide the world into learners and nonlearners.

There are people who learn, who are open to what happens around them, who listen, who hear the lessons. When they do something stupid, they don't do it again. And when they do something that works a little bit, they do it even better and harder the next time.

The question to ask is not whether you are a success or a failure, but whether you are a learner or a nonlearner.

Most of the people in this book have been learners. They have pulled themselves out of their setbacks and continued their lives, armed with new knowledge. Nonlearners have gotten "stuck" in a stage of failure, mired in feelings of anger or blame or shame, preferring to complain about the past rather than learn from it. These people, in our view, are the real failures—not because of the events that happened to them, but because of their inability to learn from them.

232

It is not the event itself, but rather how you cope with it that determines the kind of person you become.

Learners versus nonlearners. Consider the idea for a moment, and you quickly arrive at what seems like a radical notion: *If we learn from an experience, there can be no such thing as failure.*

There are events, to be sure, ones that may be unpleasant and hard to bear. But failure does not lie in the event; it lies in the *judgment* of that event. And if you are a learner—if you gain something from your supposed loss—then what others may deem a failure will not be one to you yourself.

If you are a learner, it is possible—without changing the events—to make the concept of failure disappear.

THE LESSONS OF FAILURE

What are the lessons of failure? What do we gain from the pain and the shock, the defeats that take little pieces of us (for there is no denying that along with the benefits come the scars of loss as well)?

We learn compassion and humility. Failure is a great leveler, stripping away our veneer of pretense, dissolving those outer shells that keep us from feeling the pain of others.

The former king of Silicon Valley, Nolan Bushnell, appeared remote and untouchable when he was successful. He was on a winning streak, and the rules that applied to mere mortals seemed not to apply to him. Other people worried about paying the rent, doubted their abilities, felt insecure about their future—not successful people like Nolan Bushnell. But when his empire crashed, when Nolan Bushnell was dethroned as king of Silicon Valley, when the winning streak ended, he could no longer view himself as different from other people. For the better part of a year he stayed inside his study, thinking and rethinking his past, reexamining the isolation from other people that had characterized his life. Finally he was able to whisper to himself one morning, "Yes, Nolan, you too are mortal."

Like so many of the fast-track failures we interviewed, Bushnell then became compassionate almost with a vengeance. He threw himself into community work, spoke to others about what he had experienced, and felt the pain of the world with newly sensitized skin.

If success isolates us from the human condition, failure reintroduces us to our humanity. This overdue reminder that we are part of the pain and suffering that being human implies is bracing, even intoxicating. Failure is, in the best sense of the word, democratizing. It makes us reassess our place in the universe.

We learn a new attitude toward risk. For some people, failure produces a greater sense of caution. Real estate developers Mona Rockwell and Doug Tyson and investment banker William Ivers learned to be more prudent. Over-enamored of risk, they never believed in their own vulnerability. Failure taught them otherwise. It checked their natural flirtation with extreme risk and imprinted them with greater caution.

But most people were emboldened by failure. Like someone who all his life has been afraid of swimming and is suddenly pushed into deep water, only to discover that indeed he *can* swim, the person who survives failure learns that risk is not so terrifying. Having survived once, why not try more next time?

Several years after the failure of his first Broadway show, playwright Larry Atlas describes his current state of mind:

I can fail, but I won't fail for lack of trying. As a writer I take big chances, and when that happens you are bound to fail. I have a draft of my new play now that is all wrong—but I'm so proud of what I'm attempting to do that I'm thrilled. I will not pull back from the attempt. If I had had a big success the first time, I'm convinced I never would have done this one. Tennessee Williams had a huge failure on his first play, and he said that if he had not had a failure, he would never have written *Glass Menagerie.*

What is the worst that can happen? Larry Atlas asks himself. He has already failed. And survived. He has nothing to lose and everything to gain by risking.

As director Peter Schifter says, "There are really two kinds of failure: passive failure—not daring to risk at all—which is criminal; and active failure, which is noble." Knowing you can survive defeat makes you risk active failure, and that also can lead to greatness.

We reorder our priorities. If success makes us think we will live forever, failure makes us realize we are mortal. In the recesses of our souls, setbacks are "little deaths," losses, omens of our final failure, death. If we are healthy, we do not often think that way; but there is something about failure that says to us, "Time is fleeting—hurry,

hurry." As we reinvent ourselves, prodded now by the nagging reminder of our finite lives, we ask questions we never dared ask before. Are we doing anything that matters? Are we pleased with ourselves? Have we loved and lived well, or have we been consumed by the drive for success? As somebody once said, "No one on their deathbed ever regrets that they didn't work more." Where is the balance in our lives? Are there fundamental shifts to be made? Are we in touch with *all* sides of our nature?

Change can occur only when we are open. By bringing to the surface questions that most of us bury in the accretions of success, failure promotes "the examined life." We may choose to go on as before, but we cannot do so blindly. We have been stopped. Failure is a marker, a turning point.

For many, the change involves developing other "legs," new sources of strength and balance. Some turn toward religion and long-neglected spiritual concerns, balancing what was an exclusively outer-directed life with strengthened inner values. Many choose to broaden their sources of pleasure, turning to reading, art, sports, and other hobbies. These people will never again "be" their jobs. From failure they learned that it is wiser to spread the investment of self. Almost all reappraise friends, discarding the fair-weather ones and appreciating all the more those friends of the heart who love us even when we are down. As Rob Cohen puts it, failure gives us "clarity of vision."

We gain a sense of power. This is perhaps the most curious and paradoxical lesson of all. That which seems to render us powerless can, if viewed rightly, bequeath a newfound sense of power—an inner power that no one can touch.

When you have lost money, self-esteem, and approval in the eyes of others, what kind of power can you have?

You have the power of your mind.

You have the power to figure out what went wrong and to correct it.

You have the power to reinterpret what happened to you and put it in the most enabling scenario possible.

You have options before you if you choose to see them. And therefore you have the power to change.

You have the power to reinvent yourself.

You have the power to declare yourself the judge of what you do. By changing the judgment of success and failure from one that others impose on you to one you impose on yourself, you have another important power: you have the power to forgive yourself.

Failure can only render us powerless if we let it. It's all too easy to *see* our lack of power. What is more urgent is to *feel* the power we do have. This requires a reorientation of thought. If you refuse to feel like a victim, if you take responsibility for your life, if you understand that you *can* change, you begin to act differently. And once you begin to act differently, other people begin to perceive you in a powerful, not powerless, way.

•   •   •

Years ago, Samuel Beckett was asked how he felt about the failure of *Waiting for Godot*. This man, perhaps the preeminent playwright of the twentieth century, looked at his questioner and replied, "Don't worry about me—I have breathed the vivifying air of failure many times."

Beckett understood. Nothing promotes self-confidence more than the knowledge that you are a survivor.

Suggestions for Further Reading

Averill, J. R. "The Functions of Grief." *Emotions in Personality and Psychopathology.* New York: Plenum Press, 1979

Bardwick, Judith M. *The Psychology of Women: A Study of Biocultural Conflicts.* New York: Harper and Row, 1971.

Basowith, H., et al. *Anxiety and Stress.* New York: McGraw-Hill, 1955.

Beck, Aaron T. *Depression.* Philadelphia: University of Pennsylvania Press, 1967.

Becker, Ernest. *The Denial of Death.* New York: The Free Press, 1973.

Bettelheim, Bruno. *Symbolic Wounds.* Glencoe, Ill.: The Free Press, 1954.

Blake, Robert R., and Mouton, Jane Srygley. *The New Managerial Grid.* Houston: Gulf Publishing, 1978.

Bloch, Arthur. *Murphy's Law Book Two.* Los Angeles: Price/Stern/Sloan, 1980.

Blotnick, Scully. *Otherwise Engaged: The Private Lives of Successful Career Women.* New York: Penguin Books, Inc., 1985.

Bowlby, John. *Attachment.* New York: Basic Books, Inc., 1969.

———. *Loss.* New York: Basic Books, Inc., 1980.

———. *Separation.* New York: Basic Books, Inc., 1972.

Bramson, R. M. *Coping with Difficult People.* New York: Doubleday, 1981.

Brown, B. B. *Stress and the Art of Biofeedback.* New York: Bantam Books, 1977.

Caplan, G., and Killilea, M., eds. *Support Systems and Mutual Help.* New York: Grune and Stratton, 1976.

Catalyst Staff. *Upward Mobility.* New York: Warner Books, 1982.

Clark, Ann. *New Ways to Work: A Gestalt Perspective.* San Francisco: Vitalia, 1975.

Cousins, N. *Anatomy of an Illness As Perceived by the Patient: Reflections on Healing and Regeneration.* New York: Norton, 1979.

Crystal, John, and Bolles, Richard N. *Where Do I Go from Here with My Life?: The Crystal Life Planning Manual.* Berkeley: Ten Speed Press, 1980.

De Bono, Edward. *New Think.* New York: Avon, 1971.

Deal, Terry, and Kennedy, Allan. *The Rites & Rituals of Corporate Life.* New York: New American Library. 1982.

Drucker, Peter, *Management: Tasks, Responsibilities, Practices.* New York: Harper and Row, 1973.

Dubos, R. *Man Adapting.* New Haven: Yale University Press, 1965.

Eastman, M. *The Enjoyment of Laughter.* New York: Johnson, 1971. (Reprint of 1937 edition.)

Ellis, Albert, and Harper, Robert A. *A Guide to Rational Living.* North Hollywood, Calif.: Wilshire Book Company, 1960.

237

Fensterheim, Herbert. *Help Without Psychoanalysis.* New York: Stein and Day, 1971.

Figler, Howard E. *The Complete Job Search Handbook: Presenting the Skills You Need to Get Any Job, and Have a Good Time Doing It.* New York: Holt, Rinehart and Winston, 1979.

Freud, Anna. *The Ego and the Mechanisms of Defense.* New York: International Universities Press, 1966.

Freud, Sigmund. "Mourning and Melancholia." *Standard Edition of the Complete Psychological Works of Sigmund Freud.* London: Hogarth Press, 1957.

Friedman, Martha. *Overcoming the Fear of Success.* New York: Warner Books, 1981.

Gaylin, Willard, M.D. *Feelings.* New York: Harper and Row, 1979.

Gillies, Jerry. *Money-Love.* New York: Warner Books, 1981.

Gilligan, Carol. *In a Different Voice.* Cambridge, Massachusetts: Harvard University Press, 1982.

Girdano, D. A., and Everly, G. S., Jr. *Controlling Stress and Tension: A Holistic Approach.* Englewood Cliffs, N.J.: Prentice-Hall, 1979.

Glick, I. O., et al. *The First Year of Bereavement.* New York: Wiley Interscience, 1974.

Goldberger, M. R., and Breznitz, S., eds. *Handbook of Stress: Theoretical and Clinical Aspects.* New York: The Free Press, 1982.

Gould, Roger. *Transformations.* New York: Simon and Schuster. 1978.

Haldane, Bernard. *Career Satisfaction: How to Make a Habit of Success.* Washington, D.C.: Acropolis Books Ltd., 1975.

Half, Robert. *The Robert Half Way to Get Hired in Today's Job Market.* New York: Bantam Books, 1981.

Hall, Francis S., and Hall, Douglas T. *The Two-Career Couple.* Reading, Mass.: Addison-Wesley Pub. Co., 1979.

Harper, Maxwell J., and Pell, Arthur R. *How to Get the Job You Want After Forty.* New York: Pilot Books, 1967.

Harragan, Betty L. *Games Mother Never Taught You.* New York: Warner Books, 1978.

Heard, G. *Five Ages of Man.* New York: Julian Press, 1963.

Hennig, Margaret, and Jardin, Anne. *The Managerial Woman.* Garden City, N.Y.: Anchor Press, 1977.

Holland, John L. *Making Vocational Choices: A Theory of Careers.* Englewood Cliffs, New Jersey: Prentice-Hall, Inc., 1973.

Horney, Karen. In Kelman, Harold, ed. *Feminine Psychology.* New York: Norton, 1967.

———. *Our Inner Conflicts.* New York: Norton, 1945.

Howard, Jane. *Families.* New York: Simon and Schuster, 1978.

Hyatt, Carole. *The Woman's Selling Game.* New York: Warner Books, 1979.

———. *Women & Work.* New York: M. Evans and Company, Inc., 1980.

Isaacson, Lee E. *Career Information in Counseling and Teaching.* Boston: Allyn and Bacon, Inc., 1971.

Jackson, Tom. *Guerrilla Tactics in the Job Market.* New York: Bantam Books, 1980.

James, Murial, and Jongeward, Dorothy. *Born to Win.* New York: Signet Books, 1978.

Jaques, Elliott. "The Midlife Crisis." *The Course of Life.* Vol. 3, 1981.
Jobfinding Techniques for Mature Women. Washington D.C.; U.S. Department of Labor, Women's Bureau, 1970.
Jung, Carl G. *Memories, Dreams, and Reflections.* New York: Random House, 1961.
————. *Modern Man in Search of a Soul.* New York: Harcourt Brace Jovanovich, 1933.
Kalins, Dorothy. *Cutting Loose: A Civilized Guide for Getting Out of the System.* New York: Saturday Review Press, 1973.
Kaufman, H. G. *Obsolescence and Professional Career Development.* New York: Amacom, 1974.
Kennedy, Marilyn Moats. *Office Politics: Seizing Power, Wielding Clout.* New York: Warner Books, 1980.
Keyes, Ralph. *Why We Take Risks.* Boston: Little, Brown and Co., 1985.
Kiechel, Walter, III. *Starting Over.* New York: Time Inc., 1984.
Kiesler, C. A., ed. *The Psychology of Commitment.* New York: Academic Press, 1971.
Klantz, Pauline. *If I'm So Successful Why Do I Feel Like a Fake.* New York: Peach Tree Press, 1985.
Klausner, S. Z. *Why Man Takes Chances: Studies in Stress-Seeking.* New York: Anchor Books, 1968.
Kübler-Ross, Elisabeth. *On Death and Dying.* London: Collier-Macmillian Ltd., 1969.
Kushner, Harold S. *When All You've Ever Wanted Isn't Enough.* New York: Summit Books, 1985.
————. *When Bad Things Happen to Good People.* New York: Aron Books, 1981.
LeShan, Eda J. *The Wonderful Crisis of Middle Age: Some Personal Reflections.* New York: David McKay Company, Inc., 1973.
Levinson, D. J. "The Mid-Life Transition: A Period in Adult Psychological Development." *Psychiatry* 40 (1977): 99–112.
Maslow, Abraham H. *The Farther Reaches of Human Nature.* New York: Viking, 1971.
————. *New Knowledge in Human Values.* New York: Harper and Brothers, 1959.
Masters, William H., and Johnson, Virginia E. *Human Sexual Inadequacy.* Boston: Little, Brown and Co., 1970.
Miller, Alice. *Prisoners of Childhood.* New York: Basic Books, Inc., 1981.
Miller, Arthur F., and Mattson, Ralph T. *The Truth About You: Discover What You Should Be Doing with Your Life.* Simsbury, Conn.: People Management Incorporated, 1977.
Monat, Alan, and Lazarus, Richard S., eds. *Stress and Coping.* New York: Columbia University Press, 1985.
Moore, Charles G. *The Career Game.* New York: The National Institute of Career Planning, 1975.
Morin, William J., and Cabrera, James C. *Parting Company.* New York: Harcourt Brace Jovanovich, 1984.
National Academy of Sciences. *Research on Stress in Health and Disease.* Washington, D.C.: Institute of Medicine, 1982.
Nierenberg, Gerard I. *How to Give & Receive Advice.* New York: Editorial Correspondents, Inc., 1975.

Noer, David. *How to Beat the Employment Game.* Berkeley: Ten Speed Press, 1978.

Oech, Roger von. *A Whack on the Side of the Head: How to Unlock Your Mind for Innovation.* New York: Warner Books, 1983.

O'Neil, Nena. *The Marriage Premise.* New York: Bantam Books, 1978.

Planning for Work. New York: Catalyst, 1973.

Rachman, Stanley J. *Fear and Courage.* San Francisco: W. H. Freeman, 1978.

Raphael, Beverly. *The Anatomy of Bereavement.* New York: Basic Books, Inc., 1983.

Riskind, J. "The Client's Sense of Personal Mastery." *Counseling on Personal Decisions.* New Haven, Conn.: Yale University Press, 1982.

Scarf, Maggie. *Unfinished Business.* New York: Doubleday, 1980.

Seligman, Martin. *Helplessness.* San Francisco: W. H. Freeman and Company, 1975.

Sheehy, Gail. *Passages.* New York: E. P. Dutton and Co., Inc., 1974.

———. *Pathfinders.* New York: William Morrow and Co., Inc., 1981.

Skinner, B. F. *Beyond Freedom and Dignity.* New York: Alfred A. Knopf, 1971.

Stearns, Ann Kaiser. *Living Through Personal Crisis.* New York: Ballantine Books, 1984.

Steinmetz, J., et al. *Managing Stress: Before It Manages You.* Palo Alto, Calif.: Bull Publishing, 1980.

Stone, Hal, and Winkelman, Sidra. *Embracing Our Selves.* Marina del Rey, Calif.: De Vorss and Co., 1985.

Toynbee, A. *Man's Concern with Death.* New York: McGraw-Hill, 1969.

Vaillant, G. *Adaptation to Life.* Boston: Little, Brown and Co., 1977.

Viorst, Judith. *Necessary Losses.* New York: Simon and Schuster, 1986.

Wallach, Ellen J., and Arnold, Peter. *The Job Search Companion: The Organizer for Job Seekers.* Boston: The Harvard Common Press, 1984.

Weaver, Peter. *YOU, INC.: A Detailed Escape Route to Being Your Own Boss.* Garden City, N.Y.: Doubleday, 1973.

Weisinger, Hendrie, and Lobsenz, Norman M. *Dr. Weisinger's Anger Work-Out Book.* New York: Quill, 1985.

Welch, Mary Scott. *Networking.* New York: Warner Books, 1981.

Willi, Jurg. *Couples in Collusion.* New York: Jason Aronson, 1982.

Wolfenstein, N. *Disaster.* New York: The Free Press, 1957.

Yankelovich, Daniel. *New Rules: Searching for Self-Fulfillment in a World Turned Upside Down.* New York: Random House, 1981.

Your Job Campaign. New York: Catalyst, 1975.